The Complete Book of
GREEK COOKING

The Complete Book of
GREEK COOKING

THE RECIPE CLUB OF
SAINT PAUL'S
GREEK ORTHODOX CATHEDRAL

DRAWINGS BY MANNY MALHADO

1817

HARPER & ROW, PUBLISHERS, NEW YORK
GRAND RAPIDS, PHILADELPHIA, ST. LOUIS, SAN FRANCISCO
LONDON, SINGAPORE, SYDNEY, TOKYO, TORONTO

FIRST EDITION

Designer: Helene Berinsky

Library of Congress Cataloging-in-Publication Data

St. Paul's Greek Orthodox Cathedral (Hempstead, N.Y.). Recipe Club.
  The complete book of Greek cooking/the Recipe Club of Saint Paul's Cathedral.
    p. cm.
  ISBN 0-06-016259-7
  1. Cookery, Greek.   I. Title.
TX723.5.G8S7   1990
641.59495—dc20   89-45708

90 91 92 93 94 DT/MP 10 9 8 7 6 5 4 3 2 1

CONTENTS

FOREWORD

Thirty years ago, a group of women from Saint Paul's Church decided to put together a Greek cookbook to preserve some of the traditional recipes and at the same time raise money for their church. They called themselves "the Recipe Club." That first book had all the "old" family recipes, tested and updated and presented in a very straightforward manner. The book became a bestseller; it was so successful that a second book was written, this one including more modern techniques, such as use of a food processor, as well as carefully tested and updated recipes. That book, too, became a bestseller, proving that Greek cuisine was popular even with non-Greeks.

This book presents the best recipes from the previous two, both now unavailable. Hearty, delicious home-style Greek cooking has wide appeal. It is based on wholesome ingredients, with the emphasis on fresh vegetables, olive oil, and other natural foods.

The aim of this book is to present a wide array of Greek foods. Since most of us move at a hectic pace, many recipes are included that can successfully be prepared ahead, frozen, and reheated. Whenever possible, quicker cooking preparations replace some of the more time-consuming techniques. Many of the recipes have been streamlined and simplified, and, in the dessert section in particular, calories have been trimmed.

Through the years, the Recipe Club has actively promoted Greek cooking through many demonstrations and lectures. Club members provide the delicious pastries sold at church festivals. Recently the church was elevated to the status of a cathedral. Nevertheless, the original reason for writing a cookbook has remained the same: to help our beloved parish of Saint Paul's in Hempstead, New York. All the royalties from our books have gone to the church, as will the earnings from this one.

We believe that this volume will once again become the definitive book that correctly presents the wonderful recipes of Greece.

    With these thoughts in mind, we offer our reader *kalli orexi,* meaning "good appetite!"

Katherine R. Boulukos

THE RECIPE CLUB OF
SAINT PAUL'S GREEK ORTHODOX CATHEDRAL

Katherine R. Boulukos, Chairperson

Tina Barbatsuly	Mary Mormanis
Lydia S. Baris	Helen Pappas
Nina Bendo	Athena Philippides
Sandy Cidis	Polidora C. Prieston
Carol Efthimiou	Maria Prois
Dede Yale Hirsch	Irene Skeados
Theodora Lourekas	Epiphany Touris
Helen Manis Milukas	Ethel Wiley

The Recipe Club of Saint Paul's Cathedral would like to acknowledge the help of the past club members who contributed to our three books.

Special thanks to Samantha Boulukos for her help in the preparation of this book.

The Complete Book of
GREEK COOKING

Greece

CUSTOMS, TRADITIONS, AND RELIGIOUS HIGHLIGHTS

Greek customs and traditions remain an important part of modern life, whether one is in the homeland or has been transplanted to places around the world. Second-, third-, and fourth-generation ethnic Greeks renew the bond to these traditions and keep them alive in their families, as do many who intermarry.

Religion plays a major role in the life of a Greek, beginning at the time of birth. Food is tied to religion, as it is in most cultures, since specific foods are served at key religious observances through the year.

With the birth of a baby, rich desserts are served to all who come to pay their respects. A newborn is first permitted to attend church forty days after its birth. At that time, the priest brings the child before the holy altar and offers special prayers and blessings. The baby's baptism is held sometime after that, at no specific time, but generally after the child has reached three or four months of age. The baptism is the first important religious event for the child. At that time, three Holy Sacraments are administered: Baptism, Chrismation, and Holy Communion. Baptism is the triple immersion of the baby in water. Chrismation is the anointing of the child with holy oil so he may be strengthened and grow up to become a Christian. Holy Communion is the symbolic partaking of the body and soul of Christ. The child is given a Christian name, usually one of the many saints and martyrs of the church. The child is anointed with oil, as were the kings upon their coronation, symbolizing that he, too, is entering a new kingdom, the Kingdom of God. The oil symbolically prevents the devil from grasping the child as he forgoes all

evil and adopts Christianity. A tiny lock of the child's hair is snipped off by the priest. This symbolizes the child's first donation to the church: he is giving something of himself. The baby's clothes are exchanged for all new ones, all white, a symbol of purity. The baby is given a gold cross by his godparent, as well as the baptismal clothes. At the end of the service, the child is returned by the godparent to the parents, who in turn promise to raise the child in the Orthodox church. The godparent, called a *koubaro* or *koubara,* then passes out to the guests *koufeta,* white Jordan almonds, which symbolize a wish for nothing but sweetness in their lives.

Since the child is named after a saint or martyr of the church, he should celebrate his name day. In Greece, people celebrate name days instead of birthdays; gifts are given, festive meals and desserts are prepared, and special preparations are made for an open house. Friends and relatives arrive to extend their wishes of *hronia polla,* which means "many years." Many Greeks in other parts of the world follow this tradition.

Another important event in an individual's life is the wedding. The Greek Orthodox ceremony is a long one, and in the end, the couple feel that they have been joined together for a lifetime. Double rings are blessed and exchanged. The couple sip wine from the same cup to signify the joy and bitterness they will share in life. The best man, called *koubaro,* crosses wreaths or crowns three times over their heads to symbolize the Trinity. (The same word, *koubaro,* is used for the best man as for the godparent because in the old tradition, the same person would often perform both functions in a child's life.) The crowns on the couple's heads symbolize their elevation to the sovereignty of their home as king and queen. They must keep these crowns in their homes, and when one of them dies, the crowns are buried with the body. The couple circles around the wedding table in a ceremonial wedding "dance." This circling represents a circle of eternity. At the end of the service, *koufeta,* the white Jordan almonds, are distributed to the guests.

Death is also marked by special rituals. After the burial, a memorial meal is served, called a *makaria.* The phrases *"Theos Horestone,"* "May God forgive him," and *"Eonia sou in Mneme,"* "Eternal be his memory," are spoken over and over. The traditional meal includes fish, usually fried or sautéed, salad, and dry toast, called paximadia. Forty days after the death, a second memorial service and *makaria* are held. Another memorial service is held one year after the death, another after three years. Kolyva, a traditional dish made of boiled wheat, white raisins, spices and sugar, is prepared at each of these services, called *mnemosino* (which means "in memory"). Kolyva symbolizes the resurrection, the wheat signifies everlasting life, and raisins represent sweetness, and the spices are symbols of plenty.

The Greek calendar is dotted with various important religious observances, some festive and some with deep religious significance. All give the homemaker an opportunity to use various foods as part of the observances of the day.

The most important religious events during the calendar year are:

January 1: New Year's Day, the Name Day of Saint Basil

Saint Basil is known as the donor of wishes and blessings. On this day, a special Vasilopeta, or New Year's cake, is prepared. *Vasilopeta* means "Basil's cake." As the highlight of the meal, the cake is blessed and cut by the head of the household. The first piece is set aside for Saint Basil, since the cake is made in his honor; subsequent pieces are served to each member of the family, beginning with the eldest. In one piece a silver or gold coin is hidden, and there is then great excitement to see who will get that piece. The winner is believed to get extra luck for the forthcoming year. Another custom is for the head of the house to break open a pomegranate on the doorstep of his home. If the fruit is full of seeds, the year will be good, prosperous, and happy. Saint Basil is the symbol of philanthropy, so gifts are exchanged on that day.

January 6: Epiphany Day

On this day, the church commemorates Christ's baptism in the River Jordan. Priests bless the water in the font with special prayers and sing the baptismal hymn as they immerse the cross in the holy water. They then bless their congregations and give each member a vial of holy water to take home. A portion of this holy water is drunk after fasting and a little is sprinkled in each room of the person's home. In some communities, the priest throws a cross into a body of water and hardy swimmers retrieve it for good luck.

Apokries: Pre-Lenten Observances

Before the start of Lent, a carnival spirit prevails in Greece. It begins with the observance of Meat Fare Sunday (the word *apokries* means "abstinence from meat"). The following Sunday, called Cheese Fare Sunday, is the last day when cheese, butter, and eggs may be eaten. On that day, a typical meal includes pasta, salads, and sweets. The following day is Pure Monday, the first day of the forty-day fast, when a strict fast is supposed to be observed. No meat, fish, milk, butter, cheese, or eggs are to be eaten until Easter Sunday. Today, few follow this fast totally; instead, they hold to it on Wednesdays, Fridays, and Sundays. However, all comply with this strict diet during Holy Week, the week preceding Easter.

March 25: Annunciation of the Virgin Mary

This holy day has double significance for the Greek Orthodox. The divine liturgy of the day commemorates the message from the Archangel Gabriel to the Virgin Mary that she is blessed among women. In addition, a special doxology follows the liturgy to commemorate Greek Independence Day, when Greece fought for and won its freedom from Ottoman Turkey in 1821. On this day, the strict Lent is lifted and fish is eaten.

Holy Week

The service on Palm Sunday, which begins Holy Week, rejoices in the entrance of our Lord into Jerusalem. Palms are distributed to the congregation after the liturgy. The Lenten fast is lifted, and the traditional meal is fish.

During Holy Week, the events of our Lord's life are relived through readings from the Gospel. The faithful are expected to attend services and to follow the events of Christ's life.

On Holy Thursday morning, hard-boiled eggs are dyed red, to signify the blood of Jesus. They are set aside to be eaten after the Resurrection Service, at midnight on Easter. Since eggs are the last things to be eaten before the start of the great fast, they are the first to be eaten to break the fast. The cracking of the egg represents Christ's emergence from the tomb.

On Holy Friday, the body of Christ is taken down from the cross, carried around the church in the Holy Shroud, and placed in the sepulcher, called the *Epitaphios,* to signify the burial of Christ. The *Epitaphios* is adorned with flowers, and the faithful file past the symbolic tomb, receiving a flower to take home. The traditional meal on this day is lentil soup with vinegar, the lentils symbolizing the tears of the Holy Mother.

On Holy Saturday, there are church services in the morning and then the midnight service. Homemakers are busy preparing for the feast that follows the midnight Resurrection Service. Special appetizers, breads, and desserts must be prepared for the midnight meal after church, and for the Easter Sunday celebration.

Easter

By canon law, the observance of Holy Easter in the Orthodox church is not simultaneous with that of the Western church. (Every four years, however, the holiday is celebrated at the same time.) The Resurrection Service in the Orthodox church begins shortly before midnight. The congregation gathers, each member holding a white candle, waiting to receive the Resurrection light from the holy altar. At midnight, all lights but the flame of the eternal vigil light are extinguished. The priest lights his candle from the flame and leaves through the royal altar doors, chanting, "Receive ye the light, from the light that never wanes, and glorify Christ, who has risen from the dead." The light is transferred to the candles held by the altar boys and, one by one, to those of the whole congregation. The words *"Christos anesti,"* or "Christ is risen," are spoken over and over. The reply is *"Alithos anesti,"* or "Truly He has risen." The congregation then carries its flickering candles home. The head of the house enters the house, making a cross on the threshold to bring good luck. The festive meal begins with the cracking of the red eggs. Everyone selects an egg, and a little game is played in which each person cracks his or her egg against another person's: the back of the egg to the back of someone else's and the front of the egg to someone else's. (The object of the game is to see who has the strongest egg. The person whose egg remains unbroken is thought to be assured of good luck for the year.) The midnight meal usually includes Easter soup and lamb.

The formal Easter meal is eaten on Sunday. The traditional roasted

lamb is served, along with various vegetables, and many desserts. The customary Easter bread is served, adorned with red eggs. In the afternoon the Agape Service, a special service of love, is held, with readings of the Resurrection Gospel in various foreign languages to signify the universality of the Christian faith.

Ascension Day

On the fortieth day after Easter, a special Divine Liturgy is held to commemorate Christ's last appearance on earth.

Pentecost Sunday

Pentecost, from the Greek word for "fiftieth," signifies the fiftieth day after Easter, when three thousand people were baptized. It is regarded as the beginning of the Christian church, and special services are held on that day.

August 15: The Dormition (or Falling Asleep) of the Virgin Mary

This day, considered one of the most important holidays in the Orthodox church, commemorates the day on which the Virgin Mary died. The preceding fifteen days are an important fast; many faithful observe this fast and receive Communion on Assumption. In order for the faithful to receive Communion, they must fast for at least three days before receiving.

September 8: The Nativity of the Virgin Mary

In the Orthodox church, this date is extremely important because it commemorates the birth of the Virgin Mary to Joachim and Anna. *Theotokos* is the name given to the Virgin Mary, meaning "God given."

September 14: The Elevation of the Holy Cross

On this day, the Holy Cross was found by Saint Helen, on a hill that was covered with basil bushes. For this reason, the basil plant is treasured and is not used in Greek cooking. It is grown and admired, and many bring their basil plants as gifts to the church on this particular day.

Customs and Traditions

December 25: Christmas

The day of the birth of our Lord is a joyous one in the Orthodox church. Beginning on November 15th, many follow a forty-day fast in preparation for the Nativity. It is expected that all Orthodox receive Holy Communion at Christmas. The Christmas meal is a festive one, and includes a special Christmas bread.

Throughout the year, each individual is expected to live a devout Christian life. Although people live far from their native land, many try to follow the traditions of their heritage. Despite the changes and modifications that take place, particularly with the numerous intermarriages, people adapt and try to follow the teaching of the church and the customs and traditions of their ancestors.

APPETIZERS

HOT APPETIZERS

MEAT PHYLLO ROLLS	*Bourekakia me Kreas*
ARTICHOKE PHYLLO TRIANGLES	*Bourekakia me Anginares*
SHRIMP PHYLLO TRIANGLES	*Bourekakia me Garides*
SPINACH CHEESE PHYLLO TRIANGLES	*Spanakopetes*
CHICKEN PHYLLO ROLLS	*Bourekakia me Kota*
CHEESE PHYLLO TRIANGLES	*Tiropetes*
CHEESE PHYLLO PIE	*Tiropeta*
MUSHROOM PHYLLO TRIANGLES	*Bourekakia me Manitaria*
CRABMEAT WRAPPED IN PHYLLO	*Kavouri Bourekakia*
CHICKEN LIVER PHYLLO TRIANGLES	*Bourekakia me Sikotakia*
FRIED CHICK-PEA PATTIES WITH SESAME SEED SAUCE	*Revithokeftedes me Tahini Saltsa*
FRIED SMELTS	*Marithes Tiganites*
MARINATED COCKTAIL MEATBALLS	*Keftedakia me Saltsa*
MARINATED LAMB LIVER	*Sikoti Marinato*
COCKTAIL MEATBALLS	*Keftedakia*
COCKTAIL SHISH KEBAB	*Souvlakia Meze*
LEMON-FLAVORED SOUZOUKAKIA	*Souzoukakia Lemonata*
PUMPKIN PATTIES	*Kolokithokeftedes*
SAGANAKI CHEESE	*Saganaki*
SPINACH BALLS	*Spanakokeftedes*

COLD APPETIZERS

CUCUMBER AND YOGURT DIP	*Tzatziki*
CHICK-PEA AND TAHINI DIP (L)	*Revithia me Tahini Alima*
CUMIN STICKS	*Koulourakia me Kimino*
EGGPLANT SPREAD (L)	*Melitzanosalata*
EGGPLANT AND YOGURT DIP	*Melitzanes me Yiaourti*
FETA DIP	*Feta Meze*
FETA MOLD	*Feta se Kaloupi*
MARINATED LAMB BRAINS IN LEMON SAUCE	*Miala me Lemoni*
FISH ROE SPREAD (L)	*Taramosalata*
MOLDED FISH ROE SALAD	*Taramosalata Sti Forma*
MEATLESS STUFFED GRAPE LEAVES (L)	*Dolmadakia Yialandji*
PEPPER SALAD APPETIZER (L)	*Piperies Orektiko*
MUSSELS WITH MUSTARD (L)	*Midia me Moustartha*
STUFFED MUSSELS (L)	*Midia Yemista*
MARINATED SHRIMP (L)	*Garides se Lathoxitho*
TUNA FISH WITH CHICK-PEAS	*Tonos me Revithia*

Mezedakia, or mezedes, are the appetizers so popular in Greek cuisine. The variety of both hot and cold food in this category is considerable. These mezedakia can be prepared ahead of time, and are suitable for both large and small gatherings, formal or informal. Mezedakia suitable for Lenten meals are designated (L).

A whole meal could be planned using only hot and cold mezedakia. The assortment could include such hot items as phyllo puffs filled with cheese, spinach, or crabmeat, spicy meatballs, and flaming cheese. Among the cold mezedakia could be the traditional tarama dip, eggplant spread, and marinated shrimp. Hot crusty bread, shiny Kalamata black olives, and a glass of white wine would complete the meal. Furthermore, many mezedakia can be served as a first course, such as stuffed grape leaves, fried smelts, tuna fish with chick-peas, or stuffed mussels.

HOT APPETIZERS

꧁꧁꧁꧁꧁꧁꧁꧁꧁꧁꧁

MEAT PHYLLO ROLLS
Bourekakia me Kreas

YIELD: 72 PIECES

2 pounds ground chuck or
   ground lamb
2 tablespoons butter, plus 2
   sticks (½ pound) butter,
   melted, for brushing
   phyllo
½ cup red wine

1 cup raisins or currants
½ cup pine nuts
2 teaspoons ground
   cinnamon
1 teaspoon grated nutmeg
1 pound phyllo pastry

Preheat oven to 375 degrees.

Sauté ground beef or lamb in 2 tablespoons butter over medium heat until browned. Add wine, raisins, pine nuts, and spices; stir until liquids have been absorbed. Cool.

Prepare bourekakia according to directions and diagrams in "How to Work with Phyllo" (p. 312). Use 1 teaspoon filling for each roll. Place rolls seam side down on ungreased cookie sheets. Brush tops with melted butter and bake for 30 minutes, or until golden. Serve warm.

Note: Meat rolls may be prepared ahead of time and frozen, unbaked. When ready to use, preheat oven to 350 degrees. Bake without prior thawing for about 45 minutes, or until golden. Serve warm.

Artichoke Phyllo Triangles
Bourekakia me Anginares

YIELD: 72 PIECES

THICK BÉCHAMEL SAUCE

2 tablespoons butter
2½ tablespoons flour
1 cup hot milk

1 egg yolk (optional)
salt and pepper to taste

two 10-ounce packages
   frozen artichoke hearts
½ cup minced onions
1 stick butter or margarine,
   plus 2 sticks butter,
   melted, for brushing
   phyllo (¾ pound)

2 tablespoons finely minced
   fresh dill
½ cup grated kefalotiri or
   Parmesan cheese
1 pound phyllo pastry

Prepare the béchamel sauce

Melt butter in a saucepan and slowly add flour. Blend well over low heat. Add hot milk, stirring it in rapidly with a whisk or wooden spoon until sauce thickens. Remove from heat and, stirring rapidly, add optional yolk, salt, and pepper. Cool for 15 minutes.

Let artichokes thaw, and drain well. Cut into small pieces. In a small saucepan sauté onion in 1 stick of butter or margarine. Add dill and artichoke pieces and sauté for 3 to 5 minutes. Simmer until all the liquid has evaporated. Remove from heat and add grated cheese and béchamel sauce. Blend well. Place in refrigerator for at least an hour to cool.

Preheat oven to 375 degrees.

Prepare triangular puffs according to directions and diagram 2 in "How to Work with Phyllo" (p. 312). Use 1 teaspoon filling for each puff. Place puffs on ungreased cookie sheets. Brush tops with melted butter. Bake for 15 minutes, or until golden. Serve warm.

Note: These triangles can be prepared ahead of time and frozen, unbaked. When ready to use, preheat oven to 375 degrees. Bake without prior thawing for 30 minutes, or until golden. Serve warm.

SHRIMP PHYLLO TRIANGLES
Bourekakia me Garides

YIELD: 36 TO 40 PIECES

½ cup minced onion
4 tablespoons butter, plus
   1 stick (¼ pound) butter,
   melted, for brushing
   phyllo
1 pound raw medium
   shrimp, cleaned and
   chopped

¼ cup minced parsley
salt and pepper to taste
1 egg
¼ cup grated kefalotiri
   cheese
½ pound phyllo pastry

Preheat oven to 375 degrees.

Brown onion in 4 tablespoons butter. Add shrimp, parsley, salt, and pepper. Sauté briefly until shrimp turn pink. Cool. Beat egg and add grated cheese to it; combine with cooled shrimp mixture.

Prepare triangles according to directions and diagrams in "How to Work with Phyllo" (p. 312). Use 1 teaspoon of filling for each triangle. Place on ungreased cookie sheets. Brush tops with melted butter. Bake for 20 minutes, or until golden. Serve warm.

Note: Triangles can be frozen before baking. When ready to use, preheat oven to 350 degrees. Bake without prior thawing for 25 minutes, or until golden. Serve warm.

SPINACH CHEESE PHYLLO TRIANGLES
Spanakopetes

YIELD: 75 PIECES

2 pounds spinach, or three
    10-ounce packages frozen
    chopped spinach, thawed
1½ cups finely chopped
    onion
½ cup chopped scallion
¼ cup olive oil
¾ pound feta cheese
1 pound cottage cheese
5 eggs, beaten

¼ cup breadcrumbs
½ cup finely chopped
    parsley
½ cup chopped dill
3 sticks (¾ pound) butter,
    melted, for brushing
    phyllo (half margarine
    can be used)
1 pound phyllo pastry

If fresh spinach is used, wash, clean, and chop. Steam in a covered saucepan for 2 to 3 minutes. Drain all water from spinach and then squeeze dry. If frozen spinach is used, thaw and remove all moisture.

Sauté onion and scallion in olive oil for 5 minutes. Add spinach. Simmer over low flame, stirring occasionally, until most of the moisture has evaporated.

Crumble feta. Add cottage cheese and blend well. Add beaten eggs and mix well. Toss breadcrumbs, parsley, and dill into spinach-onion mixture and add to cheese. Stir until well blended.

Preheat oven to 375 degrees.

Prepare triangles according to directions and diagrams in "How to Work with Phyllo" (p. 312). Use 1 teaspoon filling for each triangle. Place on ungreased baking sheets. Brush tops with melted butter. Bake for 20 minutes, or until golden. Let cool about 5 minutes before serving. Serve warm.

Note: Puffs can be prepared ahead of time and frozen, unbaked. When ready to use, preheat oven to 350 degrees. Bake without prior thawing for 35 to 40 minutes, or until golden. Serve warm.

CHICKEN PHYLLO ROLLS
Bourekakia me Kota

YIELD: 72 PIECES

2 pounds skinless, boneless chicken cutlets or chicken breasts
3 onions, quartered
3 stalks celery, chopped
3 to 4 peppercorns
1 teaspoon salt
2 to 3 sprigs parsley
1 stick butter, plus 2 sticks butter, melted, for brushing phyllo (¾ pound)

2 tablespoons minced fresh dill
½ cup grated kasseri cheese
1 teaspoon ground pepper
2 eggs
1 pound phyllo pastry

Poach chicken cutlets by placing them in a large pot with onions, celery, peppercorns, salt, and parsley. Add water to cover. Simmer for about 20 minutes, until breasts are cooked. Remove from liquid and cool. Chop chicken into small pieces, or shred in a food processor.

Chop onions, celery and parsley by hand or in a food processor. Combine with the chicken. Sauté chicken and vegetables in 1 stick butter for 2 to 3 minutes. Add dill and sauté for 1 minute; then add cheese and ground pepper. Cool completely. Add eggs and blend thoroughly.

Preheat oven to 375 degrees.

Prepare phyllo rolls according to directions and diagrams in "How to Work with Phyllo" (p. 312). Use 1 teaspoon filling for each roll. Brush tops with melted butter. Place rolls, seam side down, on an ungreased baking sheet. Bake for 20 minutes, or until golden. Serve warm.

Note: Rolls can be prepared ahead of time and frozen, unbaked. When ready to use, preheat oven to 350 degrees. Bake without prior thawing for 40 minutes, or until golden. Serve warm.

CHEESE PHYLLO TRIANGLES
Tiropetes

YIELD: 75 PIECES

1 pound feta cheese
12 ounces cottage cheese
5 eggs
½ cup finely chopped
   parsley or dill

2 sticks (½ pound) butter,
   melted, for brushing
   phyllo (half margarine
   can be used)
1 pound phyllo pastry

Preheat oven to 375 degrees.

Crumble feta cheese into small pieces. Add cottage cheese and blend well. Add eggs and beat thoroughly. Mix in parsley or dill.

Prepare cheese triangles according to directions and diagrams in "How to Work with Phyllo" (p. 312). Use 1 teaspoon filling for each triangle. Place triangles on ungreased cookie sheets. Brush tops with melted butter. Bake triangles for 15 to 20 minutes, or until golden. Let cool about 5 minutes before serving.

Note: Triangles can be prepared ahead of time and frozen, unbaked. When ready to use, preheat oven to 350 degrees. Bake without prior thawing for 35 minutes, or until golden. Serve warm.

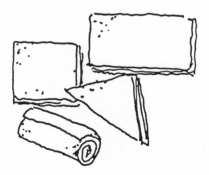

CHEESE PHYLLO PIE
Tiropeta

YIELD: 16 PIECES

12 eggs
1 pound feta cheese,
  crumbled
1 pound ricotta or soft fresh
  mizithra cheese

2 sticks butter, melted and
  cooled, plus 2 sticks
  butter, melted, for
  brushing phyllo (1
  pound)
½ pound phyllo pastry

Preheat oven to 375 degrees.

Beat eggs until thick. In another bowl mix cheese with 2 sticks melted butter. Add eggs to cheese-butter mixture.

Line an 11 x 14 x 2-inch pan with 10 buttered sheets of phyllo pastry. See "How to Work with Phyllo" (p. 312). Add egg-cheese mixture. Top with 8 buttered sheets of phyllo pastry. Using a sharp knife, score top sheets into sixteen squares.

Bake for about 30 minutes, or until golden. Cut into squares. Serve warm.

Note: This dish freezes well. It can be prepared ahead of time and frozen, unbaked. When ready to use, preheat oven to 350 degrees. Bake without prior thawing for 45 minutes, or until golden. Serve warm.

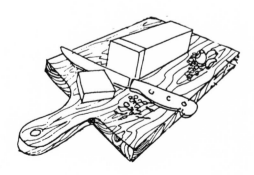

MUSHROOM PHYLLO TRIANGLES
Bourekakia me Manitaria

YIELD: 72 PIECES

3 pounds fresh mushrooms
½ cup minced onion
1 stick buttter, plus 2 sticks
   butter, melted, for
   brushing phyllo
   (¾ pound)

½ cup grated kefalotiri or
   Parmesan cheese
salt and pepper to taste
¾ cup breadcrumbs,
   preferably seasoned
1 pound phyllo pastry

Preheat oven to 375 degrees.

Clean mushrooms thoroughly and chop fine. Sauté onion in 1 stick butter until soft and golden. Add mushrooms and stir to blend. Cook until all liquid from mushrooms has evaporated. Remove from heat and add cheese, salt, pepper, and breadcrumbs.

Fold triangles according to directions and diagrams in "How to Work with Phyllo" (p. 312). Use 1 teaspoon filling for each triangle. Place on ungreased cookie sheets. Brush tops with melted butter. Bake for 15 to 20 minutes, or until golden. Serve warm.

Note: Triangles can be prepared ahead of time and frozen, unbaked. When ready to use, preheat oven to 350 degrees. Bake without prior thawing for 30 minutes, or until golden. Serve warm.

CRABMEAT WRAPPED IN PHYLLO
Kavouri Bourekakia

YIELD: 36 ROLLS

¼ cup minced onion
5 tablespoons butter, plus 1
   stick (¼ pound) butter,
   melted, for brushing
   phyllo
2 tablespoons flour
2 cups lukewarm milk
1 tablespoon minced parsley
1 tablespoon minced dill

½ cup fine breadcrumbs
½ cup chopped mushrooms
2 hard-boiled eggs, chopped
1 teaspoon dry sherry
salt to taste
1½ pounds lump crabmeat,
   picked over
½ pound phyllo pastry

Sauté onion in 5 tablespoons butter until wilted, about 5 minutes. Add flour and mix. Slowly add milk, stirring until the mixture is creamy. Remove from heat. Add remaining ingredients except phyllo pastry and melted butter. If the consistency is too thin, add more breadcrumbs. If too thick, add more milk.

Preheat oven to 375 degrees.

Prepare stuffed phyllo rolls according to directions and diagrams in "How to Work with Phyllo" (p. 312). Use 1 teaspoon filling per roll. Place rolls seam side down on an ungreased cookie sheet. Brush tops of rolls with melted butter. Bake for 30 to 35 minutes, or until golden. Serve warm.

Note: These rolls can be prepared ahead of time and frozen, unbaked. When ready to use, preheat oven to 350 degrees. Bake without prior thawing for 45 to 50 minutes, or until golden. Serve warm.

CHICKEN LIVER PHYLLO TRIANGLES
Bourekakia me Sikotakia

YIELD: 36 PIECES

4 tablespoons butter, plus 1 stick (¼ pound) butter, melted, for brushing
1 cup chopped onion
1 pound chicken livers, coarsely chopped
½ cup grated kefalotiri or Parmesan cheese
⅛ teaspoon grated nutmeg
2 tablespoons cognac
salt and pepper
½ pound phyllo pastry

Preheat oven to 375 degrees.

Melt 4 tablespoons butter, add onion and sauté until soft, about 5 minutes. Add chicken livers and continue cooking until they are browned. Remove from heat and add cheese, nutmeg, cognac, salt, and pepper.

Prepare stuffed phyllo triangles according to directions and diagrams in "How to Work with Phyllo" (p. 312). Use 1 teaspoon filling per triangle. Place on ungreased baking sheets and bake for 15 to 20 minutes, or until golden. Serve warm.

Note: These triangles can be prepared ahead of time and frozen, unbaked. When ready to use, preheat oven to 350 degrees. Bake without prior thawing for 40 minutes, or until golden. Serve warm.

Fried Chick-Pea Patties with Sesame Seed Sauce
Revithokeftedes me Tahini Saltsa

SESAME SEED SAUCE

YIELD: 1½ CUPS

1 tablespoon minced garlic
½ cup tahini (sesame seed paste)
6 tablespoons fresh lemon juice

approximately ⅓ cup cold water
½ teaspoon ground cumin
salt to taste

Hand method

Beat garlic into tahini, then gradually beat in lemon juice and enough cold water to make a smooth, creamy dressing. Add cumin and salt.

Food processor method

Combine garlic and tahini in work bowl. Pulse briefly. Add remaining ingredients and blend quickly.

CHICK-PEA PATTIES

YIELD: ABOUT 24 PATTIES

one 20-ounce can chick-peas
½ cup minced onion
2 tablespoons butter
1 egg, beaten
2 tablespoons minced parsley
salt and pepper to taste

dash of dried oregano
2 tablespoons grated sharp cheese, such as kefalotiri
1 to 2 tablespoons water (if needed)
flour for rolling
vegetable oil for frying

Drain and rinse chick-peas with cold water. Mash with a fork or in a blender or food processor. Sauté onion in butter until soft and golden; remove from heat. Add chick-peas, beaten egg, parsley, salt, pepper, oregano, and grated cheese. Add 1 to 2 tablespoons water, if necessary, to form soft mixture. Shape into 2-inch patties. Roll in flour and fry in oil until golden. Serve with Sesame Seed Sauce.

Appetizers

Note: The patties can be made larger and served as an entrée.

FRIED SMELTS
Marithes Tiganites

YIELD: 6 SERVINGS

The tiny smelt is plentiful in Greek waters and is a favorite seaside summer snack. Caught in large nets close to shore, they are then deep-fried and eaten whole much as Americans consume French fries or potato chips. Here in the United States, smelts are also plentiful and very popular among the Greeks.

2 pounds smelts (about 3 dozen)	1 cup olive oil
salt to taste	3 tablespoons fresh lemon juice
flour for coating	

Clean, wash, and drain smelts. (If smelts are large, cut heads off. Leave tiny smelts whole.) Make a small incision on one side of each smelt. Under cold running water, clean smelts by squeezing out innards. Drain. Sprinkle with salt. Coat with flour. Heat olive oil in a large frying pan. Fry smelts until golden brown and crisp on both sides. Sprinkle with lemon juice and serve hot.

Note: Smelts are sometimes called silversides.

MARINATED COCKTAIL MEATBALLS
Keftedakia me Saltsa

YIELD: 2 TO 2½ DOZEN MEATBALLS

1¼ pounds ground chuck
½ cup breadcrumbs
1 egg
1 teaspoon prepared
 mustard
1 tablespoon chopped
 parsley
pinch oregano
½ cup grated onion

salt and pepper to taste
1 teaspoon dried mint
dash each of ground
 allspice, cinnamon, and
 cloves
1 teaspoon minced garlic
½ cup tomato sauce
¼ cup water

Preheat oven to 450 degrees.

Combine all ingredients except tomato sauce and water and shape into 1-inch balls. Put in a lightly greased baking pan and bake for 20 minutes. Turn halfway through the baking time. Drain on absorbent paper. In a saucepan simmer tomato sauce with ¼ cup water for 5 minutes. Correct seasonings. Add meatballs to sauce and marinate in the refrigerator overnight. Heat in covered casserole and serve hot.

MARINATED LAMB LIVER
Sikoti Marinato

YIELD: ABOUT 24 PIECES

¼ cup plus 2 tablespoons
 fresh lemon juice
1 teaspoon minced garlic
1 teaspoon dried oregano
salt and pepper to taste

½ cup white wine vinegar
1 pound lamb liver, sliced
 ½ inch thick
½ cup flour, or as needed
1 cup olive oil

Combine ¼ cup lemon juice, garlic, oregano, salt, pepper, and wine vinegar. Marinate liver slices in the refrigerator several hours or overnight.

When ready to serve, dip liver pieces in flour and sauté in olive oil. Cut into 1-inch-square pieces, sprinkle with remaining lemon juice, and serve immediately.

Note: Do not cut liver into small pieces until ready to fry because it will dry out.

Appetizers

COCKTAIL MEATBALLS
Keftedakia

YIELD: 1½ TO 2 DOZEN

Keftedes, or keftedakia, are Greek meatballs. Small keftedakia are used as appetizers for parties and festivities of every sort. Since they are equally good at room temperature, they are a fine picnic dish. Large keftedes, with pilaf, vegetable, and salad, make a tasty family dinner.

1 pound ground round
½ cup grated onion
1 tablespoon minced garlic
salt and pepper to taste
¼ teaspoon dried oregano
⅛ teaspoon dried mint

1 or 2 slices white bread
½ cup dry white wine or
  water
1 egg
flour for rolling
vegetable oil for frying

Mix meat, onion, garlic, salt, pepper, oregano, and mint. Remove crusts from bread slices and moisten in wine or water. Add bread and egg to meat. Knead mixture. Shape into 1-inch balls, dust with flour, and sauté in hot vegetable oil. When meatballs are cooked and browned on all sides, place immediately in covered casserole and keep warm until ready to serve.

COCKTAIL SHISH KEBAB
Souvlakia Meze

YIELD: ABOUT 2 DOZEN SKEWERS, 1 PER PERSON

Souvlakia is the Greek word for small pieces of meat threaded on a skewer with vegetables and then, generally, grilled over charcoal. This is the traditional souvlakia recipe adapted as an appetizer, without vegetables.

one 6- to 8-pound leg of
    lamb, boned and trimmed

MARINADE

½ cup olive oil
1 teaspoon ground cumin
  (optional)
1 teaspoon dried oregano
2 bay leaves, crushed
1 tablespoon minced garlic

1 cup chopped green pepper
1 cup chopped onion
¼ cup port wine
¼ cup white vinegar
¼ cup fresh lemon juice
salt and pepper to taste

Cut leg of lamb into 1-inch cubes. Combine all marinade ingredients. Stir to blend. Add lamb cubes and marinate several hours or overnight. (The longer the ingredients marinate, the better the recipe will taste.)

Preheat oven to 375 degrees.

When ready to serve, thread meat on 5- or 6-inch-long wooden skewers. Bake for 12 to 15 minutes, turning frequently, until nicely browned. Serve the souvlakia on the skewers.

LEMON-FLAVORED SOUZOUKAKIA
Souzoukakia Lemonata

YIELD: 2 DOZEN MEAT ROLLS

Souzoukakia are meatballs flavored with cumin and garlic and shaped like little sausages.

1 pound ground round	salt and pepper to taste
½ teaspoon ground cumin	1 stick (¼ pound) butter
¼ cup breadcrumbs	3 tablespoons fresh lemon
1 clove garlic, minced	juice
1 egg	¼ cup water

Combine meat, cumin, breadcrumbs, garlic, egg, salt, and pepper. Shape teaspoonfuls of the meat mixture into oval or oblong shapes (wetting your hands to facilitate handling). Fry in butter over medium heat, turning frequently. Combine lemon juice and water and pour over the souzoukakia.

Note: Instead of frying the souzoukakia, you can place them in a single layer in a pan and brush with olive or vegetable oil. Broil on both sides until brown. Top with lemon sauce. They can also be served over rice as an entrée.

PUMPKIN PATTIES
Kolokithokeftedes

YIELD: ABOUT 40 SMALL PATTIES

Pumpkin is a popular vegetable that is grown in the northern part of Greece.

2½ cups grated pumpkin
   pulp, strained
½ cup chopped onion
4 eggs
2 tablespoons minced garlic
2 tablespoons minced
   parsley

1 tablespoon ground cumin
2 cups breadcrumbs
salt and pepper to taste
2 cups flour
1 cup vegetable oil for
   frying
Sesame Seed Sauce
   (optional; see p. 22)

Combine all ingredients except flour, oil, and Sesame Seed Sauce; blend well. Shape into 2-inch patties, and roll in flour. Fry in vegetable oil until golden brown. Drain on paper towels. Serve warm accompanied by Sesame Seed Sauce (optional).

SAGANAKI CHEESE
Saganaki

YIELD: 20 TO 24 PIECES

1 pound cheese, such as
   kasseri, feta, kefalotiri, or
   kefalograviera
1 stick (¼ pound) butter

3 tablespoons fresh lemon
   juice
2 tablespoons brandy
   (optional)

Slice cheese into ¾- to 1-inch-thick cubes or slices. Melt butter and fry cheese for 3 minutes on each side, or until melted and lightly brown. Sprinkle with lemon juice. Serve hot with crusty bread.

Note: Cheese can be broiled instead of fried. If broiled, do not use any butter. Place cheese in an ovenproof dish. Broil approximately 3 minutes without turning. Sprinkle with lemon juice.

Optional: Just before serving, pour 2 tablespoons brandy over hot cheese and ignite. Serve after flame extinguishes.

Appetizers

SPINACH BALLS
Spanakokeftedes

YIELD: ABOUT 24 BALLS

2 pounds fresh spinach
3 eggs
3 tablespoons melted butter
1 cup grated kefalotiri or
    Parmesan cheese
½ cup crumbled feta cheese

½ cup minced dill
salt and pepper to taste
1 cup breadcrumbs
vegetable oil for frying

Wash and clean spinach, removing the stems. Do not drain. Place in a large saucepan, cover, and steam over high heat until wilted, about three minutes. Drain and chop. Mix all ingredients except breadcrumbs and oil. Shape the mixture into 1-inch balls. Roll in breadcrumbs and deep-fry in hot oil. Drain on paper towels. Serve warm.

Note: Three 10-ounce packages of frozen chopped spinach can be used in place of the fresh spinach. It is not necessary to precook the frozen spinach. Simply thaw, drain well, and proceed with the recipe.

COLD APPETIZERS

CUCUMBER AND YOGURT DIP
Tzatziki

YIELD: 2 CUPS

This dip is extremely popular throughout Greece and is almost always included in the assorted appetizers served in restaurants and tavernas.

2 cups plain yogurt	1 tablespoon white vinegar
2 large cucumbers	2 tablespoons olive oil
1 tablespoon minced garlic	salt and pepper to taste

Put yogurt in a cheesecloth-lined sieve over a bowl. Drain several hours or overnight in the refrigerator.

Hand method

Peel, seed, and coarsely grate cucumbers. Drain well. Add garlic, vinegar, olive oil, salt, and pepper to cucumbers and mix well. Add drained yogurt and blend. Serve with toast points or crackers.

Food processor method

Grate peeled and seeded cucumber; set aside to drain. Add garlic, vinegar, olive oil, salt, and pepper. Pulse with a quick on-off. Place in a bowl and combine with cucumber and yogurt.

[LENTEN]

CHICK-PEA AND TAHINI DIP
Revithia me Tahini Alima

YIELD: 2 CUPS

one 12-ounce can chick-
  peas, drained and rinsed
  under cold water
2 to 3 teaspoons tahini
⅓ cup water
3 tablespoons fresh lemon
  juice
¼ cup olive oil
1 tablespoon minced garlic

½ teaspoon ground
  coriander (optional)
½ teaspoon ground cumin
  (optional)
salt and pepper to taste
1 tablespoon minced
  parsley, plus minced
  parsley for garnish

Hand method

Mash chick-peas with a fork. Place tahini and water in a small bowl
and beat until dissolved, using a whisk or fork. Add tahini mixture, a
teaspoonful at a time, to chick-peas, alternating with equal quantities of
lemon juice and olive oil. When all has been added, add garlic, spices,
salt, and parsley. Beat for a minute or so until well blended; then taste
for seasonings and adjust if necessary. Chill several hours or overnight.
Serve at room temperature, sprinkled with additional minced parsley, if
desired.

Food processor method

Pulverize chick-peas and garlic in a food processor, using pulse on-
off method. Combine tahini, water, lemon juice, and olive oil and add
in a stream, pulsing a few seconds more. Add spices, salt, and parsley
and pulse to a smooth mixture. Place in serving bowl, cover and refrigerate several hours or overnight.

CUMIN STICKS
Koulourakia me Kimino

YIELD: 4 TO 5 DOZEN STICKS

2 cups all-purpose flour
1 teaspoon salt
½ teaspoon dry mustard
½ cup grated kefalotiri
   cheese
2 sticks (½ pound) butter or
   margarine, melted

1 egg yolk
2 tablespoons ouzo
4 tablespoons water
1 egg white
2 teaspoons cumin seeds

Preheat oven to 350 degrees.

Blend together flour, salt, mustard, and cheese. Add melted butter, egg yolk, ouzo, and water, mixing to form a soft dough. Roll out dough to a thickness of ¼ inch and cut into 3 × ½-inch strips, or cut into various shapes with a cookie cutter. Place on a greased cookie sheet. Brush with egg white and sprinkle with cumin seeds. Bake for 15 minutes or until light brown.

[LENTEN]
EGGPLANT SPREAD
Melitzanosalata

YIELD: 4 CUPS

2 medium eggplants, about
   1 pound each
¼ cup olive oil
½ cup minced onion
1 medium ripe tomato,
   peeled, seeded, and
   chopped

3 tablespoons fresh lemon
   juice
salt and pepper to taste
6 pitted black Kalamata
   oil-cured olives
3 tablespoons chopped
   flat-leaf parsley

Preheat oven to 450 degrees.

Prick eggplants in a few places and put on a square of aluminum foil in pan. Bake about 40 minutes, or until soft. Cool. Remove stems and peel eggplants, scraping any flesh from skin. Remove excess seeds, discard skin, and chop eggplant. Place in a bowl. Blend in olive oil and onion well with eggplant. Add chopped tomato. Season with lemon juice, salt, pepper, 3 pitted olives, sliced, and 2 tablespoons parsley. Mix thoroughly. Refrigerate, preferably overnight. Garnish with remaining 3 olives, sliced, and chopped parsley. Serve with crusty bread or crackers as an appetizer or over lettuce as salad.

EGGPLANT AND YOGURT DIP
Melitzanes me Yiaourti

YIELD: 4 TO 6 SERVINGS

2 cups plain yogurt
1 eggplant, about 2 pounds
3 tablespoons olive oil
3 tablespoons minced fresh
  dill
2 cups chopped scallion
1 teaspoon minced garlic

1½ tablespoons fresh lemon
  juice
salt to taste
tomato wedges and
  imported black Greek
  olives for garnish

Preheat oven to 350 degrees.

Line a mixing bowl with cheesecloth and empty yogurt into it. Bring the edges of the cheesecloth up to make a bag; tie with string and suspend over the bowl to let yogurt drip. Let stand in a cool place for 2 to 3 hours. The yogurt will become as thick as sour cream.

Meanwhile, prick eggplant, place on a square of aluminum foil in a baking pan, and bake for 1 hour, or until very soft. Split in half lengthwise and cool. Remove as many seeds as possible, and scrape pulp well from skins. Place pulp in a colander and let drain.

Put eggplant pulp in a bowl and add yogurt. Mix well. Add remaining ingredients and chill thoroughly. Garnish, if desired, with tomato wedges and olives.

FETA DIP
Feta Meze

YIELD: 2 CUPS

Feta, the best-known Greek cheese, is a white goat's milk cheese. It is usually served as an appetizer and as a table cheese, and it is used in many phyllo recipes. This recipe and the one that follows use it in new and interesting ways.

½ **pound feta cheese**
2 **tablespoons olive oil**
8 **tablespoons milk**

1 **cup walnuts**
dash of cayenne
2 **teaspoons minced parsley**

Taste feta; if too salty, soak in cold water and cover; refrigerate for several hours. Drain cheese and break into chunks. Put 1 tablespoon oil and 4 tablespoons milk in blender. Add half of the feta and half of the walnuts. Blend to a smooth consistency. Empty the blender container and repeat with the rest of the feta, oil, milk, and walnuts. Combine the two batches in a large bowl, add cayenne, blend, and refrigerate several hours or overnight. Sprinkle with parsley; serve with crackers.

FETA MOLD
Feta se Kaloupi

YIELD: 2 CUPS

½ **pound feta cheese**
1 **stick (¼ pound) unsalted butter, softened**
12 **black oil-cured Kalamata olives, pitted and chopped**
¼ **cup finely minced onion**

1 **red or green pepper, minced fine**
celery sticks, carrot sticks, and pepper strips for garnish

Taste feta; if too salty, soak in cold water in the refrigerator for several hours. Drain and break into chunks.

Blend cheese and butter to the consistency of whipped cream, using an electric mixer or food processor. Stir in olives, onion, and pepper. Pack mixture solidly into an oiled 2-cup mold and refrigerate until firm. When ready to serve, unmold in the center of a large platter. Garnish with celery sticks, carrot sticks, and pepper strips. Serve with crackers.

MARINATED LAMB BRAINS IN LEMON SAUCE
Miala me Lemoni

YIELD: 8 SERVINGS

Lamb brains are available in Greek meat markets.

2 lamb brains (1 pound)	salt and pepper to taste
2 tablespoons white vinegar	½ cup finely chopped dill or
¼ cup olive oil	flat-leaf parsley
3 tablespoons fresh lemon juice	

Wash brains thoroughly and soak in lukewarm water for 10 minutes. With sharp knife, remove membranes. Rinse. Place brains in boiling salted water to cover; add vinegar and simmer, covered, for 20 to 30 minutes, or until soft. Drain. Cut into ½-inch cubes and let cool. Add olive oil, lemon juice, salt, pepper, and dill or parsley. Marinate 4 hours or overnight. Serve at room temperature or cold.

The Complete Book of
GREEK COOKING

FISH ROE SPREAD
Taramosalata

YIELD: 1½ CUPS

Taramosalata, the famous Greek fish roe spread, is considered "poor man's caviar." The secret of its success lies in mashing together the fish roe and the bread to form a paste before the lemon juice, olive oil, and onion are added. Tarama is salt-cured carp roe. The eggs are small and pale orange.

4 tablespoons tarama
8 slices white bread, crusts
    removed
¾ cup olive oil

4 tablespoons fresh lemon
    juice
1 teaspoon grated onion

Hand method

Place tarama in a mortar and pound it until the roe splits. Moisten bread under running water; squeeze out any excess. Add bread to tarama in the mortar and pound until they are completely blended, about 5 minutes. Put this mixture in a mixing bowl and beat with an electric mixer or a wooden spoon, adding small amounts of olive oil alternately with lemon juice. Beat for 5 minutes. Add onion and mix well. Serve in a bowl surrounded by crackers. Keep refrigerated.

Blender or food processor method

Moisten bread under running water. Squeeze out any excess. Place tarama in bowl and process for 1 minute. With motor running, add bread, all the olive oil, lemon juice, and onion alternately to form a creamy mixture.

MOLDED FISH ROE SALAD
Taramosalata Sti Forma

YIELD: 12 TO 16 SERVINGS

2 tablespoons unflavored
   gelatin
¼ cup cold water
2 cups boiling water
½ cup tarama (4 ounces)
1 cup mayonnaise
1 tablespoon fresh lemon
   juice
1 cup fresh breadcrumbs

dash of cayenne
½ cup grated onion
salt to taste
4 black olives, pitted
4 ounces pimiento
8 ounces cream cheese
2 cups chopped parsley,
   whole olives, and pickles
   for garnish

Chill a metal 6-cup fish mold in the freezer. Sprinkle gelatin over ¼ cup cold water to soften. Add the boiling water and stir until gelatin dissolves. Put in the refrigerator to cool, about 5 minutes. (Do not allow gelatin to set.)

Blend tarama, mayonnaise, lemon juice, breadcrumbs, cayenne, onion, and salt in a blender or electric mixer. Mix 1 cup of gelatin liquid into tarama mixture and put in refrigerator. Cut olives into slices and pimientos into narrow strips. Pour ½ cup of gelatin liquid into fish mold and tip it to spread into all the crevices. Arrange olive and pimiento slices as scales, eyes, and tail. Place mold in freezer for 15 minutes. Pour ¼ cup more of gelatin mixture into mold and return to freezer. Beat or blend cream cheese and add remaining ½ cup gelatin liquid to it. Place in refrigerator for 15 minutes. Do not let it set completely. Spread cheese mixture over bottom and sides of mold. Return to freezer for 15 minutes to set. Fill mold with tarama mixture. Refrigerate to set for 4 hours, or overnight. Chill serving platter in refrigerator.

To serve, dip bottom of mold in hot water. Place serving platter over mold and turn mold over quickly. Garnish with chopped parsley, olives, pickles, and any other vegetables desired. Serve with bread or crackers.

[LENTEN]

MEATLESS STUFFED GRAPE LEAVES
Dolmadakia Yialandji

YIELD: 3 DOZEN

2 cups minced onion
1 teaspoon salt
⅔ cup converted rice
¾ cup olive oil
3 cups chopped scallion,
  including greens
6 tablespoons fresh lemon
  juice
½ cup chopped parsley
  (reserve stems for lining
  pot)

½ cup chopped dill (reserve
  stems for lining pot)
salt and pepper to taste
one 12-ounce jar grape
  leaves
1 cup boiling water
parsley and lemon wedges
  for garnish

Sweat onion over very low heat with 1 teaspoon salt for 5 to 10 minutes, until wilted. Increase heat and add rice, ½ cup of the olive oil, scallion, and 1½ tablespoons lemon juice. Sauté for 2 minutes. Add parsley, dill, salt, and pepper. Sauté for 4 minutes. Set aside to cool.

Wash grape leaves under cold running water to thoroughly remove all brine. Separate leaves carefully. Remove thick stem portions. Cut large leaves in half. Place 1 tablespoon filling on underside of leaf. Starting at base, fold over, and fold in sides, rolling tightly toward point. (See illustration.)

Place parsley and dill stalks on bottom of a saucepan. Arrange dolmadakia in layers. Add remaining ¼ cup oil and 1½ tablespoons lemon juice. Weigh down dolmadakia with a heavy plate. Cover with boiling water to the level of the plate. Bring to a boil, reduce heat, and simmer for 45 minutes, or until water is absorbed. Remove plate, and sprinkle 3 tablespoons fresh lemon juice over dolmadakia. Let cool thoroughly in pot. Remove to a serving plate and garnish with parsley and lemon wedges.

Note: Fresh or frozen grape leaves can be used instead of jarred ones. See "How to Use and Freeze Fresh Grape Leaves" (p. 311).

[LENTEN]

PEPPER SALAD APPETIZER
Piperies Orektiko

YIELD: 1 CUP

6 large sweet peppers
½ cup coarsely chopped
   onion
salt and pepper to taste

3 tablespoons white vinegar
¼ cup olive oil
chopped fresh parsley to
   taste

Preheat oven to 450 degrees.

Roast peppers for about 20 minutes, or until wilted and soft. Place in a brown bag and cool for 20 minutes. Remove seeds and outer skin. Cut in pieces and put in a bowl. Add onion, salt, and pepper. Combine vinegar and olive oil and add to peppers. Sprinkle with parsley. Adjust seasonings if necessary.

[LENTEN]

MUSSELS WITH MUSTARD

Midia me Moustartha

YIELD: ABOUT 24 PIECES

**one 16-ounce jar of cleaned
mussels (see note)**

SAUCE

**1½ tablespoons fresh lemon
juice
5 tablespoons reserved
mussel liquid**

**2½ tablespoons olive oil
2½ tablespoons prepared
mustard**

Drain mussels and reserve 5 tablespoons of the liquid.

Prepare the sauce

Alternately add lemon juice, mussel broth, and olive oil to mustard, beating after each addition, until all ingredients are used and mixture is thickened. Pour sauce over mussels and serve cold, accompanied with crackers or crusty bread.

Note: If fresh mussels are used, follow this procedure for 2 dozen mussels:

Clean mussels according to technique given in "How to Clean Fresh Mussels" (p. 310).

Steam mussels in 2 cups simmering water until shells open, about 3 to 5 minutes. Discard any that do not open. Reserve the broth. Remove mussels from shells and place in a jar. Strain broth through a cheesecloth and add to the mussels. Add enough water (if necessary) to cover the mussels. Add 2 tablespoons olive oil and refrigerate. When ready to serve, drain mussels, reserving 5 tablespoons of the liquid. Follow recipe above to add mustard sauce to mussels.

[LENTEN]
STUFFED MUSSELS
Midia Yemista

YIELD: 24 MUSSELS

24 fresh mussels
salt
½ cup dry white wine
approximately 1 cup water
2 cups chopped onion
¼ cup olive oil
½ cup raw converted rice

1 teaspoon ground allspice
¼ cup pine nuts
¼ cup currants
black pepper to taste
2 tablespoons chopped
  parsley

Clean mussels according to technique given in "How to Clean Fresh Mussels" (p. 310).

Place mussels in a large pot, sprinkle with salt, and pour in wine and enough water to cover. Cover the pot and simmer for 5 minutes, or until the shells open. Discard any that do not open. Remove mussels from shells, reserving shells. Pour broth through cheesecloth and save liquid.

In a separate pan, cook onion in olive oil until soft. Add rice and cook 3 minutes longer, stirring constantly. Add 1 cup of strained mussel liquid. Cover pot and cook for 15 minutes. Add remaining ingredients, cover, and cook 5 minutes longer, or until rice is done. Add mussels and cook over low heat until just heated through. Fill 24 mussel shells with mixture. (Be sure that each mussel shell gets one mussel.) Serve hot or cold.

[LENTEN]

MARINATED SHRIMP
Garides se Lathoxitho

YIELD: 16 TO 20 SERVINGS

MARINADE

2 large red onions, sliced
    thin
3 tablespoons capers,
    drained and rinsed
3 bay leaves
1½ cups white vinegar

1½ cups water
1½ cups olive oil
1 teaspoon salt
½ teaspoon pepper
½ teaspoon dried oregano

3 pounds medium-sized
    shrimp, cooked, peeled,
    and deveined
½ pound small mushrooms,
    wiped clean

1 pound canned artichoke
    hearts, drained and cut
    into thirds

Combine all marinade ingredients. Refrigerate overnight. On the second day add cooked shrimp, mushrooms, and artichoke hearts. Refrigerate overnight and serve on the third day.

TUNA FISH WITH CHICK-PEAS

Tonos me Revithia

YIELD: 4 TO 6 SERVINGS

This makes an excellent luncheon main course.

one 20-ounce can chick-peas
two 6½-ounce cans tuna
   fish

4 scallions, white parts only,
   minced
1 tablespoon minced celery

DRESSING

½ cup olive oil
4 tablespoons fresh lemon
   juice
¼ cup chopped fresh parsley
1 tablespoon chopped fresh
   dill

½ teaspoon salt
½ teaspoon pepper
2 teaspoons minced garlic
¼ teaspoon dry mustard

Drain chick-peas and tuna. Mix together with chopped vegetables. In a screw-top jar, combine dressing ingredients and shake well. Pour dressing over chick-pea-tuna mixture and stir well. Chill for several hours for the flavors to blend.

Eggs, Pasta, and Rice and Grain

EGGS

EGGS WITH TOMATOES AND ONIONS	*Avga me Domates ke Kremidia*
POACHED EGGS WITH YOGURT	*Tsilbiri*
EGGS AND CHICKEN LIVERS	*Sikotakia me Avga*
OMELET WITH FETA	*Omeleta me Feta*

PASTA

BAKED ZITI WITH FETA	*Makaronia sto Fourno*
CABBAGE, CELERY, AND ORZO CASSEROLE	*Lahano me Kritharaki*
MACARONI WITH FETA	*Makaronia me Feta*
ORZO WITH ZUCCHINI	*Kritharaki me Kolokithakia*
SPAGHETTI WITH BROWNED BUTTER SAUCE	*Makaronia me Kavourdismeno Voutero*

RICE AND GRAIN

RICE PILAF	*Rizi Pilafi*
PILAF WITH ARTICHOKES	*Pilafi me Anginares*
LENTILS AND RICE PILAF	*Fakorizo*
RICE AND ORZO PILAF	*Kritharaki me Rize*
PILAF WITH CREAM SAUCE AVGOLEMONO	*Pilafi me Aspri Saltsa Avgolemono*
BAKED RICE	*Rize sto Fourno*
BAKED EGGPLANT AND RICE CASSEROLE	*Melitzana ke Rize sto Fourno*
BULGUR	*Pligouri*

Eggs, Greek-style, mean an omelet filled with vegetables, chicken livers, or cheese. An old, unusual poached-egg-with-yogurt dish, tsilbiri, is included, since it has been handed down through the generations, with no thought about cholesterol.

Pasta is a staple starch that is included as an accompaniment to both fish and meat. There are certain dishes, such as Spaghetti with Browned Butter Sauce (see p. 54), that evoke fond childhood memories. Orzo, or kritharaki, is another popular pasta. It has a distinctive tiny almond shape, and is used in such combinations as Orzo with Zucchini, as well as in such dishes as Lamb or Beef Casserole with Orzo (see p. 141). Although different in texture, orzo is frequently used in recipes that call for rice.

Rice (rizi) and rice dishes are so popular in Greece that it is sometimes served along with potatoes. During the Lenten fast, Spinach and Rice (see p. 197) is a typical one-dish meal.

EGGS

EGGS WITH TOMATOES AND ONIONS
Avga me Domates ke Kremidia

YIELD: 4 TO 6 SERVINGS

4 tomatoes, peeled, seeded, and chopped
½ cup minced onion
4 tablespoons butter (or 2 tablespoons butter plus 2 tablespoons olive oil)

8 eggs
salt and pepper to taste

In a skillet, sauté tomatoes and onion in 2 tablespoons of the butter over low heat until moisture has evaporated and onion is tender. Beat eggs and season with salt and pepper. In another skillet, melt remaining butter, add eggs, and cook, stirring, over low heat until eggs begin to set. Pour tomato-onion mixture on top of eggs and continue to cook, stirring lightly, until eggs are set.

POACHED EGGS WITH YOGURT
Tsilbiri

YIELD: 4 SERVINGS

This is a favorite traditional dish.

2 pints plain yogurt, at
   room temperature
8 poached eggs, hot

1 stick butter (¼ pound),
   melted and browned
salt and pepper to taste

Spoon 1 cup yogurt into each of 4 ramekins or soup bowls. Carefully place 2 poached eggs on top of yogurt in each ramekin. Spoon browned butter over all. Sprinkle with salt and pepper. Serve with garlic bread and a cooked vegetable.

Note: Butter can be reduced by half; use 1 tablespoon per 2 eggs.

EGGS AND CHICKEN LIVERS
Sikotakia me Avga

YIELD: 2 TO 3 SERVINGS

2 chicken livers (1½ ounces
   each)
2 tablespoons butter

¼ cup minced onion
salt and pepper to taste
4 eggs, well beaten

Cut livers into small pieces and set aside. In a skillet heat 1 tablespoon of the butter and in it sauté onion until tender and lightly browned. Add chicken livers, salt, and pepper, and brown lightly. Melt remaining butter in the same skillet. Add eggs and cook over low heat, stirring constantly, until eggs are set but still creamy. Turn onto serving platter and serve.

OMELET WITH FETA
Omeleta me Feta

YIELD: 2 SERVINGS

4 eggs
2 tablespoons crumbled feta
   cheese

1 tablespoon minced parsley
2 tablespoons butter
salt and pepper to taste

Beat eggs. Add feta and parsley. In a large frying pan, melt butter, add eggs, and season with salt and pepper. Cook for several minutes. Fold omelet into thirds, and serve immediately.

Variation: Vegetables can be used in this omelet: artichokes, asparagus, potatoes, and zucchini are among the traditional favorites. Add vegetables as follows:

---

one 10-ounce package frozen artichoke hearts, thawed and well drained, combined with 1 tablespoon finely chopped dill. In a small skillet, sauté in 1 tablespoon butter for 1 minute. Once eggs are set, place artichoke hearts in center of omelet, fold into thirds, and serve.

---

one 10-ounce package frozen asparagus, thawed, parboiled, well drained, and cut into 1-inch pieces. In a small skillet, sauté in 1 tablespoon butter for 1 minute. Once eggs are set, place asparagus in center of omelet, fold into thirds, and serve.

---

2 medium potatoes, sliced thin. In a small skillet, melt 1 tablespoon butter and add potatoes. Sauté for 4 minutes. Once eggs are set, place potatoes in center of omelet, fold into thirds, and serve.

---

2 medium zucchini, cut into ½-inch-thick slices. In a small skillet, sauté zucchini in 1 tablespoon vegetable oil until lightly browned, about 2 minutes. Once eggs are set, place zucchini in center of omelet, fold into thirds, and serve.

PASTA

꧁꧁꧁꧁꧁꧁꧁꧁꧁꧁

Baked Ziti with Feta
Makaronia sto Fourno

YIELD: 6 TO 8 SERVINGS

1 pound ziti
1 pound feta cheese
6 eggs
1 quart milk

2 tablespoons minced onion
6 tablespoons grated
    kefalotiri cheese

Preheat oven to 350 degrees.

Cook ziti according to package directions and drain well. Crumble feta. Separate eggs and beat whites until frothy. Beat egg yolks until creamy. Fold yolks into whites, and add feta, milk, and onion. Spread the ziti in a buttered 10 × 14-inch pan. Pour egg mixture over pasta and sprinkle kefalotiri cheese over the mixture. Bake for 1 hour or until golden and bubbly.

CABBAGE, CELERY, AND ORZO CASSEROLE
Lahano me Kritharaki

YIELD: 6 SERVINGS

½ cup vegetable oil
1 cup finely minced onion
1 small head of cabbage, about 2 pounds, sliced thin (about ¼-inch-thick slices)
8 stalks celery, cut into 1-inch pieces

one 8-ounce can tomato sauce
1 tablespoon tomato paste
salt and pepper to taste
¼ pound orzo
½ cup grated kefalotiri cheese (optional)

Heat oil in a 5-quart Dutch oven and sauté onion, cabbage, and celery until lightly browned or limp. Add tomato sauce and tomato paste (if mixture seems too thick add a little water) and simmer over medium heat until vegetables are almost cooked, about 15 minutes, adding more water if necessary. Add salt, pepper, and orzo and simmer, covered, until orzo is cooked, about 15 minutes. Remove from heat and sprinkle with cheese.

MACARONI WITH FETA
Makaronia me Feta

YIELD: 4 TO 5 SERVINGS

5 tablespoons butter, melted
½ cup breadcrumbs
½ cup grated kefalotiri cheese
½ pound macaroni, cooked and drained

½ pound feta cheese, crumbled
1½ cups milk
4 eggs, well beaten

Preheat oven to 350 degrees.

Grease a 10- or 12-inch square or round pan with 1 tablespoon butter. Sprinkle pan with half the breadcrumbs and half the grated cheese. Combine macaroni with melted butter and crumbled feta. Pour into the pan and sprinkle with remaining breadcrumbs. Combine milk with eggs and pour over the macaroni mixture. Sprinkle with remaining grated cheese. Bake for 30 minutes, or until brown.

Eggs, Pasta, and Rice and Grain

Orzo with Zucchini
Kritharaki me Kolokithakia

YIELD: 4 TO 6 SERVINGS

⅓ cup orzo
4 to 5 medium zucchini
(about 3 pounds),
scrubbed, trimmed, and
diced

¼ cup vegetable or olive oil
salt and pepper to taste
½ teaspoon dried oregano

Fill a large pot with water, bring to a boil, and add orzo. Reduce heat, and cook for 15 minutes, until tender, stirring occasionally to prevent sticking. While orzo cooks, in a large heavy pot, sauté zucchini in oil until brown, about 5 minutes. Add drained orzo to zucchini; season with salt, pepper, and oregano. Cover and cook over low heat for 10 minutes. Shake the pot a few times to prevent mixture from becoming lumpy (stirring can mash the zucchini). Serve hot or cold.

SPAGHETTI WITH BROWNED BUTTER SAUCE
Makaronia me Kavourdismeno Voutero

YIELD: 4 TO 5 SERVINGS

This Greek recipe is simple to make. The browned butter is the "secret ingredient."

1 pound spaghetti (#8 or #9) or 1 pound macaroni

1 stick (¼ pound) butter

½ cup grated kefalotiri cheese

Cook spaghetti according to package directions and drain well. Meanwhile, melt butter in a small frying pan. Add 2 or 3 tablespoons of grated cheese to butter and allow both butter and cheese to brown lightly, stirring all the while. Put drained spaghetti into a serving bowl. Sprinkle with remaining grated cheese and keep tossing so that cheese penetrates throughout. When butter and cheese mixture is lightly browned, pour over spaghetti.

Variation: 2 finely minced cloves garlic can be added to the browned butter. Plain yogurt can also be added as a topping. For a richer taste, double the amount of butter.

RICE AND GRAIN

𐃏𐃏𐃏𐃏𐃏𐃏𐃏𐃏𐃏𐃏𐃏

RICE PILAF
Rizi Pilafi

YIELD: 4 TO 6 SERVINGS

4 tablespoons butter　　　**2¼ cups boiling chicken**
1 cup raw converted rice　　**stock**

Melt butter in a heavy casserole. Add rice and sauté, stirring, over medium heat for 3 minutes, or until rice is opaque. Add boiling stock and stir. Cover casserole and simmer, without stirring, for about 20 minutes, or until rice has absorbed all the liquid. A linen towel can be placed over the casserole after rice is cooked to absorb excess moisture. Replace cover and let casserole stand for five minutes.

Variation: ¼ cup minced onion can be added with rice to melted butter and sautéed as above. For a tomato flavor, add one tablespoon tomato paste or ½ cup tomato sauce to stock. If a richer flavor is desired, increase butter by 4 tablespoons.

PILAF WITH ARTICHOKES
Pilafi me Anginares

YIELD: 8 TO 10 SERVINGS

1½ sticks (6 ounces) butter
  or margarine
½ cup minced onion
1 tablespoon dried dill, or
  ½ cup minced fresh dill
two 10-ounce packages
  frozen artichoke hearts,
  thawed

2 cups raw converted rice
5 cups chicken stock
one 8-ounce can tomato
  sauce
salt and pepper to taste

Melt 4 tablespoons butter in a deep pot. Add onion, dried dill, and artichokes and brown. (If fresh dill is used, add before the browned butter.) Add rice and sauté until opaque, about 2 minutes. In a saucepan bring the chicken stock and tomato sauce to a boil and add to rice and artichokes. Cover and simmer over low heat for 20 minutes, or until liquid has been absorbed. Brown remaining 8 tablespoons butter, pour over rice mixture, and season with salt and pepper. Stir to blend. Remove from heat and let stand for 5 minutes before serving.

LENTILS AND RICE PILAF
Fakorizo

YIELD: 6 SERVINGS

1 cup lentils, picked over
5 cups chicken stock
1 cup raw converted rice
salt to taste
½ cup minced onion

½ cup vegetable or olive oil
1 cup canned plum
  tomatoes, drained and
  chopped
black pepper to to taste

Wash lentils. Boil them in chicken stock in a deep pot for 5 minutes. Add rice and salt and simmer, covered, until all liquid has been absorbed, about 30 minutes. In the meantime, prepare the sauce. Sauté onion in oil for 3 minutes. Add tomatoes and simmer for 10 minutes. As soon as lentil-rice mixture is cooked, remove from heat and add sauce. Sprinkle with pepper.

Eggs, Pasta, and Rice and Grain

Note: This can be served as a Lenten dish if plain water is substituted for chicken stock.

Variation: If orzo is used instead of rice, increase the amount of chicken stock by ½ cup.

RICE AND ORZO PILAF
Kritharaki me Rize

YIELD: 4 TO 5 SERVINGS

2 tablespoons butter or
   margarine
⅔ cup raw converted rice
½ cup orzo

3 cups boiling chicken stock
grated kefalotiri cheese or
   Eggplant-Tomato Sauce
   (see p. 176)

In a medium-sized saucepan melt butter and lightly brown rice and orzo. Add stock, cover tightly, and simmer for 20 minutes, or until all the liquid has been absorbed. This can also be baked in a 350 degree oven for 30 minutes. Serve with grated cheese and/or Eggplant-Tomato Sauce.

PILAF WITH CREAM SAUCE AVGOLEMONO

Pilafi me Aspri Saltsa Avgolemono

YIELD: 15 TO 20 SERVINGS

10 cups chicken stock or
water
4 cups raw converted rice
1 cup milk
2 sticks (½ pound) butter
¼ cup flour

3 egg yolks
3 tablespoons fresh lemon
juice
½ pound kefalotiri or
Parmesan cheese, grated

Put 9 cups of stock into a large pot and bring to a boil. Add rice and stir with a fork. Cover and cook until fluffy and soft, about 20 minutes. While rice cooks, heat remaining cup of broth and the milk. Melt 1 stick of butter in a saucepan, add flour, and blend well. Slowly add hot broth and milk. Cook over low heat until sauce thickens, stirring constantly to prevent lumping or burning. Remove from heat.

Beat egg yolks with lemon juice and slowly add to the sauce, stirring constantly. Return to the heat, and stir until thickened. Remove from heat, and add half the grated cheese. In a small saucepan, melt 1 stick of butter until lightly browned. Pour over rice. Pack rice in a 10-inch mold and turn onto a platter. Pour hot sauce over rice. Sprinkle with remaining cheese. Serve hot.

Note: This recipe can be successfully halved. Use 2 egg yolks.

BAKED RICE
Rize sto Fourno

YIELD: 4 SERVINGS

4 tablespoons butter
1 cup minced onion
¼ cup chopped green
  pepper
1 cup sliced mushrooms

1 cup raw converted rice
2 cups boiling chicken stock
1 teaspoon salt
¼ teaspoon pepper
dash of dried thyme

Preheat oven to 350 degrees.

Melt 2 tablespoons butter in a 1-quart Dutch oven. Add onion and sauté until soft. Add green pepper and mushrooms and sauté for 5 minutes. Remove mixture and set aside.

In same pot melt remaining 2 tablespoons butter. Add rice and sauté until opaque. Add stock and salt, and stir. Add reserved vegetables and season with pepper and thyme. Cover and bake for 30 to 40 minutes, or until all the liquid has been absorbed and rice is done.

BAKED EGGPLANT AND RICE CASSEROLE
Melitzana ke Rize sto Fourno

YIELD: 8 SERVINGS

2 eggplants, about 1½
  pounds each
1 teaspoon salt
¼ cup vegetable or olive oil
3 cups finely minced onion
1 tablespoon minced garlic
1 green pepper, seeded and
  cut into 1-inch cubes
1 teaspoon dried oregano
1 bay leaf

3 tomatoes, peeled, seeded,
  and chopped
1 cup raw converted rice
2¼ cups boiling chicken
  stock
salt and pepper to taste
½ cup grated kefalotiri
  cheese
2 tablespoons butter

Preheat oven to 400 degrees.

Slice unpeeled eggplants and cut into 1-inch cubes. Place in a colander, sprinkle with salt, cover with a weighted plate, and let stand for 30 minutes.

Heat oil in a heavy skillet. Carefully dry eggplant pieces and add to the skillet. Cook over high heat, stirring occasionally, until lightly browned. Add onion, garlic, green pepper, oregano, and bay leaf while stirring. Stir in tomatoes and reduce heat. Simmer for 5 minutes, or until most of the liquid has evaporated. Pour vegetable mixture into a casserole and stir in the rice and boiling chicken stock. Season with salt and pepper. Sprinkle with cheese and dot with butter. Bake, uncovered, for 30 minutes, or until the liquid has been absorbed by the rice.

BULGUR
Pligouri

YIELD: 4 SERVINGS

1½ cups rich chicken stock
salt to taste
1 cup bulgur

4 tablespoons butter,
melted and browned

Bring stock to a boil. Add salt and bulgur. Cover and cook over low heat for about 25 minutes, or until bulgur is cooked. Correct seasoning and add butter.

Variation: Brown 1 medium onion, chopped, in 2 tablespoons butter until soft. Add 1 cup bulgur and stir to coat. Add 1½ cups rich chicken stock and bring to a boil. Continue as above.

Soups

Chicken Soup with Avgolemono Sauce	*Soupa Avgolemono*
Bean Soup	*Fassoulada*
Meatball Avgolemono Soup	*Giouvarlakia*
Mock Mageritsa	*Apli Mageritsa*
Tahini Soup (L)	*Tahinosoupa*
Fish Soup	*Psarosoupa*
Kakavia	
Lentil Soup (L)	*Faki*
Summer Cucumber Soup	*Kalokerini Soupa me Angourakia*

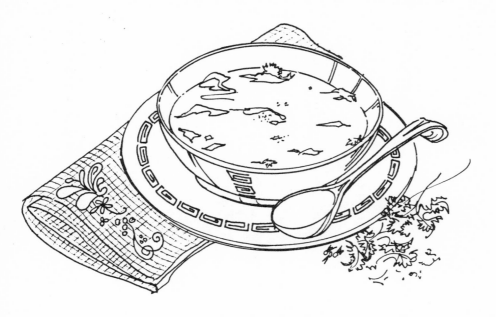

The range of Greek soups goes far beyond the well-known Avgolemono, the egg-and-lemon-flavored chicken soup. From the hearty Kakavia of the islands (actually a Greek version of the French bouillabaisse) to the cold soups, the many varieties are a significant part of the Greek diet. Soup plays an important role during the various religious holidays, particularly Lent and Easter. Lentil Soup, a favorite from the time of the ancient Greeks, is still served on Holy Friday, the lentils signifying the tears of the Virgin Mary. Mageritsa, or tripe soup, is traditional fare at the Easter meal. (Included in this section is a simplified version of this soup.) Bean Soup is the mainstay of the Greek villager, who usually eats it every Friday.

The Complete Book of
GREEK COOKING

CHICKEN SOUP WITH AVGOLEMONO SAUCE
Soupa Avgolemono

Avgolemono is a staple in Greek cuisine, used in soups and as a sauce for stews, vegetables, and meats.

CHICKEN SOUP

one 3- to 3½-pound roasting chicken	1 onion
2 to 2½ quarts water	1 stalk celery
a few peppercorns	salt to taste
1 small carrot	1 cup raw converted rice, orzo, or kritharaki

AVGOLEMONO SAUCE

2 eggs	3 tablespoons fresh lemon juice

Wash chicken and place in heavy kettle in water to cover. Add peppercorns, carrot, onion, and celery. Bring to a boil, cover, and simmer over low heat for 2 hours, or until chicken is tender, adding salt to taste during last hour of cooking. Remove chicken and keep warm. Strain broth and remove as much fat as possible. Add rice, orzo, or kritharaki and simmer, covered, until rice or pasta is tender, 15 to 20 minutes.

Make the Avgolemono Sauce

Hand method

Beat eggs well and gradually beat in lemon juice. Add two cups hot, strained broth slowly to egg sauce, beating constantly. Return soup to heat and stir vigorously until thickened.

Blender or food processor method

Blend eggs with lemon juice. With motor running, very slowly add 2 to 3 cups of hot, strained broth. When combined, pour egg-lemon mixture from bowl into remaining broth, stirring briskly. After all the liquid has been combined, reduce heat and continue to stir until thickened.

To serve, ladle into soup bowls and add slices of cooked chicken, if desired.

Note: A 46-ounce can of chicken broth can be used. Bring to a boil and add rice or orzo. Simmer for 15 to 20 minutes, or until rice or pasta is tender. Remove from heat and prepare Avgolemono Sauce as explained above. Combine with hot soup, stir, and serve.

BEAN SOUP
Fassoulada

YIELD: 6 TO 8 SERVINGS

Fassoulada is nourishing, tasty, and economical, and, together with a salad, crusty bread, and a simple dessert, provides a complete meal.

1 pound navy beans	2 stalks celery, chopped
½ cup olive oil	one 6-ounce can tomato
2 cups chopped onion	puree
2 teaspoons minced garlic,	3 quarts water
optional	1 cup chopped parsley
1 large carrot, chopped	salt and pepper to taste

Soak beans in hot water to cover for 30 minutes. Sauté onion, garlic, carrot, and celery in oil until limp. Add tomato puree and water. Bring to a boil. Add drained beans and salt and pepper. Simmer for about 2 hours, or until beans are tender. Add parsley after 1¾ hours.

MEATBALL AVGOLEMONO SOUP
Giouvarlakia

YIELD: 4 SERVINGS

Some people consider Giouvarlakia a "meatball soup"; others consider it meatballs with avgolemono sauce. Whichever you think it is, this is a quick, delicious entrée. Serve with a green salad.

1 cup minced onion	¼ cup chopped parsley
1 pound ground beef	salt and pepper to taste
¼ cup raw converted rice	½ cup flour for coating
3 tablespoons fresh lemon juice	5 cups chicken stock
1 teaspoon chopped fresh mint leaves or ½ teaspoon dried mint	

AVGOLEMONO SAUCE

2 eggs	3 tablespoons fresh lemon juice
2 tablespoons cold water	

Combine onion with ground beef. Add raw rice, lemon juice, mint, parsley, salt, and pepper. Make small meatballs and dip lightly in flour to coat. Bring chicken stock to a boil. Add meatballs and simmer for about 30 minutes. (These can be made ahead of time.) Before serving, reheat broth and meatballs.

Prepare the Avgolemono Sauce

Beat eggs with water. Add lemon juice slowly, stirring constantly. Add all the hot broth from the meatballs, stirring constantly to avoid curdling. When all the liquid has been added to egg-lemon mixture, return to the pot, pouring over meatballs. Cook gently until sauce has thickened. Serve at once in soup bowls.

MOCK MAGERITSA
Apli Mageritsa

YIELD: 6 TO 8 SERVINGS

The traditional Mageritsa recipe calls for lamb tripe, lungs, and heart. The following simplified version substitutes more readily available ingredients.

3 pounds lamb shoulder, whole	salt and 8 whole peppercorns
2 pounds lamb bones	3 quarts water
2 stalks celery	8 scallions, finely minced
1 carrot, scraped	1 cup finely minced dill
2 small onions, peeled	½ cup raw converted rice

AVGOLEMONO SAUCE

4 eggs	6 tablespoons fresh lemon juice

Simmer meat and bones, celery, carrot, onions, and salt and peppercorns in 3 quarts water for 2 hours. Strain and skim broth and reserve. Remove meat from bones and dice. Add meat, scallions, dill, and rice to broth and simmer for 20 minutes, or until rice is tender.

Strain broth again and use to prepare Avgolemono Sauce

In a blender or food processor, beat eggs thoroughly. Slowly add lemon juice and hot broth and continue beating. If there is more liquid than the blender will hold, empty half of egg mixture into a saucepan and continue beating in the blender, slowly adding the rest of the liquid. Mix all the sauce together in the saucepan, add the meat and gently reheat.

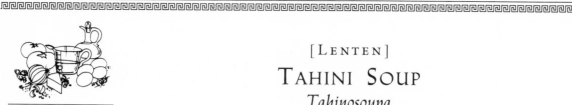

[LENTEN]
TAHINI SOUP
Tahinosoupa

YIELD: 6 SERVINGS

2 quarts plus ½ cup cold
  water
salt to taste
1 cup raw converted rice
6 ounces tahini (¾ cup)

6 tablespoons fresh lemon
  juice
1 teaspoon tomato paste
  (optional)

Bring 2 quarts salted water to a boil, add rice, and cook, covered, for 20 minutes. While rice is cooking, mix tahini in a bowl with ½ cup cold water. Add lemon juice and mix well. Slowly add 1 or 2 full ladles of rice water to tahini. Remove rice from the heat and pour all the tahini mixture into it. Add optional tomato paste, stir and serve.

FISH SOUP
Psarosoupa

YIELD: 6 SERVINGS

6 cups fish stock
½ cup raw converted rice
1 egg

2 tablespoons fresh lemon
  juice

Bring fish stock to a boil. Add rice and reduce heat. Cook, covered, for 15 to 20 minutes on low heat, until rice is tender. Prepare egg-lemon sauce by beating egg with lemon juice in a medium-sized bowl. Slowly add 2 cups hot liquid, stirring constantly. Pour back into pot and simmer for 3 minutes to incorporate.

KAKAVIA

YIELD: 12 SERVINGS

What the French call bouillabaisse, the Greeks call kakavia, a name with an interesting derivation. When fishermen gathered on the beach after their daily catch, they would make a huge fire and place all the fish they could not sell into a large kettle, or *kakavia*. Hence the name of this hearty fish soup, which is still a favorite main meal among Greek islanders. The following is an adaptation of the traditional recipe.

4 to 6 pounds whole cleaned fish: striped bass, sea bass, or red snapper
½ cup olive oil
4 cups chopped onion
2 stalks celery, cubed
1 tablespoon minced garlic
2 leeks, sliced
3 large carrots, pared and cubed
1 tablespoon salt
1 teaspoon pepper
3 tablespoons fresh lemon juice
one 1-pound can plum tomatoes with liquid
4 cups water
12 clams, scrubbed
12 shrimp, shelled and deveined
12 mussels, scrubbed and cleaned
1 cup white wine
3 bay leaves
½ teaspoon dried thyme
1 tablespoon minced parsley

Clean fish and cut into small pieces. Heat oil in a large pot. Sauté onion, celery, garlic, and leeks over medium heat for 5 minutes. Add carrots, salt, pepper, lemon juice, tomatoes, and 4 cups water. Add fish and cook for 15 minutes. Add shellfish, wine, bay leaves, thyme, and parsley and simmer for 5 minutes, or until clams and mussels open. Serve in deep bowls with crusty garlic bread.

Variation: 12 baby lobster tails (about ½ pound each) can be added with the other shellfish.

[LENTEN]
LENTIL SOUP
Faki

YIELD: 6 TO 8 SERVINGS

1 pound lentils
2 quarts water
1 cup chopped onions
2 stalks celery, chopped
1 carrot, chopped
2 teaspoons minced garlic
½ cup olive oil

1 tablespoon tomato paste
¼ cup chopped fresh parsley
bay leaf
salt to taste
3 tablespoons wine vinegar
    or lemon juice

Rinse lentils in cold water in colander; drain. Sauté vegetables and garlic in olive oil for 2 to 3 minutes, until wilted. Add lentils and water along with tomato paste, parsley, and bay leaf. Bring to a boil and simmer covered 45 minutes, or until lentils are tender. In last 15 minutes of cooking add a big pinch of salt. Stir in vinegar before serving.

Variation: One-half teaspoon oregano and ½ cup cooked tomatoes can be added just before soup is served.

SUMMER CUCUMBER SOUP
Kalokerini Soupa me Angourakia

YIELD: 4 SERVINGS

The Greeks have long had a love affair with yogurt, which is the basis of this delicious and refreshing soup.

3 cups yogurt
1½ cups peeled, seeded, and
   grated cucumber
½ teaspoon salt
¾ cup cold water

¼ teaspoon pepper
1 tablespoon minced dill
3 tablespoons minced chives
1 tablespoon minced garlic

Place all the ingredients in a mixing bowl. Stir until well blended. Serve in chilled bowls with garlic bread.

Fish and Shellfish

BROILED FILLETS WITH KASSERI AND TOMATOES	*Fetes Psari me Kasseri kai Domates*
BAKED CODFISH CAKES	*Bakaliaros Keftedes*
BROILED FISH	*Psari Tis Skaras*
POACHED FISH WITH MAYONNAISE	*Psari me Mayoneza*
PORGIES WITH AVGOLEMONO SAUCE	*Tsipoures Avgolemono*
CODFISH STEW (L)	*Bakaliaro Yahni*
FRIED COD	*Bakaliaro Tighanito*
FRIED FISH WITH ROSEMARY SAUCE	*Psari Savoro*
FISH PATTIES WITH ROSEMARY SAUCE	*Psarokeftedes me Savoro*
FISH PLAKI	*Psari Plaki*
STEWED FISH WITH ONION	*Bourtheto*
ROLLED STUFFED FILLETS WITH AVGOLEMONO SAUCE	*Fetes Psari Gemistes Avgolemono*

SQUID IN WINE	*Kalamarakia me Krassi*
STUFFED SQUID	*Kalamarakia Yemista*
FRIED BABY SQUID	*Kalamarakia Tighanita*
MUSSELS WITH WINE SAUCE (L)	*Midia Krassata*
MUSSELS PILAF WITH PINE NUTS (L)	*Midia Pilafi me Koukounaria*
BAKED LOBSTER TAILS WITH FETA	*Astakos Psitos me Feta*
SHRIMP SCORPIO	*Garides me Saltsa*
OCTOPUS IN RED WINE SAUCE	*Oktapodi Krassato*

Although Greece's mountainous, arid terrain makes it less than ideal for large-scale agriculture, its thousands of miles of coastline and hundreds of islands make it a fisherman's paradise. Think of a Greek island and the emerald-blue Aegean, and your next thought inevitably will be of a luxuriant array of fish and shellfish. Here we present the pick of the catch, from Baked Lobster Tails with Feta to such island specialties as Shrimp Scorpio. (Dishes suitable for Lenten use are designated L.)

In general, the Greeks prefer cooking fish at high heat in hot oil to the more gentle poaching or sautéing. They frequently marinate the fish in oil and lemon juice before frying it in olive oil. After centuries of preparing fish, the Greeks have developed many interesting dishes to contribute to the world's cuisine.

BROILED FILLETS WITH KASSERI AND TOMATOES
Fetes Psari me Kasseri kai Domates

YIELD: 4 SERVINGS

2 pounds skinless flounder
  or other fish fillets
2 tablespoons grated onion
1½ teaspoons salt
¼ teaspoon pepper

3 tomatoes, chopped
1 stick (¼ pound) butter,
  melted
1 cup grated kasseri cheese

Preheat broiler.

Place fillets in a single layer in a well-greased shallow baking dish. Sprinkle with onion, salt, pepper, and tomatoes. Sprinkle tomatoes lightly with additional salt and pepper (optional). Drizzle butter over all. Broil 4 inches from heat for 5 minutes, or until fish flakes easily. Sprinkle with cheese and broil 2 minutes more.

BAKED CODFISH CAKES
Bakaliaros Keftedes

YIELD: 4 TO 6 SERVINGS

1 pound dried salt cod
4 medium potatoes, cooked
  and mashed (dry, without
  milk or butter)
¼ cup milk

1 tablespoon minced onion
cayenne to taste
1 egg
Garlic Sauce (see page 177)

Soak cod in cold water for six hours, changing water several times. Drain.

Place cod in a pan and cover with boiling water. Cover pan and let stand for 20 minutes; drain. Cover fish with more boiling water and let stand for another 20 minutes; drain.

Preheat oven to 350 degrees.

Flake fish with a fork. Mix flaked fish with mashed potatoes, milk, onion, cayenne, and slightly-beaten egg. Shape into 2-inch cakes, place in a well-greased baking pan, and bake for 35 minutes or until light brown. Serve with Garlic Sauce.

Fish and Shellfish

BROILED FISH
Psari Tis Skaras

YIELD: 4 SERVINGS

2 porgies (2 pounds each) or 3-pound sea bass or 2- to 3-pound whole flounder or 3-pound whole red snapper

salt to taste
olive oil for brushing

SAUCE

1 cup olive oil
½ teaspoon pepper
½ cup fresh lemon juice
1 tablespoon chopped fresh or 1 teaspoon dried oregano

2 tablespoons thinly sliced onion
1 tablespoon chopped parsley

Clean, wash, and salt fish. Brush with oil. Barbecue or broil, about 10 minutes on each side.

Prepare the sauce

Combine oil, pepper, lemon juice, and oregano. Whisk until thick and almost white in color. Add sliced onion and parsley.

Place fish on serving platter and pour sauce over fish.

POACHED FISH WITH MAYONNAISE
Psari me Mayoneza

YIELD: 6 TO 8 SERVINGS

8 cups water
½ cup olive oil
4 carrots, peeled and cut
   into chunks
3 onions
3 celery stalks with leaves,
   cut into chunks
salt to taste
5 pounds cleaned whole
   fish: sea bass, striped bass,
   red snapper, or blackfish

4 potatoes, peeled and
   quartered
3 tablespoons fresh lime
   juice
parsley for garnish
Homemade Mayonnaise
   (see p. 182)

Bring water to a boil in a fish poacher. Add olive oil, carrots, onions, and celery. Boil for 10 minutes. Lightly salt fish. Place in the boiling water, making sure that it covers the fish (add more water, if necessary). Add potatoes. Cover pot, lower heat, and simmer for 15 minutes, or until fish is cooked and opaque. Remove from water carefully and let cool. Cut head and tail off and set aside. When cool, remove skin and lift out the center bone and all other bones. Squeeze fresh lime juice over fish.

Reassemble fish on a fish-shaped platter, adding the head and tail for decoration. Cover with Homemade Mayonnaise. Decorate with the cooked sliced carrots and potatoes. Garnish with parsley. Chill several hours and serve cold.

Note: The fish stock can be used to prepare Fish Soup (see recipe on p. 70).

PORGIES WITH AVGOLEMONO SAUCE
Tsipoures Avgolemono

YIELD: 6 SERVINGS

1 bunch celery
2 cups boiling water
2 cups finely minced onion
½ cup vegetable or olive oil
3 to 4 whole porgies (about
   1 pound each), cleaned
salt and pepper to taste

1 cup water
2 eggs
6 tablespoons fresh lemon
   juice
1 tablespoon flour
fresh parsley or dill for
   garnish

Cut celery into 3-inch pieces. Blanch in 2 cups boiling water for 5 minutes. Drain.

In a large skillet, sauté onion in oil until soft. Place celery on top of onions; place the fish on top of the celery and sprinkle with salt and pepper. Add 1 cup water, cover, and simmer for 20 minutes, or until fish flakes. Remove fish and vegetables, place on a heated platter, and keep warm.

Strain broth in which the fish cooked, measure, and add enough water to make 1 cup. Heat the broth. Beat eggs, lemon juice, and flour in a blender. Gradually beat in the heated broth. Pour into a saucepan and heat gently until slightly thick. Pour over fish. Garnish with parsley or dill. Serve immediately.

Variation: Striped bass, sea bass, or red snapper can be substituted for porgies, about 3 pounds, cleaned. Increase water to 1½ cups, cooking time to 30 minutes.

[LENTEN]
CODFISH STEW
Bakaliaro Yahni

YIELD: 6 SERVINGS

2 pounds dried salt cod
1 bay leaf
2 pounds small white
   onions
½ cup olive oil
3-ounce can tomato paste
¾ cup water

salt and pepper to taste
1 tablespoon minced garlic
½ cup red wine
2 pounds small potatoes,
   peeled

Soak cod in cold water for six hours, changing water several times.
   Put all ingredients except potatoes in a Dutch oven, cover, and bring to a boil. Add potatoes. Cook over low heat for about 1 hour, or until potatoes are cooked and fish flakes easily with a fork. If liquid cooks away, add a little more water.

FRIED COD
Bakaliaro Tighanito

YIELD: 4 TO 6 SERVINGS

2 pounds dried salt cod
1½ cups all-purpose flour
½ teaspoon salt
dash of pepper
1 teaspoon double-acting
   baking powder

water
vegetable oil for frying
Garlic Sauce (see p. 177)

Soak codfish in cold water for six hours, changing water several times.

Drain cod and cut into 8 to 10 pieces. Combine flour, salt, pepper, and baking powder with enough water to make a batter the consistency of a thin white sauce. Dip pieces of cod in batter and fry in 1 inch hot oil until golden brown. Drain on absorbent paper and serve with Garlic Sauce.

Fish and Shellfish

FRIED FISH WITH ROSEMARY SAUCE
Psari Savoro

YIELD: 4 TO 6 SERVINGS

Although bony, the porgy, called *tsipoura* in Greek, is considered by many to be the favorite fish of Greece. The following recipe can be prepared with whole porgies or fish fillets.

4 small porgies, cleaned, about 1½ pounds each, or 4 to 6 fillets, such as flounder, lemon sole, or gray sole, about 3 to 4 pounds total	all-purpose flour for dredging salt and pepper to taste olive oil for frying Rosemary Sauce (see p. 181)

Dip fish in flour and sprinkle with salt and pepper. Fry in 1 inch hot oil in a large skillet until brown on both sides. Remove from pan and keep warm.

Return fish to skillet and cover with Rosemary Sauce.

Cover immediately and let stand at least 1 hour before serving. Serve at room temperature or reheat gently.

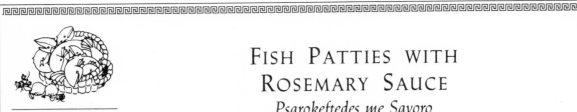

FISH PATTIES WITH ROSEMARY SAUCE
Psarokeftedes me Savoro

YIELD: 5 TO 6 SERVINGS

6 cups water
1 stalk celery, cut into 8 pieces
½ cup chopped parsley
1 onion, quartered
3 pounds whole fish (cod or flounder), cleaned
1 tablespoon minced mint leaves
½ cup minced onion
2 eggs
1 cup breadcrumbs

⅓ cup grated kefalotiri cheese
salt and pepper to taste
¾ cup water
1 cup all-purpose flour for coating
vegetable oil for frying
6 tablespoons fresh lemon juice
Rosemary Sauce (see page 181)

Bring 6 cups water to a boil. Add celery pieces, parsley, and onion; boil for 10 minutes. Reduce heat and add whole fish; cook, covered, for 20 minutes. Strain, reserving liquid. Cool fish and debone. Remove head and skin, and discard.

Mash fish with a fork. (You should have 2 cups.) Add mint, onion, eggs, breadcrumbs, grated cheese, salt, pepper, and ¾ cup water. Mix thoroughly. Form into small patties. Coat each patty in flour and fry in hot oil until golden brown. Sprinkle with lemon juice. Serve with Rosemary Sauce.

Note: Both the fish and the sauce are served at room temperature.

The strained fish stock can be used to prepare Fish Soup (see p. 70).

FISH PLAKI
Psari Plaki

YIELD: 6 SERVINGS

Plaki is a method of cooking, usually with onions, tomatoes, parsley, and olive oil. Though *plaki* is usually associated with fish, beans *plaki* and vegetable *plaki* are also made.

2 large onions, sliced into
   rings
½ cup olive oil
1 cup coarsely chopped
   celery
3 scallions, chopped
1 cup chopped parsley
3 fresh tomatoes, sliced
1 tablespoon finely minced
   garlic
1 bay leaf

2 to 3 pounds fish fillets:
   striped bass, sea bass,
   bluefish or tilefish
2 teaspoons dried oregano
salt and pepper to taste
2 whole lemons, sliced into
   thin rings
½ cup white wine
3 tablespoons fresh lemon
   juice
¼ cup breadcrumbs

Preheat oven to 350 degrees.

Sauté onions in oil until soft. Add celery, scallions, parsley, tomatoes, garlic, and bay leaf. Simmer until liquid has evaporated. Place fish in greased baking pan and sprinkle with oregano, salt, and pepper. Cover fish with cooked vegetables. Decorate with lemon slices. Add wine and lemon juice. Top with breadcrumbs. Bake for 45 minutes, or until fish flakes easily.

STEWED FISH WITH ONION
Bourtheto

YIELD: 6 SERVINGS

3½ pounds red snapper,
    cod, turbot, or haddock
1½ cups water
½ cup olive oil
1 teaspoon salt

1 teaspoon pepper
1 teaspoon paprika, or to
    taste
⅛ teaspoon cayenne
2 cups sliced onions

Cut the fish in to six serving pieces. Put water, oil, seasonings, and onions in a saucepan and simmer for 15 minutes. Add fish and cook over low heat for 15 minutes, or until fish flakes easily with a fork. Serve with Rice Pilaf (see p. 55).

ROLLED STUFFED FILLETS WITH AVGOLEMONO SAUCE
Fetes Psari Gemistes Avgolemono

YIELD: 4 SERVINGS

3 cups water
1 carrot, chopped
1 cup chopped onions
1 bay leaf
a few peppercorns
12 shrimp, shelled and
    deveined
6 tablespoons butter or
    margarine

2 teaspoons minced garlic
¼ cup minced onion
¼ cup minced green pepper
¼ cup flavored breadcrumbs
1 tablespoon minced parsley
½ teaspoon salt
⅛ teaspoon pepper
4 fillets of sole or flounder
    (about 1½ to 2 pounds)

AVGOLEMONO SAUCE

3 eggs
1 cup broth, reserved from
  cooking shrimp

6 tablespoons fresh lemon
  juice

Bring 3 cups of water to a boil in a large pot. Add carrots, onions, bay leaf, and peppercorns, and boil for 5 minutes. Reduce heat, and add shrimp. Cook for 3 minutes, or until they turn pink. Remove shrimp and reserve 1 cup of the broth for the Avgolemono Sauce.

Preheat oven to 350 degrees.

Melt 2 tablespoons butter in a large skillet. Stir in garlic, onion, and green pepper and sauté until onion is golden. Dice 8 shrimp and add to the skillet with the breadcrumbs, parsley, salt, and pepper. Stir and remove the skillet from heat.

On boned side of each fillet spread 2 tablespoons of shrimp mixture. Roll fillets carefully and tuck any extra mixture into end of rolled fillets.

Melt 4 tablespoons butter. Use 2 tablespoons to coat a 10 x 6 x 2-inch baking dish. Arrange fillets flat side down in the dish. Brush with remaining melted butter. Bake for 25 to 30 minutes.

Prepare the Avgolemono Sauce

Beat the eggs until creamy. Add lemon juice and beat. Very slowly add warm broth reserved from cooked shrimp; beat until thick. When fish is baked, place on a platter and pour sauce over all. Garnish each fillet with a whole shrimp.

SQUID IN WINE
Kalamarakia me Krassi

YIELD: 6 SERVINGS

3 pounds cleaned squid (see
 "How to Prepare Fresh
 Squid," p. 310)
2 cups chopped onion
½ cup vegetable or olive oil
1 cup chopped parsley

1 tablespoon chopped garlic
½ cup dry sherry or red
 wine
2 cups crushed tomatoes
1 teaspoon salt
½ teaspoon pepper

Blanch squid in boiling water for 5 minutes. Drain well and cut
into ringlets.

Sauté onion in oil until soft. Do not brown. Add parsley, garlic,
sherry or wine, tomatoes, squid, salt, pepper, and ink sacs. Simmer
slowly for 30 minutes, or until squid is fork tender. Serve over rice.

Note: You can use frozen, cleaned squid. Thaw and proceed with
the recipe, adding ½ cup clam juice with parsley, garlic, and sherry.

STUFFED SQUID
Kalamarakia Yemista

YIELD: 4 TO 6 SERVINGS

½ cup chopped onions
1 tablespoon chopped garlic
½ cup plus 1 tablespoon
 olive oil
salt and pepper to taste
1 cup tomato sauce
1 bay leaf, crumbled
½ cup raw converted rice
¼ cup currants (optional)

½ cup chopped parsley or
 dill
1 pound small, cleaned
 squid, about 3 to 4 inches
 long (see "How to
 Prepare Fresh Squid"
 p. 310)
1½ cups boiling water

Brown onions and garlic in ½ cup oil. Add salt and pepper, tomato sauce, bay leaf, rice, currants, parsley or dill, and the chopped tentacles. Cook for approximately 10 minutes, until liquid has been absorbed.

Lightly brush a medium-sized casserole with 1 tablespoon olive oil. Using a teaspoon, fill each squid cavity with the onion mixture. Do not overstuff, or squid will burst during cooking. Place squid in casserole and pour any remaining stuffing mixture on top. Add water, cover, and simmer for 25 minutes, or until squid is fork tender.

Fish and Shellfish

FRIED BABY SQUID
Kalamarakia Tighanita

YIELD: 4 TO 6 SERVINGS

Squid is well liked by Greeks. The baby squid are considered more tender and tastier. Today frozen, cleaned squid is available at many fish stores. Thaw at room temperature before cooking.

3 pounds cleaned squid (see "How to Prepare Fresh Squid," p. 310), about 3 to 4 inches long salt and pepper to taste	flour for coating vegetable oil for frying 3 tablespoons fresh lemon juice

Season squid lightly with salt and pepper. Dip in flour and shake off excess. Heat 1 inch of oil in a frying pan. Fry squid in batches so as not to crowd. Cook until golden. Remove as they are done. When all the pieces are fried, return to frying pan to reheat. Transfer to a serving platter, sprinkle with fresh lemon juice, and serve immediately.

[LENTEN]

MUSSELS WITH WINE SAUCE
Midia Krassata

YIELD: 4 TO 6 SERVINGS

½ cup chopped onion
2 teaspoons minced garlic
3 tablespoons vegetable or
  olive oil
3 quarts mussels, cleaned
  and bearded (see "How to
  Clean Fresh Mussels,"
  p. 310)
1 cup dry white wine
4 sprigs parsley
1 sprig fresh thyme, or ½
  teaspoon dried thyme

1 bay leaf
½ teaspoon pepper
¼ cup white vinegar
2 tablespoons prepared
  mustard
½ teaspoon salt
1 cup olive oil
¾ cup diced, blanched
  celery
1 tablespoon minced fresh
  parsley
1 teaspoon dried tarragon

In a Dutch oven, sauté onion and garlic in oil until soft. Add well-scrubbed mussels, wine, parsley sprigs, thyme, and bay leaf. Sprinkle with ¼ teaspoon pepper. Bring to a boil, cover, lower heat, and simmer for 6 to 7 minutes, shaking pan, until mussels open. Transfer mussels to a large bowl. Strain cooking liquid through cheesecloth, and boil to reduce to 1 cup.

In another bowl, combine ¼ teaspoon pepper, vinegar, mustard, and salt. Pour in olive oil in a slow stream. Add celery, parsley, and tarragon, and stir the mixture into the reduced cooking liquid. Pour over the mussels and serve at room temperature.

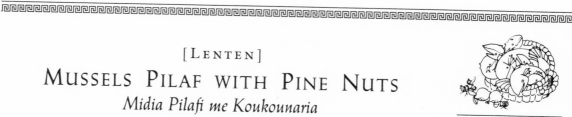

[LENTEN]
MUSSELS PILAF WITH PINE NUTS
Midia Pilafi me Koukounaria

YIELD: 4 TO 6 SERVINGS

2 to 3 dozen mussels, cleaned and bearded (see "How to Clean Fresh Mussels," p. 310)
½ cup dry white wine
1 teaspoon tomato paste
½ cup chopped onion or scallion
½ cup olive oil
1 cup raw long-grain rice
½ cup pine nuts
½ cup dried currants (optional)
¼ cup chopped parsley

Steam cleaned mussels in wine for 5 minutes. Remove from shells, discarding any unopened mussels. Set aside.

Strain mussel broth; dissolve tomato paste into the broth. Add water to make 2½ cups liquid. Sauté onion in olive oil until translucent. Add liquid and bring to a boil. Add rice, reduce heat, and simmer, covered, for 20 minutes. Add mussels, pine nuts, currants, and parsley. Cook for an additional 5 minutes, until liquid has been absorbed.

BAKED LOBSTER TAILS WITH FETA
Astakos Psitos me Feta

YIELD: 6 SERVINGS

Lobster is available off the southern islands of Greece. This recipe comes to us from Leon Lionides, owner of New York's famed Coach House Restaurant.

3 tablespoons olive oil
2 cups chopped onions
2 teaspoons minced garlic
3 cups crushed canned plum
   tomatoes
½ teaspoon dried oregano
dash of dry mustard
dash of sugar
¼ cup finely minced parsley
1 tablespoon finely minced
   dill

pepper to taste
12 frozen baby lobster tails,
   thawed
1 cup all-purpose flour
1 stick (¼ pound) butter
4 large tomatoes, peeled and
   cut into ¼-inch-thick
   slices
¾ pound feta cheese,
   crumbled

Preheat oven to 375 degrees.

Heat oil in a saucepan. Add onion and gently sauté until wilted. Add garlic, plum tomatoes, oregano, mustard, sugar, parsley, dill, and pepper. Simmer for 30 minutes, or until sauce is moderately thick. Thaw lobster tails and shell them, taking care to remove the meat in one piece. Roll lobster tails in flour; sauté briskly in butter, stirring, for 2 minutes, or just until firm. Remove to a shallow baking dish. Pour sauce over lobster tails and arrange tomato slices on top. Cover with feta and bake 15 minutes, or until cheese melts. Serve with Rice Pilaf (see p. 55).

SHRIMP SCORPIO
Garides me Saltsa

YIELD: 4 SERVINGS

3 tablespoons olive oil
2 cups minced onion
2 teaspoons minced garlic
¼ cup finely minced parsley
1 tablespoon finely minced
   dill (optional)
¼ teaspoon dry mustard

¼ teaspoon sugar
2 cups fresh or canned
   peeled tomatoes, chopped
½ cup tomato sauce
1 pound medium shrimp,
   peeled and deveined
1 cup crumbled feta cheese

Preheat oven to 425 degrees.

Heat oil in a saucepan and add onions. Cook, stirring, until the onion starts to brown. Add garlic, parsley, dill, mustard, sugar, tomatoes, and tomato sauce; simmer for 30 minutes. (Do not add salt at any time.) Add shrimp to sauce and cook for 3 minutes. Pour the mixture into a 1½-quart casserole and sprinkle with crumbled cheese. Bake for 5 minutes, or until cheese melts. Serve immediately.

OCTOPUS IN RED WINE SAUCE
Oktapodi Krassato

YIELD: 4 SERVINGS

Octopus has a flavor resembling lobster and is even more tender. It must be slowly pounded against a rock when first caught, as the flesh can be very tough, and this tenderizes it. Since the fisherman does the pounding, the octopus purchased in a fish market should be ready to cook.

2 pounds fresh octopus	**salt and pepper to taste**
4 cups chopped onions	**1 bay leaf, crushed**
½ cup olive oil	**1 cup red wine**

Wash octopus carefully and discard the ink sac. Cut octopus into bite-sized pieces. Sauté onions in olive oil until soft and golden. Add octopus, salt, pepper, and bay leaf, and simmer for 10 minutes. Add wine and enough water to cover. Bring to boil, cover, and simmer for about 1 hour, or until octopus is tender. Serve with Rice Pilaf (see p. 55).

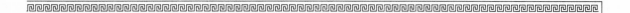

POULTRY

BROILED CHICKEN OREGANO	*Kotopoulo Riganato tis Skaras*
CHICKEN KAPAMA	*Kota Kapama*
CHICKEN BREASTS IN PHYLLO	*Kotopites*
CHICKEN-ARTICHOKE CASSEROLE	*Kota me Anginares Plaki*
CHICKEN WITH ORZO	*Kritharaki me Kota*
CHICKEN SOUVLAKIA	*Souvlakia me Kota*
CHICKEN STEFADO	*Kotopoulo Stefado*
CHICKEN WITH SCALLIONS AND AVGOLEMONO	*Kotopoulo me Avgolemono*
CHICKEN WITH SPINACH AVGOLEMONO	*Kota me Spanaki Avgolemono*
CHICKEN PILAF	*Kotopoulo Pilafi*
STUFFING FOR 12- TO 16-POUND TURKEY OR LARGE ROASTING CHICKENS	*Yemises Yia Galopoula-Kotas*

Chicken, although not too plentiful, is a favorite dish in Greece. It is sautéed, broiled, and stewed with many vegetables in savory sauces. The most popular way to roast a bird is to stuff it with a robust mixture of chopped vegetables combined with nuts, or fruit, or chopped meat, or rice, and seasoned with several herbs and aromatic spices. This will be a new taste experience for anyone who has never enjoyed a roast chicken or turkey à la Grecque.

Lemon plays an important role in the cooking of fowl in Greece. The cut-up bird is frequently marinated in olive oil and lemon juice and flavored with oregano before it is broiled or pot-roasted, and a bird is never oven-roasted without having its skin liberally rubbed with lemon juice both before and during cooking.

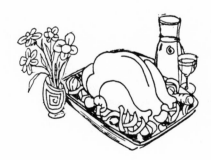

BROILED CHICKEN OREGANO
Kotopoulo Riganato tis Skaras

YIELD: 6 SERVINGS

MARINADE

½ cup olive oil
½ cup dry white wine
2 tablespoons dried oregano

1 tablespoon salt
1 teaspoon pepper
1 tablespoon minced garlic

one 2½- to 3-pound chicken,
  cut into serving pieces

Combine marinade ingredients in a bowl. Marinate chicken pieces for 2 hours in the refrigerator. Before broiling, bring to room temperature.

Remove chicken from marinade and put on a hot grill. Barbecue over charcoal or under oven broiler for 15 minutes on each side, or until golden brown, basting often with marinade.

CHICKEN KAPAMA
Kota Kapama

YIELD: 6 SERVINGS

one 3- to 4-pound chicken,
   cut into serving pieces
salt and pepper to taste
¼ teaspoon ground
   cinnamon
6 tablespoons butter
2 cups canned crushed
   tomatoes
one 6-ounce can tomato
   paste

1 teaspoon sugar
¾ cup water
3 sticks cinnamon
1 bay leaf
1 cup minced onions
1 tablespoon minced garlic
1 pound macaroni
1 cup grated kefalotiri
   cheese

Sprinkle chicken with salt, pepper, and cinnamon. In a Dutch oven, melt 2 tablespoons butter and brown chicken until golden on all sides.

In a bowl combine tomatoes, tomato paste, sugar, and water and pour mixture over chicken. Add cinnamon sticks and bay leaf.

In a medium-sized frying pan, melt 2 tablespoons butter and sauté onions and garlic until onions are wilted. Add to chicken. Bring to a boil, cover, and simmer until chicken is tender, 50 to 60 minutes.

In the last 20 minutes, cook macaroni according to package directions. Drain and empty into serving dish. Brown remaining butter and pour over macaroni.

Place macaroni on a large serving platter. Place chicken and sauce over macaroni and sprinkle with grated cheese.

CHICKEN BREASTS IN PHYLLO
Kotopites

YIELD: 4 SERVINGS

6 tablespoons butter, plus 1
  stick (¼ pound) butter,
  melted, for brushing
  phyllo
½ cup minced onions
½ pound mushrooms,
  minced fine
2 tablespoons minced
  parsley
1 teaspoon minced garlic
1 tablespoon all-purpose
  flour

¼ cup dry white wine
salt and pepper to taste
2 tablespoons vegetable oil
2 whole skinless, boneless
  chicken breasts, halved (4
  pieces), or 4 chicken
  cutlets
8 sheets phyllo pastry
1 cup breadcrumbs
½ pound feta cheese,
  crumbled

Preheat oven to 350 degrees.

In a skillet, heat 2 tablespoons butter and sauté onions until golden; remove and set aside. Heat 2 more tablespoons butter and sauté mushrooms until all juices have evaporated. Add onions, parsley, and garlic and sauté for 1 minute. Stir in flour and blend well. Add wine and stir over moderate heat until thickened. Season with salt and pepper to taste. Remove and set aside.

In the same skillet, melt 2 more tablespoons butter with oil and sauté chicken breasts (or cutlets) until lightly browned, about 1 minute on each side. Remove from heat.

Brush one sheet of phyllo at a time with melted butter (keep remaining sheets from drying out by covering with plastic wrap; see "How to Work with Phyllo," p. 312). Sprinkle with breadcrumbs, place a second sheet of phyllo on top of first, butter and sprinkle with breadcrumbs. Place chicken breast on the lower half of phyllo. Put a quarter of mushroom mixture and a quarter of feta over chicken. Fold up sides of phyllo over chicken, envelope-style. Repeat with remaining breasts. Butter chicken rolls well and place seam side down on an ungreased baking sheet. Bake for 35 minutes, or until golden. Serve warm.

Note: Recipe can be prepared and frozen, unbaked. To serve, bake unthawed in a preheated 350-degree oven for 50 minutes, or until golden.

CHICKEN-ARTICHOKE CASSEROLE
Kota me Anginares Plaki

YIELD: 6 SERVINGS

one 3-pound chicken, cut
   into serving pieces
½ cup minced onions
6 tablespoons butter
1½ teaspoons salt
½ teaspoon pepper
½ pound fresh mushrooms,
   cleaned and sliced

2 tablespoons flour
1 cup chicken stock
¼ cup dry white wine
one 15-ounce can artichoke
   hearts or two 10-ounce
   packages frozen artichoke
   hearts, thawed

Preheat oven to 375 degrees.

In a large skillet, brown chicken and onion in 4 tablespoons butter. Season with salt and pepper. Remove chicken and onions and put in a 2-quart casserole. Add remaining 2 tablespoons butter to the skillet and sauté mushrooms for 5 minutes. Sprinkle flour over mushrooms and stir in stock and wine. Simmer for 5 minutes, stirring constantly, until thickened and smooth. Arrange artichokes among chicken pieces. Pour mushroom sauce over chicken and artichokes. Cover and bake for 40 minutes, or until chicken pieces are tender.

CHICKEN WITH ORZO
Kritharaki me Kota

YIELD: 4 SERVINGS

1 stick (¼ pound) butter
½ cup minced onion
one 4-pound frying chicken,
 cut into serving pieces
2 cups water

1 cup orzo
salt and pepper to taste
½ cup grated kefalotiri
 cheese
2 cups plain yogurt

In a large skillet, melt butter, add onion, and cook slowly until soft. Add chicken and brown on all sides. Add water and bring to a boil. Add orzo, salt, and pepper. Lower heat and simmer, covered, for 30 to 40 minutes, or until chicken is tender and all the liquid is absorbed. Sprinkle with grated cheese and serve with plain yogurt on the side.

CHICKEN SOUVLAKIA
Souvlakia me Kota

YIELD: 6 SERVINGS

MARINADE

½ cup olive oil
¼ cup fresh lemon juice or
 wine vinegar

¼ cup red wine
½ tablespoon minced garlic
1 teaspoon dried oregano

3 whole chicken breasts,
 skinned and boned, or 6
 chicken cutlets, cut into
 bite-size squares
1 pound chicken livers
 (optional)

2 green peppers, each cut
 into 6 squares, for a total
 of 12 pieces
6 large mushroom caps, cut
 in half, or 12 small ones
12 cherry tomatoes

Combine marinade ingredients in a bowl. Add chicken and livers and marinate in the refrigerator for 3 hours. Using 12 long (8- to 9-inch) skewers, arrange alternating pieces of chicken, green pepper, mushroom, chicken liver, and the tomatoes. Brush with some of the marinade. Barbecue over charcoal or under broiler in the oven for 15 to 20 minutes, brushing with marinade and turning frequently.

Poultry

CHICKEN STEFADO
Kotopoulo Stefado

YIELD: 4 TO 6 SERVINGS

one 3- to 4-pound chicken, cut into serving pieces
4 tablespoons olive oil
½ cup minced onions
one 6-ounce can tomato paste
2 bay leaves
1 tablespoon whole allspice berries
1 tablespoon whole peppercorns
2 pounds small white onions, cleaned, or 2 pounds frozen onions, thawed

Brown chicken in oil in Dutch oven. Add minced onions and tomato paste; add enough water to cover ingredients. Place bay leaves, allspice, and peppercorns in a square of cheesecloth and tie into a pouch. Add to chicken, cover pot, and cook for 30 minutes. Add whole white onions to chicken and simmer until tender, about 30 minutes longer.

CHICKEN WITH SCALLIONS AND AVGOLEMONO
Kotopoulo me Avgolemono

YIELD: 4 TO 6 SERVINGS

one 3 to 4-pound chicken,
   cut into serving pieces
4 tablespoons butter
salt and pepper to taste
1 cup hot water
2 cups chopped scallions (in
   1-inch pieces), including
   green part

3 eggs
3 tablespoons fresh lemon
   juice
2 tablespoons chopped dill
   (optional)

In a Dutch oven melt butter and brown chicken until golden on all sides. Sprinkle with salt and pepper; add hot water and scallions. Cover and cook over low heat for 40 minutes.

In a small bowl, beat eggs, adding lemon juice slowly. Slowly add 1 cup hot broth from pot, beating eggs constantly to prevent curdling. Reduce heat to a simmer. Pour egg-lemon mixture into pot, stirring for a minute or so to keep it from curdling. Remove from heat, and place on serving platter. Add (optional) chopped dill.

CHICKEN WITH
SPINACH AVGOLEMONO
Kota me Spanaki Avgolemono

YIELD: 4 SERVINGS

4 tablespoons butter or
olive oil
one 4-pound frying chicken,
cut into serving pieces

1 cup chopped onions
1 cup water
salt and pepper to taste
3 pounds fresh spinach

AVGOLEMONO SAUCE

3 eggs
2 tablespoons flour

6 tablespoons fresh lemon
juice

Melt butter in a large skillet. Add chicken and onions, and brown lightly. Add water, salt, and pepper. Bring to a boil, cover, and simmer for 30 minutes. Wash spinach thoroughly and tear each leaf into 2 or 3 pieces. Scald in boiling water; remove and drain. Add spinach to chicken and cook for 15 to 20 minutes, or until chicken is tender. Remove from heat.

Prepare the Avgolemono Sauce

Beat eggs until frothy. Add flour and lemon juice, beating well. Slowly add some hot liquid from pot, beating constantly. Pour sauce into pot, shaking pot gently to distribute. Do not allow sauce to boil. Serve immediately with rice.

CHICKEN PILAF
Kotopoulo Pilafi

YIELD: 4 SERVINGS

one 2½- to 3-pound
   chicken, cut into serving
   pieces
8 tablespoons butter
salt and pepper to taste
⅛ teaspoon ground
   cinnamon
⅛ teaspoon ground cloves

⅛ teaspoon ground allspice
1 cup chopped onions
3 tablespoons tomato paste
¼ cup cold water plus 2
   cups boiling water
1 cup raw converted rice

In a Dutch oven, brown chicken in 4 tablespoons of butter with salt, pepper, and spices. Add onions and continue to brown. Dilute tomato paste in cold water and add to the chicken. Cover and simmer for about 20 minutes. Add boiling water and stir in rice. Cover and simmer for 20 minutes, or until chicken is tender.

Optional: When ready to serve, brown remaining 4 tablespoons butter and pour over chicken and rice.

STUFFING FOR
12- TO 16-POUND TURKEY OR
LARGE ROASTING CHICKENS
Yemises Yia Galopoula-Kotas

Poultry

YIELD: STUFFING FOR 12- TO 16-POUND TURKEY OR
2 LARGE CHICKENS

The traditional Greek stuffing for poultry includes chestnuts, which are plentiful in Greece.

1 cup minced onion
1 stick (¼ pound) butter
1 pound ground beef
1 chicken liver, chopped
  (optional)
2 tablespoons tomato paste
  (optional)
½ cup chopped parsley
½ cup chopped dill
½ teaspoon ground
  cinnamon

salt and pepper to taste
2 cups chicken stock
½ cup raw converted rice
2 cups water
1 pound cooked, shelled
  chestnuts, broken into
  large pieces
½ pound pine nuts
½ cup raisins or currants
1 apple, chopped (optional)

Brown onions in butter until golden. Add meat and optional liver and cook until no longer raw-looking. Add tomato paste, parsley, dill, cinnamon, salt, pepper, and chicken stock. Cover and simmer about 30 minutes, or until meat is cooked. Add rice, water, chestnuts, pine nuts, raisins, and apple. Continue to cook another 20 to 30 minutes, until liquid has been absorbed by rice. Stuff bird and truss.

Note: For one large chicken, use only half the above ingredients. Do not stuff bird until ready to roast.

MEATS

BEEF

BEEF WITH ARTICHOKES AND PINE NUTS	*Kreas me Anginares ke Koukounaria*
BEEF ONION STEW	*Stefado*
MACEDONIAN STUFFED CABBAGE WITH THICK AVGOLEMONO	*Sarmades me Avgolemono*
MEATBALLS	*Keftedes*
MANTI WITH PHYLLO	*Manti me Phyllo*
MOCK MANTI	*Aplo Manti*
BEEF WITH YOGURT IN PITA BREAD	*Fetes Vodines se Peta*
MOUSSAKA	
MOUSSAKA WITH ARTICHOKES	*Moussaka me Anginares*
STUFFED VEGETABLES	*Yemista Lahanika*
PASTITSIO	
PASTITSIO TRIANGLES	*Pastitsio Trigona*
PASTITSIO WITH EGGPLANT	*Pastitsio me Melitzana*
PASTITSIO WITH PHYLLO	*Pastitsio me Phyllo*
STUFFED GRAPE LEAVES WITH AVGOLEMONO SAUCE	*Dolmades me Avgolemono*

LAMB

TRADITIONAL ROAST LAMB WITH POTATOES	*Arni Psito me Patates*
ROLLED STUFFED LEG OF LAMB	*Gemisto Arni me Feta*

ROAST LAMB WITH ARTICHOKES	*Arni Psito me Anginares*
BARBECUED LEG OF LAMB	*Arni tis Souvlas*
ROLLED STUFFED BREAST OF LAMB	*Arnisio Rolo Gemisto*
BARBECUED WHOLE BABY LAMB	*Arni tou Galactos sti Souvla*
STUFFED CROWN ROAST OF LAMB	*Korona Arniou Gemisti*
HOLIDAY MEAT PIE	*Kreatopeta*
LAMB OR BEEF CASSEROLE WITH ORZO	*Kritharaki me Kreas*
LAMB CHUNKS IN PHYLLO	*Arni Exohiko*
LAMB AND PEAS CASSEROLE	*Arni me Araka Giouvetsi*
LAMB PIE WITH PHYLLO	*Peta me Arni*
LAMB SHANKS WITH LENTILS	*Arnisia Kotsia me Fakes*
LAMB SURPRISE	*Arni Kleftiko*
ARTICHOKES STUFFED WITH LAMB IN WINE SAUCE	*Gemistes Anginares me Saltsa Krassi*
LAMB WITH FRESH VEGETABLES	*Arni me Freska Lahanika*
LAMB WITH FRESH VEGETABLES AND AVGOLEMONO SAUCE	*Arni me Avgolemono*
LAMB WITH VEGETABLES	*Tourlou*
LITTLE SHOES	*Papoutsakia*
SHISH KEBAB	*Souvlakia*
MEAT WITH QUINCE	*Kreas me Kydonia*

PORK

ROAST SUCKLING PIG	*Ghourounaki Psito*
PORK WITH GREEN OLIVES	*Hirino me Prasines Elies*
PORK CHOPS WITH SAUERKRAUT	*Paidakia Hirina me Lahano Toursi*
FRESH HAM WITH CELERY, AVGOLEMONO	*Hirino Yahni me Selino Avgolemono*
FRESH HAM MAKARONADA	*Hirino Yahni Makaronada*
SAUSAGE SPARTAN-STYLE	*Loukaniko*

VEAL

STEWED VEAL *Sofrito*
VEAL WITH OLIVES *Kreas me Elies*

൫൫൫൫൫൫൫൫൫൫൫൫

L amb is the staple meat of Greece, and there are endless interesting and delicious ways of preparing it that are unknown today, for the most part, in America.

Spit-roasted spring lamb is traditional for the Easter feast that follows the long Lenten fasting. The lamb is often served with pilaf, and is sometimes stuffed with pilaf before it is roasted. Suckling pig is also spit-roasted over charcoal, although pork itself is not frequently used. Occasionally it is stuffed before roasting with a fascinating filling of crumbled feta cheese mixed with chopped parsley and subtly flavored with one of Greece's favorite herbs, oregano.

However, the majority of meat dishes in Greece are prepared in stews or casseroles. Cubed meat is simmered until tender with every kind of vegetable conceivable and served with the famous Greek egg-and-lemon sauce, avgolemono. Ground beef or lamb is used to stuff vegetables, grape leaves, and cabbage leaves, and is combined with eggplant in the famous moussaka.

Beef or rabbit stewed with onions in a highly seasoned sauce is called stefado. There is an interesting legend concerning this dish. Some bandits hiding on the outskirts of a mountain village smelled the mouthwatering aroma of a rabbit simmering in a pot on the outdoor stove of

a nearby cottage. The chief ordered his men to fetch the pot of stew, then proceeded to eat the entire dish while his fellow bandits looked on hungrily. (There must have been honor even among the bandits, for them not to turn on him!) The dish was so delicious that the bandit chief spared the village from plunder.

Throughout the meat chapter in this book you will find abundant use of tomatoes, onions, garlic, parsley, oregano, and cinnamon. These basic ingredients are the key to the savory, aromatic meat dishes of Greece, which could do much to provide blessed relief from the everlasting roasts, steaks, and chops served too frequently on American tables.

BEEF

BEEF WITH ARTICHOKES AND PINE NUTS
Kreas me Anginares ke Koukounaria

YIELD: 4 SERVINGS

2 tablespoons olive oil
1 tablespoon minced garlic
1½ pounds beef chuck, round, or London broil
2 cups beef stock
¼ teaspoon salt
¼ teaspoon pepper

¼ teaspoon ground cumin
one 10-ounce package frozen artichoke hearts, thawed, or one 15-ounce can, drained, rinsed, and halved
½ cup pine nuts

Heat oil in a casserole. Add garlic and beef and sauté over high heat until beef is browned on all sides. Add stock and seasonings and bring to a boil. Lower heat, cover, and simmer for 1½ to 2 hours, or until fork tender. Add artichokes and pine nuts. Simmer for 5 minutes. Slice beef and arrange on a serving plate. Garnish with artichoke hearts and pour sauce on top.

Meats

BEEF ONION STEW
Stefado

YIELD: 6 TO 8 SERVINGS

This version of stefado is delicious enough for the most demanding bandit chief!

3 tablespoons butter	3 pounds small white
3 pounds boneless beef	onions, peeled
chuck, cut into 2-inch	2 tablespoons minced garlic
pieces	1 teaspoon ground
1 cup red wine	cinnamon
2 cups tomato sauce	dash of dried oregano
4 tablespoons tomato paste	1 bay leaf, crushed
1 cup hot water	salt and pepper to taste
3 tablespoons olive oil	¼ cup minced parsley

Melt butter in a heavy casserole or Dutch oven; add meat and brown on all sides. Add ¼ cup wine and simmer for a few minutes. Add tomato sauce and tomato paste diluted in the hot water. Cover and continue to simmer.

In a skillet, heat olive oil. Add onions and brown. Transfer to the meat, along with garlic, cinnamon, oregano, bay leaf, salt, and pepper. Cover and simmer over very low heat for 1 to 1½ hours, or until meat is very tender. As the meat cooks, gradually add remaining wine. Sprinkle with parsley before serving.

MACEDONIAN STUFFED CABBAGE WITH THICK AVGOLEMONO
Sarmades me Avgolemono

YIELD: 8 TO 10 SERVINGS

This is a traditional regional dish from the northern part of Greece. The long cooking is necessary because of the pork filling.

boiling water
3 to 4 medium cabbages
  (about 40 cabbage leaves)
one 16-ounce can
  sauerkraut, drained
1½ pounds ground beef
1½ pounds ground pork

salt and pepper to taste
1 cup chopped onions
¾ cup raw converted rice
2 to 3 lemons, peeled and
  sliced

THICK AVGOLEMONO SAUCE

3 eggs
½ cup fresh lemon juice

2 cups hot chicken stock

Fill a large pot with water and bring to a boil. Remove outer leaves from cabbage heads, being careful not to tear them. Parboil about 5 minutes. Drain in a colander.

Place sauerkraut in bottom of Dutch oven. (Be sure to use a large pot, and do not fill to the top.) Cover with a few cabbage leaves. Thoroughly combine beef, pork, salt, pepper, onions, and rice. Carefully remove heavy center vein from steamed cabbage leaves and cut each leaf in half. Place 1 rounded tablespoon of meat mixture near cut end of leaf; fold over. Fold edges in toward center and roll up tightly. Place rolls in casserole with lemon slices between the layers. Cover with an inverted heavy plate to act as a weight. Add enough boiling water to cover rim of plate. Cover casserole, bring slowly to a boil, and simmer gently until liquid has been absorbed, about 1 hour.

When the rolls are cooked, prepare sauce

Beat eggs until frothy; add lemon juice. Gradually add hot stock, beating constantly. Pour into a saucepan and cook over low heat, stirring constantly, until sauce thickens. To serve, place several rolls on each dish and spoon some cooked sauerkraut over them; top with Thick Avgolemono Sauce. Serve immediately.

Note: Leftover steamed leaves can be frozen, wrapped in plastic wrap. To use, bring to room temperature.

Meats

MEATBALLS
Keftedes

YIELD: ABOUT 24 BALLS

1 pound onions, grated
1 tablespoon plus ½
   teaspoon salt
1 pound ground beef
salt and pepper to taste
1 teaspoon dried oregano
½ cup breadcrumbs

¼ teaspoon vinegar
¾ cup water
1 teaspoon dried mint
   (optional)
2 cups all-purpose flour
1 quart corn or vegetable oil
   for deep-frying

Add 1 tablespoon salt to grated onions and squeeze together. Put this pulp in a cheesecloth bag or strainer and let cold water run through it for 2 minutes. Squeeze the water from the pulp and place pulp in a bowl. Add ground beef, salt, pepper, oregano, breadcrumbs, vinegar, water, and mint. Put flour on a sheet of wax paper. Take a tablespoonful of meat mixture and drop on the flour. Roll meat in flour into a ball. Heat oil in a deep-fryer or large frying pan. Fry meatballs until golden brown. Serve warm or cold, accompanied with a green salad.

Note: This recipe can be served as an appetizer. Use 1 teaspoon rather than 1 tablespoon of meat per ball. Your yield will be about 48 balls.

MANTI WITH PHYLLO
Manti me Phyllo

YIELD: 72 PIECES

This regional dish from the north is quite unusual in that it calls for pligouri, a coarse wheat similar to bulgur, to be mixed with ground meat and covered with phyllo. Pligouri is available in Greek specialty shops.

½ cup chopped onion
2 tablespoons olive oil
1½ pounds ground beef
salt and pepper to taste
1 cup pligouri or bulgur
1 cup milk
¼ cup water

1 pound phyllo
2 sticks (½ pound) butter, melted, for brushing phyllo
2 to 3 cups hot chicken stock
2 cups plain yogurt

Preheat oven to 350 degrees.

Sauté onion in oil. Add ground beef and cook until well browned. Add salt and pepper. Add pnigouri or bulgur, milk, and water. Bring to a boil and cook until liquid has been absorbed.

Unroll the phyllo onto a flat surface. Using kitchen shears or a sharp knife, cut 4 x 4-inch squares through all the thicknesses. Take 4 squares of phyllo and cover the remainder with plastic wrap. Brush each square with melted butter and stack one on top of the other. (You are working with 4 phyllo sheets buttered together; treat as one.) Place a heaping teaspoon of the meat mixture in the center of the phyllo square; pick up the four corner edges and bring together to form a pouch. Press corners together to seal and place sack in a 10 x 16-inch baking pan. Continue this process until phyllo and/or filling are used up.

Do not crowd in the baking pan. Brush the top of each sack with more melted butter. Bake until golden, 35 to 45 minutes. As soon as the pan is removed from the oven, spoon boiling hot stock over each pouch with a baster (or use a teaspoon). Continue adding broth as long as it can be absorbed. Serve with yogurt on the side.

Note: This can be used as a first course.

Variation: Homemade dough can be used instead of phyllo. Use the following recipe:

2 cups flour	**2 tablespoons oil**
1 teaspoon salt	**¾ cup water**

Combine flour and salt. Work in oil and about ¾ cup water. Knead dough lightly. If it seems too stiff, add a little more oil and water, without making dough sticky. Set aside 1 hour to rest.

Preheat oven to 350 degrees.

Roll out dough thin on lightly floured board. Cut dough into 4 x 4-inch squares. Place a spoonful of filling in center of each square and bring corners together. Moisten edges, seal, and twist the angles. Arrange in the buttered pan. Prick pastry. Bake for 45 minutes, or until pastry is golden. Remove from oven and pour the hot chicken broth over the manti. Let stand until most of the broth is absorbed.

Mock Manti

Aplo Manti

YIELD: 6 SERVINGS

For the busy cook this Mock Manti is a simplified version of the original (see previous recipe), again using the wholesome pligouri wheat (available in Greek specialty shops) and yogurt. It is called mock because it is made without phyllo dough.

1½ pounds ground beef	1 teaspoon ground
1 cup minced onions	cinnamon
2 tablespoons butter,	1 cup pligouri or bulgur
melted	¼ cup milk
salt and pepper to taste	2 cups chicken stock
½ teaspoon ground cumin	2 cups plain yogurt

Brown meat and onions in melted butter. Add salt, pepper, cumin, cinnamon, pligouri or bulgur, milk, and stock. Cover and cook until liquid has been absorbed and grain is tender, about 30 minutes. Serve with yogurt on the side.

Beef with Yogurt in Pita Bread
Fetes Vodines se Peta

YIELD: 4 SERVINGS

A recent Greek dish called gyro is very popular in the United States. It is made with compressed meat and roasted on a vertical skewer. (Compressed meat consists of various cuts of beef that are chopped, minced, or ground, then compressed into a large cylindrical shape, put on a skewer, and broiled vertically.) This recipe is a good substitute for the commercial gyro and suitable for home preparation.

½ cup dry red wine
2 tablespoons olive or
    vegetable oil
2 teaspoons minced garlic
½ teaspoon dried oregano,
    crushed
½ teaspoon salt
dash of pepper
1 pound flank steak or
    London broil

1 tablespoon butter or
    margarine
4 pitas (see note)
3 cups chopped lettuce
1 cup peeled, seeded, and
    diced tomato
1 cup peeled, seeded, and
    diced cucumber
1 cup plain yogurt (see
    note)

Combine wine, oil, garlic, oregano, salt, and pepper. Cut steak into strips, 2 inches long by ¼ inch wide, or as thin as possible. Pour wine marinade over beef strips, and let stand for 1 hour at room temperature. Drain meat strips and cook, in two batches, in hot butter, stirring, for 2 to 3 minutes, or until brown on all sides. Serve meat in a chafing dish or on a hot tray to keep warm. Open one end of pita to make a pocket. Set out dishes of lettuce, tomato, cucumber, and yogurt. Allow each person to fill his own pita.

Note: In many cities, pita can be purchased in ethnic bakeries or in supermarkets under such names as "Syrian," "Greek," and "Arab" bread.

Note: Commercially purchased yogurt can be thickened by placing yogurt in a cheesecloth-lined sieve and letting it stand overnight in the refrigerator. Or, place a double thickness of paper towels directly over the top of yogurt to absorb the liquid. Refrigerate overnight, remove paper.

MOUSSAKA

YIELD: 10 TO 15 SERVINGS

Moussaka is a layered casserole that incorporates chopped meat and vegetables. The traditional dish is made with eggplant, but potato or zucchini can be used, either separately or combined. One variation is to make the bottom layer potato, put the meat in the center, and top with the eggplant. When potatoes are used, they are sliced, brushed lightly with oil, and broiled. Zucchini are also sliced and broiled.

5 large eggplants, about 1½ pounds each
salt
10 tablespoons butter
3 pounds ground beef
1½ cups chopped onion
2 tablespoons tomato paste
¼ cup chopped parsley
½ cup red wine
salt and pepper to taste
½ cup water
⅛ teaspoon ground cinnamon

¾ cup grated kefalotiri or Parmesan cheese
½ cup breadcrumbs
8 tablespoons all-purpose flour
4 cups hot milk
½ teaspoon salt
⅛ teaspoon pepper
⅛ teaspoon grated nutmeg
3 eggs, lightly beaten
vegetable oil for brushing eggplant

Remove ½-inch-wide strips of peel lengthwise from eggplants, leaving ½ inch peel between the strips. Cut into ½-inch rounds, sprinkle with salt, and let stand in a colander under a heavy or weighted plate for ½ hour. Rinse and dry eggplant rounds.

Melt 4 tablespoons butter in a saucepan and sauté meat and onion until brown. Add tomato paste, parsley, wine, salt, pepper, and water.

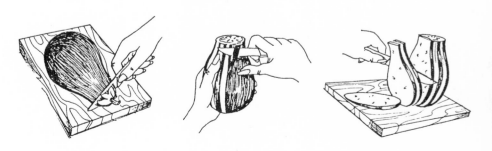

Simmer until liquid has been absorbed. Cool. Stir in cinnamon, ½ cup cheese, and half the breadcrumbs.

Meats

Prepare the sauce

Melt 6 tablespoons butter in a saucepan over low heat. Add flour and stir until well blended. Remove from heat, and gradually stir in milk. Return to heat and cook, stirring, until sauce is thick and smooth. Add salt, and pepper, and nutmeg. Combine eggs with a little of the hot sauce, then stir egg mixture into sauce and cook over very low heat for 2 minutes, stirring constantly.

Preheat broiler.

Lightly brush eggplant slices with oil on both sides. Place on an ungreased cookie sheet and broil until lightly browned. Set aside to cool.

Preheat oven to 350 degrees.

Sprinkle bottom of a 10 x 16-inch pan with remaining breadcrumbs. Place a layer of eggplant slices on the breadcrumbs, then spread meat mixture over eggplant slices. Cover meat with remaining eggplant slices. Spoon sauce over eggplant; sprinkle with remaining ¼ cup grated cheese. Bake for 40 minutes, or until golden. Cool for 10 minutes before cutting. Serve warm.

Note: Moussaka can be prepared up to the cream sauce and finished the next day. This can also be baked, cooled, frozen, and reheated.

MOUSSAKA WITH ARTICHOKES
Moussaka me Anginares

YIELD: 8 TO 10 SERVINGS

four 10-ounce packages
   frozen artichoke hearts
2 sticks (½ pound) butter
2 pounds ground beef
½ cup chopped onions
1 cup tomato sauce
½ cup white wine
2 tablespoons chopped fresh
   dill
salt and pepper to taste

6 tablespoons all-purpose
   flour
1 quart hot milk
2 eggs, lightly beaten
1 cup grated kefalotiri
   cheese
½ teaspoon white pepper
1 teaspoons salt
¼ cup breadcrumbs

Drop artichokes into boiling salted water, return to boil, and cook for 3 minutes. Drain thoroughly in a colander. Place in heatproof dish.

Brown 6 tablespoons butter. Pour over artichokes and set aside.

Sauté meat and onions in 2 tablespoons butter until lightly browned. Add tomato sauce, wine, dill, salt, and pepper; simmer for 15 minutes.

Preheat oven to 350 degrees.

Prepare the sauce

Melt 1 stick butter in a saucepan. Add flour and stir to blend. Gradually add milk and then the eggs, stirring constantly. Cook over low heat until sauce is smooth and thickened. Add ½ cup grated cheese and cook a few minutes longer, stirring constantly. Stir in white pepper and salt. Cover tightly and place over hot water to keep warm. Sprinkle the breadcrumbs over the bottom of a 9 x 13 x 1¾-inch roasting pan. Place half the artichokes over the breadcrumbs. Pour one third of the sauce over artichokes. Spread meat mixture over sauce. Pour in one third of the sauce, add the remaining artichokes, and cover with the final third of the sauce. Sprinkle with remaining grated cheese. Bake for 35 minutes, or until golden brown.

Note: Two 28-ounce cans of artichokes can be substituted for the frozen. Drain canned artichokes in a colander and rinse under cold water for 5 minutes to remove salty brine.

STUFFED VEGETABLES
Yemista Lahanika

YIELD: 6 SERVINGS

1½ cups chopped onions
5 tablespoons butter
2 pounds ground beef
salt and pepper to taste
¼ cup chopped flat-leaf
   parsley
¼ cup chopped mint
   (optional)

3 tablespoons tomato paste
3¼ cups water
1 cup raw converted rice
6 green peppers
6 tomatoes
2 potatoes, peeled and sliced
   (optional)

Preheat oven to 350 degrees.

Sauté onions in 3 tablespoons butter. Add beef and brown. Season with salt, pepper, parsley, and mint. Combine 1 tablespoon of tomato paste with 1½ cups of the water. Add rice and mix. Bring to a boil and cook until liquid has been absorbed by rice.

Cut thin slice from top of each pepper and tomato, scoop out insides, and arrange vegetables in greased baking pan. Stuff with meat and rice mixture and cap with tops of vegetables. Dilute remaining tomato paste in remaining water and add to pan. Sliced potatoes can be placed between vegetables if desired. Dot with remaining 2 tablespoons butter. Bake for about 1 hour, or until vegetables are done, basting with the pan sauce.

PASTITSIO

YIELD: 12 SERVINGS

Pastitsio is a layered pasta casserole that is extremely popular because it uses simple, basic ingredients.

THIN CREAM SAUCE

4 tablespoons butter	2 cups hot milk
⅓ cup all-purpose flour	2 egg yoks

THICK CREAM SAUCE

4 cups milk	½ cup all-purpose flour
4 eggs	

FILLING

1½ cups chopped onions	dash of ground cinnamon
2 pounds ground beef	salt and pepper to taste
4 tablespoons butter	1 tablespoon minced garlic
2 cups Italian plum tomatoes, chopped	1¼ pounds tubular pasta, such as ziti # 2
1 cup tomato sauce	½ cup breadcrumbs
1 teaspoon dried or 1 tablespoon fresh chopped oregano	1 cup grated kefalotiri or Parmesan cheese

Prepare thin sauce

Melt butter in saucepan. Stir in flour and cook until mixture turns golden. Gradually stir in hot milk and cook, stirring, until sauce is smooth and hot. In a small bowl, beat egg yolks, then briskly stir in 1 cup of hot milk mixture. Pour egg-milk mixture into remaining sauce. Stir and remove from heat without cooking the eggs.

Prepare thick sauce

Heat milk to a simmer and set aside. In a bowl, beat eggs with flour. Gradually stir hot milk into egg mixture. Return to saucepan and cook, stirring constantly, until mixture is quite thick. Do not boil after eggs have been added.

Brown chopped onions and meat in butter. Add tomatoes, tomato sauce, spices, and seasonings. Cover and simmer for 30 minutes, or until liquid has been absorbed. Cool.

Preheat oven to 350 degrees.

Cook pasta according to package directions, and drain. Sprinkle breadcrumbs into a buttered 11 x 14 x 2-inch baking pan. Place a layer of pasta in the baking pan; then add half the thin cream sauce. Add meat. Sprinkle with ¼ cup grated cheese. Add another layer of pasta and sprinkle with ¼ cup cheese. Cover with remaining thin cream sauce. Spread thick cream sauce over the top and sprinkle with remaining ½ cup cheese. Bake for 1 hour, or until golden. Let stand 15 minutes to cool, and cut into squares. (Note that you cannot cut the Pastitsio easily unless you cool it for 15 minutes.) When ready to serve, reheat in hot oven.

Note: This dish can be prepared a day in advance, adding the thick cream sauce just before baking the dish.

Meats

PASTITSIO TRIANGLES
Pastitsio Trigona

YIELD: 4 DOZEN

Pastitsio is a common Greek dish, but these turnovers are an unusual combination of pasta with phyllo. It is an excellent buffet or party dish.

1 pound large-size elbow macaroni	½ teaspoon pepper
2 sticks (½ pound) butter, plus 2 sticks (½ pound) butter, melted, for brushing phyllo	2 teaspoons cinnamon
	1 large bay leaf, crumbled
	1 cup tomato sauce
	¾ pound feta cheese, crumbled
1 cup finely minced onions	3 eggs, lightly beaten
1½ pounds ground beef	1 pound phyllo pastry
1 teaspoon salt	

Preheat oven to 350 degrees.

Cook macaroni according to package directions, rinse in cold water, and drain.

Melt 2 sticks butter in a large frying pan, add onions and meat and cook until meat has browned. Add salt, pepper, cinnamon, and bay leaf. When well browned, add tomato sauce and simmer until liquid has been absorbed.

When cool, add macaroni to the cooled meat mixture. In a separate bowl, mix feta with beaten eggs. Slowly add to macaroni mixture, mixing carefully. Cool in refrigerator for 1 hour.

Cut phyllo sheets in half, arrange in a single pile, and cover with plastic wrap. Work with one phyllo sheet at a time and leave the rest covered. Brush each sheet with butter; place a well-rounded tablespoon of the macaroni mixture (about the size of a small ice cream scoop) at the bottom of the sheet and form into a triangle (see "How to Work with Phyllo," p. 312). Place triangles on ungreased baking sheets and brush tops with melted butter. Bake for 30 minutes, or until golden.

Note: This versatile recipe can be served as a luncheon dish or first course. It can also be prepared in a 9 x 13 x 1¾-inch baking pan (layer half the buttered phyllo, all of the meat and macaroni mixture, then the remaining phyllo; brush with butter and bake until golden brown. To serve, cut into squares.) You can also cut the recipe in half or prepare it in advance and freeze before baking. To serve, bake in a preheated oven at 350 degrees, without prior thawing, for 1¼ hours, or until golden.

Meats

PASTITSIO WITH EGGPLANT
Pastitsio me Melitzana

YIELD: 6 TO 8 SERVINGS

1 cup chopped onions
4½ tablespoons butter
1 pound ground beef or lamb
2 cups crushed fresh or canned tomatoes
1 teaspoon salt
¼ teaspoon pepper
¼ teaspoon grated nutmeg
¼ teaspoon ground cinnamon
2 eggs, beaten
½ cup grated kefalotiri or Parmesan cheese

1½ cups elbow macaroni, cooked according to package directions and drained
1 medium-sized eggplant, about 1 pound, cut into ¼-inch-thick slices
1 tablespoon olive oil
1 teaspoon cornstarch
1½ cups milk, heated
3 eggs, beaten
salt and pepper to taste

Preheat oven to 350 degrees.

Sauté onions in 2 tablespoons butter until wilted. Add meat and cook until brown. Add tomatoes and cook until liquid has been absorbed. Season with salt, pepper, nutmeg, and cinnamon. Add 2 beaten eggs and ⅓ cup of the grated cheese. Combine meat mixture with macaroni and pour into a greased 13 x 9 x 2-inch pan. (Pan should be about half full.)

Preheat broiler.

(continued)

129

Brush eggplant slices with 1 tablespoon olive oil. Broil until lightly browned. Drain on paper towels, then place over the macaroni and meat mixture.

Prepare the sauce

Melt 2 tablespoons butter and blend in cornstarch. Gradually add hot milk and cook over low heat, stirring, until slightly thickened. Pour in 3 beaten eggs, stirring constantly. Season lightly with salt and pepper. Pour sauce evenly over pan ingredients. Sprinkle top with remaining butter, melted, and grated cheese. Bake for 45 minutes, or until sauce is set and golden brown. Cool about 5 minutes before slicing.

Note: This is an excellent buffet item, serving at least 16 when sliced thin.

PASTITSIO WITH PHYLLO
Pastitsio me Phyllo

YIELD: 30 SERVINGS

This variation of pastitsio is an excellent buffet or party dish because it yields a large number of pieces.

2 pounds lean ground beef	**2 tablespoons tomato paste**
1 cup chopped onions	**1 cup water**
1 stick (¼ pound) butter,	**1¼ pounds macaroni**
plus 1 stick butter (¼	**10 sheets phyllo pastry**
pound) melted, for	**3 cups grated kefalotiri**
brushing phyllo	**cheese**
2 teaspoons salt	**12 eggs**
¼ teaspoon pepper	**1 quart milk**
½ cup white wine (optional)	

Preheat oven to 350 degrees.

Sauté ground beef and onions in 4 tablespoons butter. Season with salt and pepper. Add wine, tomato paste, and water, and simmer until liquid has evaporated, about 40 minutes.

Cook macaroni according to package directions until almost done. Pour into colander; rinse with cold water and drain well. Mix with ½ cup melted butter.

Arrange 5 phyllo sheets, brushed one at a time with melted butter, in a 14 x 11-inch baking pan. Place half the macaroni in pan. Sprinkle with half of grated cheese and cover with beef mixture, spreading evenly over entire surface. Sprinkle with remaining grated cheese over meat and cover with remaining macaroni. Beat eggs until light and fluffy, and mix with milk. Carefully pour mixture over ingredients in pan. Top with 5 phyllo sheets, each brushed with the remaining melted butter. Bake for 30 to 40 minutes, or until golden on top and firm when tested with a knife. Let stand for 15 minutes before cutting into squares. (See "How to Work with Phyllo," p. 312, for cutting method.)

Note: Can be prepared a day ahead of time, baked, cooled, and cut into squares. Reheat before serving.

Meats

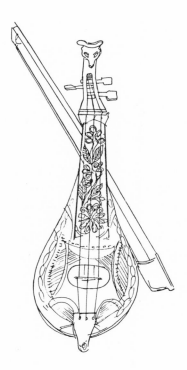

131

STUFFED GRAPE LEAVES WITH AVGOLEMONO SAUCE
Dolmades me Avgolemono

YIELD: 6 TO 8 SERVINGS

1½ pounds ground beef or lamb
1½ cups chopped onions
1 cup raw converted rice
salt and pepper to taste
1 teaspoon dried mint leaves or 3 tablespoons chopped fresh mint

¼ cup chopped fresh dill
¼ cup water
1-pound jar grape leaves
3 cups hot chicken stock
1 tablespoon butter
Avgolemono Sauce (see p. 175)

Combine meat, onions, rice, salt, pepper, mint, and dill. Add water and mix well.

Drain brine from jar of grape leaves and wash leaves well. Put 1 heaping tablespoon of meat and rice mixture in center of leaf's dull side and roll leaf tightly, folding edges over and rolling toward point of leaf.

Cover bottom of an ungreased Dutch oven or casserole with torn leaves. Arrange rolls in layers. Pour hot chicken stock over rolls and dot with butter. Cover with a heavy plate to keep rolls from opening as rice puffs. Cover casserole, and cook over low heat for 1 hour.

There should be some liquid left in casserole for Avgolemono Sauce (see p. 175). If dry when cooking time is up, add 1 cup water and simmer for a few minutes longer. Remove from heat and keep covered. Measure liquid and prepare the sauce. To serve, remove to plate and pour Avgolemono Sauce over dolmades.

Variation: Cabbage leaves can be substituted for grape leaves. The method of preparation is basically the same: Remove the core from a medium-sized round cabbage. Place whole cabbbage in boiling salted water, prying open leaves with two forks. Boil for 3 to 5 minutes. Drain off hot water and add cold water, until leaves are cool enough to work with. Cut each leaf in half, if large, and remove or trim heavy center vein. Roll as above, using the same method for cooking. Avgolemono Sauce is also poured over the stuffed cabbage. When preparing recipe with cabbage leaves, omit mint from seasoning.

LAMB

TRADITIONAL ROAST LAMB WITH POTATOES
Arni Psito me Patates

YIELD: 6 SERVINGS

one 6-pound leg of young
   spring lamb
2 to 3 cloves garlic, thinly
   sliced
salt and pepper to taste
1½ tablespoons dried
   oregano

4 tablespoons olive oil
6 tablespoons fresh lemon
   juice
20 small potatoes, peeled
2 tablespoons tomato paste,
   diluted in ¼ cup water
2 cups hot water

Preheat oven to 450 degrees.

Wash leg of lamb. Slit with a sharp knife in various places on both sides of lamb. Insert garlic slices in slits. Season with salt, pepper, and ½ tablespoon oregano, and brush with olive oil. Pour lemon juice over lamb and place in roasting pan, fat side up. Roast for about ½ hour.

While lamb is browning, combine salt, tomato paste, and water and pour over potatoes. Add to roasting pan; sprinkle with remaining oregano. Lower oven temperature to 350 degrees. Roast for 1½ hours, turning and basting the potatoes occasionally. Remove to a hot serving platter; slice and serve meat surrounded by potatoes.

ROLLED STUFFED LEG OF LAMB
Gemisto Arni me Feta

YIELD: 8 SERVINGS

MARINADE

¼ cup olive oil
3 tablespoons fresh lemon
   juice
¼ cup white wine
1 bay leaf, crushed

¼ teaspoon dried thyme, or
   ½ teaspoon dried oregano
1 tablespoon minced garlic
salt and pepper to taste

one 7- to 9-pound leg of
   lamb, boned and
   butterflied

STUFFING

8 scallions, finely chopped
1 cup chopped parsley
½ cup chopped dill

1½ tablespoons minced
   garlic
¾ pound feta cheese

GRAVY (OPTIONAL)

4 tablespoons butter
½ pound fresh mushrooms,
   sliced

3 tablespoons flour
¾ cup beef stock
1 cup water

Combine all ingredients for marinade and pour over lamb; refrigerate in a covered bowl for several hours or overnight.

When ready to bake, preheat oven to 350 degrees.

Combine chopped scallions, parsley, dill, and garlic. Crumble feta into herb-garlic mixture.

Remove lamb from marinade; reserve the marinade. Flatten lamb and spread the stuffing in the center. Fold one side of lamb over the other and tie securely. Place in roasting pan, pouring reserved marinade over. Bake for about 2½ hours. Serve with pan juices, or with gravy.

Melt butter and sauté mushrooms. Remove from pan and set aside. Add flour to pan and blend. Combine beef stock and water, add to pan, and stir over low heat until gravy thickens. Add reserved mushrooms.

Meats

ROAST LAMB WITH ARTICHOKES
Arni Psito me Anginares

YIELD: 6 SERVINGS

one 4-pound leg or
   shoulder of lamb
3 tablespoons olive oil
salt and pepper to taste
1 tablespoon dried oregano
3 tablespoons fresh lemon
   juice

2 cups water
two 10-ounce packages
   frozen artichoke hearts,
   thawed
parsley sprigs for garnish

Preheat oven to 450 degrees.

Rub meat with olive oil, salt, pepper, oregano, and lemon juice. Roast for 20 minutes, then reduce oven heat to 350 degrees. Add 1 cup water to the roasting pan, and cook 15 minutes longer. Add another cup of water to the pan and the artichoke hearts; continue cooking for 15 minutes, or until meat is done to taste. Baste occasionally with pan drippings. If necessary, add more water. Transfer meat to a serving platter and arrange the artichokes around it. Garnish with parsley.

Note: 6 fresh artichokes can be used instead of the frozen hearts. (See "How to Prepare Fresh Artichokes, p. 309.) Add two cups of water with the artichokes, and increase cooking time to 30 minutes.

BARBECUED LEG OF LAMB
Arni tis Souvlas

YIELD: 6 SERVINGS

MARINADE

1 cup olive oil
½ cup fresh lemon juice
2 cups red wine
1 tablespoon minced garlic

1 tablespoon salt
1 teaspoon pepper
2 tablespoons dried oregano

one 7-pound leg of lamb,
  boned and rolled

Combine all marinade ingredients in a bowl. Add lamb and marinate in the refrigerator for 4 hours, turning two or three times. Bring to room temperature before cooking.

Skewer lamb and place on rotisserie. Barbecue for 2½ hours, basting with the marinade to the desired degree of doneness.

Note: Lamb can be cooked in an indoor rotisserie oven. Preheat oven to 400 degrees. Bake for 2 to 2½ hours, basting frequently with marinade.

Rolled Stuffed Breast of Lamb
Arnisio Rolo Gemisto

YIELD: 6 SERVINGS

2 pieces breast of lamb, about 2 pounds each
salt and pepper to taste
8 tablespoons olive oil
½ pound ground beef or veal
½ cup minced scallion
½ cup white wine
1 pound ripe tomatoes, peeled, seeded, and chopped

2 tablespoons minced parsley
1 tablespoon minced dill
½ cup toasted breadcrumbs
½ cup grated kefalotiri cheese
3 tablespooons fresh lemon juice

Preheat oven to 400 degrees.

Dry lamb and sprinkle with salt and pepper. Set aside.

Heat 5 tablespoons oil in large skillet; add ground beef (or veal) and scallion, and brown lightly. Add wine, tomatoes, parsley, and dill. Cook over high heat for 15 minutes, or until all the liquid has evaporated. Remove from heat and cool partially. Add breadcrumbs and grated cheese.

Spread mixture on the lamb breast and roll it up carefully. Sew or tie the breast together. Rub surface of lamb with lemon juice and a little more salt and pepper. Put remaining olive oil into a baking pan; place the rolled meat in it and roast for 20 to 30 minutes, or until brown on all sides. Lower oven temperature to 325 degrees and roast for 2 hours, or until meat is tender. Cool slightly to make carving easier. Serve with green beans and sautéed carrots or other vegetables.

BARBECUED WHOLE BABY LAMB
Arni tou Galactos sti Souvla

YIELD: 12 TO 16 SERVINGS

The traditional Easter meal features a baby lamb cooked on a spit. In Greece, people go out to the countryside. Here in the States, the tradition continues.

MARINADE

2 cups olive oil

1 cup fresh lemon juice

3 tablespoons salt

1 tablespoon pepper

½ cup dried oregano

2 tablespoons minced garlic

one 12- to 16-pound baby lamb

Combine marinade ingredients in a bowl. Marinate lamb in refrigerator for several hours.

Tie legs of the lamb together. Push the hot white coals away from the center of the grill and place a sheet of aluminum foil in the free area to catch the falling fat. This will prevent the coals from igniting when the fat splatters on them. Barbecue lamb over charcoal or in an oven broiler for 3 to 4 hours, basting frequently with marinade.

STUFFED CROWN ROAST OF LAMB
Korona Arniou Gemisti

YIELD: 8 SERVINGS

one 4- to 5-pound crown
   roast of lamb
2 cloves garlic, slivered
2 tablespoons salt
½ teaspoon pepper
1½ tablespoons fresh lemon
   juice
1 small eggplant,
   approximately 1 pound
2 tablespoons vegetable or
   olive oil
½ cup minced onion
1 stalk celery, minced fine
¼ cup minced parsley
1 pound ground lean lamb
¼ teaspoon ground
   cinnamon

¼ teaspoon ground
   cardamom
¼ cup raisins
8 black Kalamata olives,
   pitted and chopped
½ cup cooked, chopped
   chestnuts, pine nuts, or
   walnuts
1 teaspoon grated lemon
   peel
1½ cups cooked rice or
   cooked orzo
salt and pepper to taste
Kalamata olives for garnish

Preheat oven to 350 degrees.

Pat meat dry. Make incisions all over the roast and insert garlic slivers. Rub with 1 tablespoon salt, pepper, and lemon juice. Put in a roasting pan.

Peel and cut eggplant into 1-inch cubes. Sprinkle with 1 tablespoon salt. Let stand for 15 minutes, then rinse and dry on paper towels. Sauté in hot oil until golden on all sides, then remove from pan. Add onion and cook until wilted, then add celery and cook until soft. Add parsley and ground meat. Sauté, separating with a fork, until golden brown. Add cinnamon, cardamom, raisins, chopped olives, chestnuts, lemon peel, rice, and cooked eggplant. Mix lightly. Season with salt and pepper to taste. Spoon into the roast. Wrap ends of bones with aluminum foil to prevent burning. Roast for 1½ hours or until meat is tender. Let stand 10 minutes before carving. Remove aluminum foil and decorate ends of bones with pitted olives.

HOLIDAY MEAT PIE
Kreatopeta

YIELD: 8 SERVINGS

This is a traditional Carnival time and Ascension Day recipe.

2½ pounds lean boneless
    shoulder or leg of lamb,
    cut into cubes
4½ cups warm water
1 cup minced onions
1½ cups chopped celery
1½ cups minced parsley
1 teaspoon minced garlic

1 teaspoon minced fresh
    mint, or ½ teaspoon
    dried mint
2 cups tomato sauce
½ cup olive oil
1 teaspoon salt
½ teaspoon pepper

CRUST

3½ cups all-purpose flour,
    sifted
1 teaspoon salt
3 tablespoons olive oil

1 egg
2 to 3 tablespoons warm
    water

4 eggs
1 cup grated kefalotiri or
    Parmesan cheese
1 teaspoon ground
    cinnamon

1 cup raw converted rice
1 tablespoon each, butter
    and olive oil for greasing
    pan
olive oil for brushing crust

Place meat in a large covered casserole with warm water; bring to a boil. Add the onions, celery, parsley, garlic, mint, tomato sauce, olive oil, salt, and pepper. Cover and cook over low heat for 1 hour.

While meat cooks, prepare the piecrust

Put sifted flour, salt, and olive oil into a bowl and mix well with a fork. Add egg. Gradually add warm water and stir until dough is well blended. Knead for 5 minutes, or until dough is firm. Chill thoroughly for at least 1 hour.

Preheat oven to 400 degrees.

Remove lamb from heat. Beat 4 eggs lightly and add grated cheese and cinnamon. Mix well, and add to meat mixture, along with rice. Divide chilled dough into two balls. Roll each ball out on a lightly floured surface to ⅛-inch thickness, making one piece big enough to line a 15 x 11-inch baking pan with a lip to turn over the top. The other piece should be large enough to fit the top of the pan. Grease pan with butter and olive oil; line with the larger piece of dough. Pour in meat mixture, spreading evenly. Cover with the second crust, turning the lip of the lower crust over, and crimp the edges. Brush lightly with olive oil. Prick with a fork. Bake for 45 minutes, or until crust is golden brown. Allow to set for a few minutes before cutting into squares.

Meats

Note: Crust can be prepared in a food processor. Combine all the ingredients and process until mixture forms a ball. Proceed as above.

LAMB OR BEEF CASSEROLE WITH ORZO
Kritharaki me Kreas

YIELD: 5 TO 6 SERVINGS

2½ pounds boneless lamb
   or beef chuck
1 stick (¼ pound) butter or
   ½ cup vegetable or
   olive oil
¼ cup minced onion
8-ounce can tomato sauce,
   or 4 to 5 medium ripe
   fresh tomatoes, peeled,
   seeded, and chopped

¼ teaspoon each salt and
   pepper
2 cups water
6½ cups boiling water
½ pound orzo
1 cup grated kefalotiri
   cheese

Preheat oven to 350 degrees.

Cut meat into bite-sized pieces. Melt butter in a large casserole. Add meat, onion, tomato sauce or tomatoes, salt, pepper, and 2 cups water; mix well. Cover and bake for 1 hour, or until meat is tender.

Add 6½ cups boiling water and orzo to meat mixture. Stir well and continue baking for ½ hour. Serve at once with grated cheese.

Lamb Chunks in Phyllo
Arni Exohiko

YIELD: 15 SERVINGS

The word *exohiko* means countryside and reveals the origins of this recipe. Easily prepared ahead of time, it is an ideal dish for picnics and cookouts.

one 6- to 8-pound leg of lamb
2 to 3 cloves garlic, slivered
salt and pepper to taste
dried oregano to taste
3 sticks (¾ pound) butter, melted
3 tablespoons fresh lemon juice
2 cups hot water
2 carrots, diced
½ cup celery, diced

4 to 5 very small onions, peeled
2 cups Béchamel Sauce (see p. 176)
2 cups cooked vegetables (such as chopped artichoke hearts, peas, or cut green beans)
1 pound phyllo pastry
2 cups fresh breadcrumbs
½ pound feta cheese, crumbled

Preheat oven to 450 degrees.

With a sharp knife make incisions all over lamb and insert garlic slivers. Season with salt, pepper, and oregano. Brush with melted butter. Pour lemon juice over lamb and place it in a roasting pan, fat side up. Roast for ½ hour. Lower oven temperature to 350 degrees and add hot water, carrots, celery, and onions. Roast for 1½ hours, adding more water if necessary. Remove from oven when lamb is done (150 degrees on a meat thermometer). Cut meat into 1-inch cubes. Make a thick Béchamel Sauce using the pan juices for stock. Add any vegetable you desire to the sauce.

Oven temperature should remain at 350 degrees.

Unwrap phyllo and quickly cover with plastic wrap (see "How to Work with Phyllo," p. 312). Brush one sheet of phyllo with melted butter, sprinkle with breadcrumbs, and place a second sheet of phyllo on top of the first; butter and sprinkle with breadcrumbs. Place several pieces of meat, 1 heaping tablespoon of sauce with vegetables, and crumbled feta on lower half of phyllo. Fold up the sides of the phyllo, envelope-style. Continue this procedure until all phyllo and/or filling ingredients are used up. You should have 15 phyllo envelopes. Brush tops with melted butter. Place on ungreased baking sheet seam side down and bake for 30 to 45 minutes, or until golden.

Note: Recipe can be prepared and frozen, unbaked. To serve, preheat oven to 350 degrees. Bake, unthawed, for 1 hour, or until golden.

LAMB AND PEAS CASSEROLE
Arni me Araka Giouvetsi

YIELD: 6 SERVINGS

4 pounds boneless chuck of lamb or ½ leg of lamb (about 4 pounds), cut into cubes
salt and pepper to taste
1½ pounds fresh tomatoes, peeled, seeded, and chopped, or 1 pound crushed canned tomatoes, drained and chopped

1 stick (¼ pound) butter, melted
3 pounds fresh peas or 2 pounds frozen peas, thawed
1 to 2 cups water
¼ cup chopped fresh dill

Preheat oven to 325 degrees.

Pat meat dry, season with salt and pepper, and put in a casserole. Add one third of the tomatoes and melted butter and bake for 1 hour, or until meat is nearly tender. Meanwhile shell, wash, and drain peas, if you are using fresh. Add remaining tomatoes and water to cover the meat, about 1 to 2 cups. When it begins to simmer, add fresh peas and dill. Sprinkle with additional salt and pepper. Cook slowly for 15 minutes, or until peas are tender. (If frozen peas are used, add during the last 5 minutes of cooking.)

LAMB PIE WITH PHYLLO
Peta me Arni

YIELD: 12 SERVINGS

1½ pounds boned lean
    shoulder of lamb
3 tablespoons butter, plus 1
    stick (¼ pound), melted,
    for brushing phyllo
1 teaspoon salt
½ teaspoon pepper
½ cup finely minced onion
1 cup diced potatoes,
    cooked until barely tender
¾ cup crumbled feta cheese
½ cup cooked rice
    (optional; if not used,
    increase amount of potato
    by ½ cup)

½ cup chopped celery
¼ cup minced parsley
¼ cup olive oil
½ teaspoon crushed dried
    mint
½ teaspoon ground
    cinnamon
salt and pepper to taste
12 sheets phyllo pastry

Wipe lamb with paper towels and cut into ½-inch cubes. Melt 3 tablespoons butter in a large skillet, add lamb cubes, and brown well. (You will probably have to do this in two batches.) Transfer cubes to a mixing bowl using a slotted spoon and sprinkle with salt and pepper. In fat remaining in the skillet, sauté onion until wilted. Toss onion with lamb and add potatoes, feta, rice, celery, parsley, olive oil, mint, and cinnamon, and more salt and pepper to taste.

Preheat oven to 350 degrees.

Brush bottom and sides of an 11¾ x 7½ x 1¾-inch baking dish with melted butter. Brush 1 phyllo sheet with melted butter and place in the pan so that half the sheet hangs over rim. Arrange 5 more sheets in pan in the same manner so that bottom and sides of pan are entirely covered with overlapping phyllo. (Butter each sheet separately; keep remaining phyllo covered with plastic wrap to prevent drying out. See "How to Work with Phyllo," p. 312.) Spread meat filling evenly over phyllo and fold overhanging edges of phyllo over the filling. Butter remaining phyllo sheets and arrange over the filling, folding where necessary to accommodate the pan. Brush top with remaining butter, and with a sharp knife score it into 12 squares, but do not cut all the way through. Bake for 45 minutes, or until golden. Let stand for 5 minutes, then cut through the squares to separate.

Note: Recipe can be prepared and frozen, unbaked. When ready to use, preheat oven to 350 degrees. Remove from freezer and bake, unthawed, for 1 hour and 15 minutes, or until golden.

LAMB SHANKS WITH LENTILS
Arnisia Kotsia me Fakes

YIELD: 6 SERVINGS

6 medium lamb shanks,
 about 8 ounces each
2 tablespoons vegetable or
 olive oil
½ cup water
2 teaspoons minced garlic
2 teaspoons salt
⅛ teaspoon dried oregano

pepper to taste
1½ cups lentils
3 cups water
1 small onion, studded with
 3 whole cloves
½ cup chopped celery
1 bay leaf
6 thin lemon slices

In a large skillet, brown lamb shanks in hot oil. Add ½ cup water, garlic, ½ teaspoon salt, oregano, and pepper. Cook, covered, over low heat for 1 hour, or until meat is tender.

Rinse lentils and drain. In a medium-sized saucepan, combine lentils with 3 cups water, onion, celery, bay leaf, and 1½ teaspoons salt. Simmer, covered, for 50 to 60 minutes, or until vegetables are tender. If mixture is too thick, add a little more water.

Preheat oven to 350 degrees.

Pour lentil mixture into a greased 10-inch baking dish. Top with meat and lemon slices. Bake 30 to 35 minutes, or until liquid is absorbed and lentils are tender. Discard onion and bay leaf before serving.

Note: This dish can be prepared ahead and baked before serving.

LAMB SURPRISE
Arni Kleftiko

YIELD: 8 SERVINGS

one 4-pound boneless leg of
   lamb or 8 shoulder lamb
   chops
8 slivers garlic
eight 1-inch cubes feta or
   kasseri cheese
8 small carrots, cut in half
8 small white onions
8 small stalks celery, cut
   into 2-inch pieces

8 small potatoes, peeled,
   halved, and buttered with
   4 tablespoons melted
   butter
3 tablespoons fresh lemon
   juice
salt and pepper to taste
1 tablespoon dried oregano
1 tablespoon dried mint

Preheat oven to 350 degrees.

If using leg of lamb, cut meat into eight 4- to 5-inch serving pieces.
Make incisions in meat and insert slivers of garlic. Place each piece of
meat on a large square of heavy-duty aluminum foil. Add 1 cube of
cheese, and distribute the vegetables evenly among the eight packets.
Add a few drops of lemon juice, salt, pepper, oregano, and mint. Fold
the foil in double fold at top and seal like a package. Arrange packages
close together in a baking pan and bake 1½ to 2 hours. Serve each foil
package, sealed, on dinner plate and let each guest open his own.

Variation: Other vegetables can be used, such as 4 small zucchini,
cut up; 4 ripe tomatoes, quartered; 4 green peppers, cut into eighths; 2
medium eggplants, peeled and cubed; 8 frozen artichoke hearts, thawed;
or 8 whole mushrooms.

ARTICHOKES STUFFED WITH LAMB IN WINE SAUCE

Gemistes Anginares me Saltsa Krassi

Meats

YIELD: 4 SERVINGS

4 whole fresh artichokes
1 pound ground lamb
¾ cup chopped onions
2 tablespoons olive oil
½ cup fine dry breadcrumbs

¼ cup minced parsley
2 eggs, beaten
½ teaspoon salt
¼ teaspoon pepper
¼ teaspoon grated nutmeg

WINE SAUCE

¼ cup white wine
1 tablespoon minced onion
½ cup olive oil
¼ cup white vinegar
2 tablespoons minced
  parsley

1 tablespoon fresh lemon
  juice
salt and pepper to taste

Preheat oven to 375 degrees.

Wash artichokes and cut off stems close to the base. Cook in boiling salted water to cover for 25 to 30 minutes, or until stalks can be pierced easily with a fork. Drain upside down. Cut off top third of leaves with kitchen shears; remove center leaves and chokes.

Lightly brown lamb and onions in oil; add breadcrumbs, parsley, eggs, salt, pepper, and nutmeg and mix well. Spread artichoke leaves slightly apart and fill centers with meat mixture. Place in a 9 x 9 x 2-inch baking dish. Pour hot water around artichokes to a depth of one inch. Bake, uncovered, for 30 to 35 minutes, or until heated through.

Prepare wine sauce

Combine wine and onion in a small saucepan. Add olive oil, vinegar, parsley, lemon juice, salt, and pepper; mix well. Cook until mixture is heated through, but do not boil. Serve the stuffed artichokes with the wine sauce.

LAMB WITH FRESH VEGETABLES
Arni me Freska Lahanika

YIELD: 6 SERVINGS

Another popular lamb casserole uses fresh vegetables with a light tomato sauce. Once again, the vegetable combinations are endless. Note that cabbage, fava beans, and brussels sprouts take the longest to cook. Eggplant, okra, celery, potatoes, and string beans take a moderate time to cook; dandelion greens, peas, spinach, and zucchini take the least time.

3 pounds boneless lean shoulder of lamb, or other lamb stew meat	1 cup water
	salt and pepper to taste
	¼ cup chopped parsley
4 tablespoons butter	your choice of vegetables
1½ cups minced onions	(see below)
1 cup tomato sauce	lemon wedges

Cut lamb into 3-inch pieces. Melt butter in a saucepan or casserole; add meat and onions and brown well over moderate heat. Add tomato sauce, water, salt, pepper, and parsley. Bring mixture to a boil, cover, and simmer for 45 minutes, or until meat is tender. Add more water if necessary. Add vegetables and cook according to instructions below. Serve with lemon wedges.

VEGETABLES

Brussels sprouts—2 pounds, cleaned. Cook 45 minutes with meat.

Cabbage—1 large head, cut into wedges. Cook 45 minutes with meat.

Celery—3 bunches, cut into 2- to 3-inch pieces. Cook 30 minutes with meat.

Dandelion greens—2 pounds, chopped. Cook 20 minutes with meat.

Eggplant—2 to 3 large, peeled and cut into 2-inch cubes. Place in large bowl or colander and lightly salt. Cover with heavy plate to drain for 15 minutes; rinse and dry. Cook 30 minutes with meat.

Fava beans—2 to 3 pounds, shelled. Any tender outer skins can be added with beans to casserole. Add ½ cup chopped fresh dill. Cook 45 minutes with meat.

Okra—2 pounds, trimmed, or two 10-ounce packages frozen okra, thawed. Cook 30 minutes with meat.

Peas—3 pounds, shelled, or 2 pounds frozen peas, thawed. Cook 5 minutes with meat.

Potatoes—6 to 8, peeled and quartered. Add 1 teaspoon cinnamon. Cook 30 minutes with meat.

Spinach—3 pounds, chopped. Cook 10 to 15 minutes with meat.

Green beans—2 pounds, trimmed. Cook 30 minutes with meat.

Zucchini—2 pounds, scrubbed well and cut into 3-inch pieces. Cook 20 minutes with meat.

Note: In Greek cooking, the vegetables are cooked to a well-done stage; they are not served crispy.

LAMB WITH FRESH VEGETABLES AND AVGOLEMONO SAUCE
Arni me Avgolemono

YIELD: 6 TO 8 SERVINGS

Lamb is the staple meat in Greece, and the combinations of meat and vegetables are endless. The general procedure is to sauté the lamb pieces, add the vegetables, and finally prepare the avgolemono, which covers the completed dish.

3 pounds lean boneless shoulder of lamb or chuck of lamb
8 tablespoons (¼ pound) butter
1½ cups minced onions
2 cups water

salt and pepper to taste
½ cup chopped dill
3 tablespoons fresh lemon juice
your choice of vegetables (see below)

AVGOLEMONO SAUCE

3 eggs
2 tablespoons flour
½ cup fresh lemon juice

1 cup hot liquid (from cooked lamb)

Cut lamb into 3-inch pieces. Melt butter in a saucepan or casserole, add meat and onions, and brown well over moderate heat. Add water, salt, pepper, dill, and lemon juice. Bring mixture to a boil, cover, and simmer for 1 hour, or until meat is tender. Add vegetables and cook according to instructions below.

Meats

Fresh artichokes—12 small artichokes and ½ cup chopped fresh dill. Cook 1 hour with meat. (See "How to Prepare Fresh Artichokes," p. 309.)

Frozen artichokes—Three 10-ounce packages frozen artichoke hearts, thawed, and ½ cup chopped fresh dill. Cook ½ hour with meat.

Broccoli—2 bunches, chopped. Cook 45 minutes with meat.

Cauliflower—2 heads, cut into florets. Cook 45 minutes with meat.

Celery—3 bunches, cut into 2- to 3-inch pieces. Cook 30 minutes with meat.

Celery and leeks—1½ bunches celery and 1½ bunches leeks. Trim and rinse celery. Slit leeks lengthwise; remove tough outer leaves. Rinse thoroughly under cold water to remove sand. Cut leeks and celery into 2-inch pieces. Cook 30 minutes with meat.

Escarole—2 pounds. Remove tough outer leaves; separate leaves and rinse to remove sand; cut up into bite-size pieces. Cook 15 minutes.

Leeks—2 bunches. Slit leeks lengthwise; remove tough outer leaves. Rinse thoroughly under cold water to remove sand and cut into 2-inch pieces. Cook 30 minutes with meat.

Spinach—3 pounds, chopped. Cook 10 minutes with meat.

When vegetables are cooked, remove casserole from heat.

Prepare the Avgolemono Sauce

Beat eggs until light; add flour and lemon juice and mix well. Add about 1 cup of hot liquid from casserole to egg mixture very slowly, stirring constantly. Pour into stew slowly, shaking pan until sauce mixes with liquid in casserole. Serve immediately.

LAMB WITH VEGETABLES
Tourlou

YIELD: 6 SERVINGS

Tourlou is a stew of mixed vegetables and lamb.

1 cup chopped onion
4 tablespoons butter
2 pounds lean boneless
   shoulder or leg of lamb,
   cut into 2-inch cubes
1½ cups water
3 medium tomatoes
2 small zucchini

1 medium eggplant
¼ pound okra (optional) or
   one 10-ounce package
   frozen okra, thawed
2 large green peppers
½ pound green beans
salt and pepper to taste

Sauté onion in butter in large saucepan or casserole until lightly browned. Add meat and water and simmer about ½ hour, or until nearly tender.

While meat is cooking, prepare vegetables: Peel and slice tomatoes and zucchini. Remove lengthwise 1-inch strips of eggplant skin, leaving 1-inch strips of skin between, and cut eggplant into 2-inch-thick rounds. Trim okra by removing cone-shaped portions at top. Discard seeds from green peppers and dice. Cut ends of beans, string if necessary, and slit lengthwise. When meat is nearly tender, add salt and pepper. Add beans, zucchini, eggplant, tomatoes, green pepper, and okra, in that order. Cover tightly and cook until vegetables are done, about 20 minutes. If necessary, add hot water during cooking.

LITTLE SHOES
Papoutsakia

YIELD: 6 SERVINGS

Papoutsakia is the Greek word for little shoes, which these eggplant shells filled with chopped meat resemble.

6 baby eggplants
olive oil
3 tablespoons butter
1 cup chopped onions
½ pound ground lamb or
   beef
salt and pepper to taste

1 tablespoon chopped
   flat-leaf parsley
½ cup tomato sauce
½ cup grated kefalotiri or
   Parmesan cheese
1 cup tomato sauce

Cut eggplants in half lengthwise. Scoop out pulp and chop; set aside.

Lightly brush eggplant shells with oil on both sides. Broil until they begin to soften, then transfer to a lightly greased baking dish.

Place 2 tablespoons butter in a skillet and sauté onions until golden. Add meat and continue to cook until meat is browned. Add eggplant pulp, salt, pepper, parsley, and ½ cup tomato sauce. Mix well and simmer until most of the liquid has evaporated. Cool. Add ¼ cup grated cheese and mix well.

Preheat oven to 350 degrees.

Fill eggplant shells with meat mixture and top each "little shoe" with remaining grated cheese. Dot with remaining butter. Add 1 cup tomato sauce to pan. Bake until eggplants are soft, about 15 minutes. Serve hot.

Variation: A béchamel sauce can be added to the top of the "little shoes." Use half the quantity of Béchamel Sauce (see p. 176). Stuff eggplant and spread a little of the sauce over the stuffing. Sprinkle with grated cheese. Cook in a 350-degree oven until sauce is browned and eggplant is tender.

Variation: 6 zucchini cut lengthwise can be used instead of eggplants.

SHISH KEBAB
Souvlakia

YIELD: 8 SERVINGS

one 7- to 8-pound leg of
   lamb
1 cup olive oil
⅓ cup fresh lemon juice
½ cup red wine
salt and pepper to taste
1 tablespoon fresh or 1
   teaspoon dried oregano
1 tablespoon minced garlic

2 bay leaves
24 cherry tomatoes
1 large Spanish onion,
   about ½ pound,
   quartered and separated
4 medium green peppers
   (1 pound), cut into 1-inch
   squares
24 mushroom caps

Cut lamb into 1- to 2-inch cubes. Combine olive oil, lemon juice, and wine and pour over meat. Sprinkle with salt and pepper, oregano, and garlic. Add bay leaves, tomatoes, onion, and pepper. Weigh down with a heavy plate, cover, and refrigerate several hours or overnight.

Skewer meat, alternating with tomatoes, onion, green pepper, and mushroom caps. Use 4 to 5 pieces of meat per skewer, alternating with vegetables. Cook skewers over charcoal (or in oven broiler), basting and turning occasionally, for about 20 to 25 minutes, or until cooked to taste.

Variation: Pork or beef cubes can be substituted. Marinate according to recipe. Increase cooking time approximately 20 to 40 minutes, depending on meat used.

MEAT WITH QUINCE
Kreas me Kydonia

YIELD: 6 SERVINGS

Quince is an extremely popular fruit that grows throughout Greece. This dish incorporates the unique flavor of cooked quince with the meat.

1 cup chopped onions	2 cups water
3 pounds boneless lamb or pork, cut into 2-inch cubes	4 pounds quince
	1 cinnamon stick
	salt and pepper to taste
4 tablespoons butter or olive oil	1 tablespoon sugar

Sauté onions and meat in butter until onions are soft and meat is browned. Add water, bring to a boil, cover, and simmer for about 1 hour, or until meat is almost tender.

Peel and core quince and cut into thick slices. Be sure black seeds are all removed. Add quince to meat; add cinnamon, salt, pepper, sugar, and more water if necessary. Continue to cook until meat is very tender and quince is soft, about 1 hour.

Variation: This dish can be prepared with one 4-pound chicken, quartered. Brown the chicken pieces and follow procedure above.

PORK

Roast Suckling Pig
Ghourounaki Psito

YIELD: 6 SERVINGS

1 suckling pig, 10 to 12
   pounds
salt and pepper to taste
2 lemons, halved
½ cup olive oil

¼ cup fresh lemon juice
1 tablespoon rosemary or
   thyme
1 apple

Preheat oven to 450 degrees.

Carefully clean a small suckling pig, wash inside and out with cold water, and dry thoroughly. Rub inside and out with salt, pepper, and cut lemons, saving 1 of the lemon halves. Let stand for about 1 hour.

Pull front legs of pig forward and tie together. Wedge mouth open with a small piece of wood. Combine olive oil, lemon juice, and thyme; brush pig generously with this mixture.

Place pig on a rack in roasting pan and roast for 30 minutes. Reduce temperature to 325 degrees and continue roasting for about 4 hours, or until thoroughly cooked (185 degrees on a meat thermometer). Baste often, using lemon half dipped in pan drippings as baster. To serve, untie legs and replace wedge of wood in mouth with a shiny red apple.

Note: A suckling pig prepared as above can also be skewered and cooked over charcoal. Allow 4 to 5 hours cooking time and turn often.

PORK WITH GREEN OLIVES
Hirino me Prasines Elies

YIELD: 6 SERVINGS

2 pounds pork tenderloin
2 tablespoons butter or
  margarine
1 teaspoon minced garlic
2 tablespoons slivered
  almonds
1½ teaspoons salt
¼ teaspoon pepper
1 cup sliced onions

½ pound sliced mushrooms
  (optional)
1 cup dry white wine
1 teaspoon minced mint
  (optional)
2 tablespoons minced
  parsley
12 pitted tsakistes green
  olives (see note)

Cut pork into 1-inch-thick slices; cut slices in half. Melt butter in a large Dutch oven and brown meat with garlic and almonds. Season with salt and pepper. Add onions, mushrooms, wine, mint, and parsley. Cover and simmer for 45 minutes, or until pork is tender. Add olives and heat.

Note: Tsakistes are cracked green olives that are marinated in herbs and brine. They can be purchased in Greek specialty shops.

Variation: Omit slivered almonds and tsakistes olives. Slice 12 green olives stuffed with almonds and add with 2 tablespoons fresh lemon juice to the cooked tenderloin. Heat to blend flavors.

PORK CHOPS WITH SAUERKRAUT
Paidakia Hirina me Lahano Toursi

YIELD: 4 TO 6 SERVINGS

Pork is frequently served in northern Greece, particularly in Kastoria.

2 tablespoons butter
6 to 8 pork chops, center
   cut, trimmed
2 pounds sauerkraut
2 tablespoons tomato paste,
   diluted in ½ cup water

1 tablespoon olive oil
1 teaspoon paprika or
   caraway seeds
2 cups water
salt and pepper to taste

In skillet melt butter and brown pork chops well. Drain sauerkraut and place in a casserole. Add diluted tomato paste, olive oil, and paprika or caraway seeds to sauerkraut. Place chops on top of sauerkraut and add pan drippings. Add water, salt, and pepper. Cover and simmer for about 1 hour, or until chops are very tender.

Note: The casserole can be baked in a 350-degree oven for 1 hour.

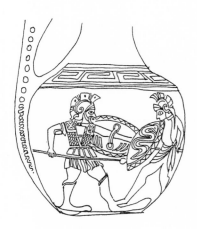

Fresh Ham with Celery, Avgolemono

Hirino Yahni me Selino Avgolemono

YIELD: 8 SERVINGS

This is the traditional Christmas dish from Sparta and Mani in the Peloponnesus.

one 4- to 5-pound fresh ham	salt and pepper to taste
4 tablespoons butter	2 bunches celery
1½ cups chopped onion	

AVGOLEMONO SAUCE

4 eggs	¾ cup fresh lemon juice
2 tablespoons flour	

Cut ham into 2-inch cubes. Brown in butter with onion. Add water to cover and salt and pepper. Bring to a boil, cover, and simmer until meat is almost done, about 1 hour.

Scrub and scrape celery and cut into 2-inch pieces. Add celery to meat and more water to cover; simmer an additional 30 minutes, until meat and vegetable are done.

Prepare the Avgolemono Sauce

Beat eggs in a small bowl until frothy. Add flour and lemon juice, beating well. Slowly add 2 cups hot liquid from the pot, beating constantly. Remove pot from heat. Pour sauce back into pot, shaking gently to distribute. Do not allow sauce to boil. Serve immediately.

FRESH HAM MAKARONADA
Hirino Yahni Makaronada

YIELD: 8 TO 10 SERVINGS

6 pounds fresh ham
2 sticks (½ pound) butter
1 teaspoon salt
½ teaspoon pepper
½ teaspoon ground
   cinnamon
1½ cups chopped onion

2 cups tomato puree
8 cups water
3 cinnamon sticks
1½ pounds macaroni
1 cup grated kefalotiri or
   Parmesan cheese, for
   topping

Cut ham into 3-inch cubes. In skillet brown meat in 4 tablespoons butter; add salt, pepper, and ground cinnamon. In a large casserole brown onion in 4 tablespoons butter. Add meat, tomato puree, water, and cinnamon sticks. Simmer about 3 hours, until sauce is thick and meat well done.

Cook macaroni according to package directions. Drain and empty into serving dish. Brown remaining ¼ pound butter in a small skillet. Pour browned butter over macaroni; add grated cheese. Pour sauce and meat over all. Serve immediately.

SAUSAGE SPARTAN-STYLE
Loukaniko

Meats

YIELD: 2 TO 3 SERVINGS

This savory luncheon dish goes well with a leafy green salad. It is also suitable as an appetizer or for a party buffet.

- 1 pound Greek "sweet" sausages (see note)
- 6 small onions, sliced
- 6 green peppers, seeded and cut into 1-inch sections
- 1 tablespoon minced garlic
- 2 to 3 whole cloves
- 2 teaspoons dried oregano
- one 8-ounce can tomato sauce
- ⅓ cup white wine
- ½ cup water

Cut sausages into 1-inch-thick slices. In an ungreased frying pan, sauté until brown. Remove and set aside. Drain all but 3 tablespoons drippings from pan. Sauté onions in drippings. Add green pepper, garlic, cloves, and oregano. Cook until onions and peppers are wilted. Add tomato sauce and browned sausage, wine, and water and simmer for 5 minutes. Serve hot with crusty bread.

Note: Greek "sweet" sausage is flavored with orange or leeks. It is sold in Greek specialty shops.

VEAL

ꙮꙮꙮꙮꙮꙮꙮꙮꙮꙮ

STEWED VEAL
Sofrito

YIELD: 4 SERVINGS

This recipe is an adaptation of the traditional sofrito from the island of Corfu.

2½ pounds fully trimmed boneless veal shoulder, cut into ½-inch-thick slices
1 cup flour
½ cup olive oil or vegetable oil

¼ cup white vinegar
approximately ½ cup water
1 tablespoon minced garlic
1 teaspoon salt
½ teaspoon pepper
½ cup minced parsley

Coat veal slices with flour. Fry meat in oil until well browned on both sides. Add vinegar, enough water (up to ½ cup) to barely cover, garlic, salt, and pepper. Cover and simmer gently until meat is tender and liquid is reduced to a thick sauce, approximately 30 minutes. Sprinkle with parsley and serve with mashed potatoes.

VEAL WITH OLIVES
Kreas me Elies

YIELD: 5 TO 6 SERVINGS

2½ pounds boneless veal,
  cut into 2-inch cubes
salt and pepper to taste
½ cup all-purpose flour
¼ cup olive oil (or half oil,
  half butter)
½ cup chopped onions

½ cup white wine
one 35-ounce can crushed
  tomatoes
2 tablespoons minced
  parsley
1 cup pitted black olives
1 cup pitted green olives

Season meat with salt and pepper and flour lightly. Heat oil in a large skillet, add meat, and brown. Add onions, wine, tomatoes, and parsley. Cover and cook for 45 minutes, or until tender. Rinse olives and drain. Add to meat and continue cooking, uncovered, until all liquid has evaporated, about 5 minutes. Serve over rice, if desired.

Variation: Beef or lamb can be used. In this case, increase cooking time by 15 minutes; add ¼ cup water with the wine.

SALADS,
SALAD DRESSINGS
AND SAUCES

SALADS

BEAN SALAD, POLITIKO-STYLE	*Fassoulada Politikia*
BEET SALAD	*Patzaria Salata*
COLD LENTIL SALAD	*Salata Faki*
CRACKED WHEAT SALAD	*Pligouri Salata*
COUNTRY-STYLE SALAD	*Horiatiki Salata*
ROMAINE AND FRESH CABBAGE SALAD	*Marouli ke Lahano Salata*
HOT POTATO SALAD	*Zesti Patatosalata*
SPRING GREENS SALAD	*Maroulosalata*
SUMMER SALAD	*Kalokerini Salata*
TOMATO SALAD	*Domatosalata*

SALAD DRESSINGS AND SAUCES

AVGOLEMONO SAUCE	*Saltsa Avgolemono*
BÉCHAMEL SAUCE	
EGGPLANT-TOMATO SAUCE	*Saltsa me Melitzana*

GARLIC SAUCE	*Skordalia*
GARLIC SAUCE WITH WALNUTS	*Skordalia me Karidia*
MEAT SAUCE FOR MACARONI	*Makaronada*
TOMATO SAUCE	*Saltsa Domates*
MARINADE	*Marinata*
OLIVE OIL AND LEMON SAUCE	*Ladolemono*
ROSEMARY SAUCE	*Saltsa Savoro*
YOGURT SALAD DRESSING	*Saltsa me Yaourti*
HOMEMADE MAYONNAISE	*Spitikia Mayoneza*
FETA DRESSING	*Saltsa me Feta*

Few dishes are as evocative of Greece as a simple assortment of lettuce, tomatoes, olives, feta, a sprinkling of oregano, some good virgin olive oil, and a splash of lemon juice—in other words, the classic Greek salad. From this very solid foundation springs a large number of regional and seasonal variations, employing anything from artichokes and cauliflower to tiny new peas, eggplants, and sweet peppers. Other more exotic salads presented in this chapter include Cracked Wheat Salad and a superb Cold Lentil Salad.

The olive tree flourishes on the rocky, arid terrain of Greece. It provides Greece not only with a thriving industry but also with a food product that is the basis of her cuisine. The olive tree is as old as the mythological history of Greece. The Greek goddess Athena, who bequeathed her name to the capital city of Athens, caused the olive tree to be born. When she and Poseidon, who had opened a salt spring with his trident in the rock on which the Acropolis was later built, fought for supremacy over the Athenians, the gods decided in favor of Athena because in their estimation the olive was a greater gift to mankind than salt.

Olive oil is used as a dressing on both vegetables and salad greens. It is combined with either lemon or vinegar. Fresh herbs, mainly dill, mint, and oregano, are often used in salads and dressings.

The Greeks pride themselves on the fact that the earliest Greeks created the truly gourmet kitchen. One of the earliest books on food and dining was written in about A.D. 190 by Athenaeus. The title, *Deipnosophistai*, literally means "experts in living and gourmets on food." Ancient tablets recorded the earliest versions of such culinary treasures as the basic white sauce, invented by the ancient sage Orion, and the basic brown sauce, formulated by Lamprikades. In the modern world, the avgolemono sauce, which is a tart, creamy sauce made with eggs and

lemon juice, runs like a golden thread through Greek cooking. It is added to soups and stews, and is served with many meat and vegetable dishes.

The other two major sauces in Greek cooking are a simple tomato sauce used in many meat and chicken dishes, and the pungent sauce called skordalia. The major ingredient is garlic, which is thickened with mashed potatoes, walnuts, or bread and served with fish, beets, cucumbers, and eggplant.

SALADS

BEAN SALAD, POLITIKO-STYLE
Fassoulada Politikia

YIELD: 6 TO 8 SERVINGS

½ pound navy pea beans
½ cup thinly sliced onions
½ cup olive oil
6 tablespoons fresh lemon juice

salt and pepper to taste
2 to 3 stalks celery, diced
½ cup chopped flat-leaf parsley

Soak beans several hours or overnight in water to cover; drain. Cover with fresh water, bring to a boil, and cook about 1 hour, or until tender. Drain beans and place in a large bowl; add onions, olive oil, lemon juice, salt, pepper, celery, and parsley. Mix well and serve at room temperature or slightly chilled.

Note: Two 20-ounce cans of cannellini beans ban be used instead. Rinse under cold water and drain.

Beet Salad
Patzaria Salata

YIELD: 6 TO 8 SERVINGS

two 1-pound cans cut red beets or 2 pounds fresh beets, cooked, drained, and sliced

3 tablespoons minced garlic
½ cup olive oil
½ cup wine vinegar
salt and pepper to taste

Combine ingredients and marinate in refrigerator several hours before serving. This salad should be well seasoned, so add a generous amount of salt and pepper. This recipe can be served with a Garlic Sauce (see p. 177).

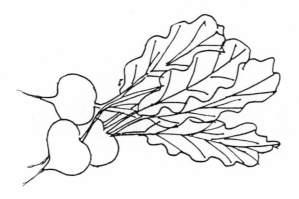

COLD LENTIL SALAD
Salata Faki

YIELD: 4 SERVINGS

1 cup lentils, rinsed
1 onion, studded with 2
  cloves
1 bay leaf
1 teaspoon salt
4 cups water
½ cup olive oil

⅓ cup wine vinegar
1 tablespoon dried oregano
1 cup minced celery
2 tablespoons minced
  scallion or onion
crisp lettuce
2 tomatoes, quartered

Place lentils, onion, bay leaf, salt, and water in a large, heavy saucepan. Bring to a boil and simmer for 30 to 40 minutes, or until tender. Drain. Discard onion and bay leaf.

Combine oil, vinegar, and oregano and pour over lentils. Let cool to room temperature and refrigerate for at least 2 hours. When ready to serve, add celery and scallion and toss. Serve in a bowl lined with lettuce. Garnish with tomatoes.

CRACKED WHEAT SALAD
Pligouri Salata

YIELD: 6 TO 8 SERVINGS

1 cup pligouri (fine cracked
  wheat) or bulgur
4 scallions, chopped
1 cup chopped curly parsley
1 pint cherry tomatoes

½ cup olive oil
¼ cup wine vinegar
1 teaspoon minced garlic
salt and pepper to taste

Soak cracked wheat in cold water to cover for 1 hour. Meanwhile combine chopped scallions and parsley; cut cherry tomatoes in half and add to scallion-parsley mixture.

Drain wheat and mix with greens and tomatoes. Combine oil, vinegar, garlic, salt, and pepper, and pour over salad. Toss, then let stand for a few minutes before serving.

COUNTRY-STYLE SALAD
Horiatiki Salata

YIELD: 4 TO 6 SERVINGS

4 cups salad greens (escarole, romaine, chicory, or other greens)

4 to 8 radishes, cut into "roses"

1 red onion, peeled and cut into rings (use according to taste)

1 small green pepper, cored, seeded, and cut into thin rings or strips

1 to 2 tomatoes, cut into wedges

½ cup feta cheese, crumbled

1 teaspoon coarse salt

1 clove garlic

8 Kalamata or other black olives

4 to 8 flat anchovy fillets (optional)

1 tablespoon dried oregano

2 tablespoons fresh lemon juice or vinegar

salt and pepper to taste

½ cup olive oil

Wash and dry salad greens; tear into bite-sized pieces. Prepare radishes, onion, green pepper, and tomatoes. Pour a little coarse salt into a salad bowl, then crush garlic clove and rub it around surface of bowl. Add salad greens, prepared vegetables, cheese, salt, olives, anchovy fillets, and oregano. Sprinkle with lemon juice, salt, and pepper; toss lightly. Add oil and toss again. Add more lemon juice or vinegar and oil to taste. Serve immediately.

ROMAINE AND FRESH CABBAGE SALAD
Marouli ke Lahano Salata

YIELD: 10 TO 12 SERVINGS

4 cups cabbage, finely
  shredded
2 cups romaine lettuce,
  finely chopped

½ cup finely chopped
  scallions (white part only)
½ cup finely chopped dill

DRESSING

¾ cup olive oil
¼ cup wine vinegar
1 teaspoon salt
½ teaspoon pepper

1 teaspoon finely minced
  garlic
2 teaspoons torn fresh
  oregano leaves

Combine cabbage, romaine, scallion, and dill. Combine dressing
ingredients and mix well. Pour over salad greens, toss well.

HOT POTATO SALAD
Zesti Patatosalata

YIELD: 6 TO 8 SERVINGS

1 large onion
1 tablespoon salt
4 to 5 large potatoes, peeled
½ cup olive oil
6 tablespoons fresh lemon
  juice

½ cup diced celery
1 teaspoon salt, or to taste
½ teaspoon pepper, or to
  taste
½ cup chopped parsley

Slice onion thin and place in a large bowl. Sprinkle with salt, cover with cold water, and let stand for about 5 minutes; drain.

Cook potatoes in boiling salted water until tender. Drain, and slice into bowl with onion. Add olive oil, lemon juice, and celery. Mix well to distribute dressing. Season with salt and pepper to taste and garnish with chopped parsley. Serve warm.

Salads, Dressings, and Sauces

SPRING GREENS SALAD
Maroulosalata

YIELD: 6 TO 8 SERVINGS

1 head romaine lettuce
½ cup finely minced scallion
½ cup finely minced dill

¼ cup grated kefalotiri cheese (optional)

DRESSING

½ cup olive oil
¼ cup wine vinegar
1 teaspoon salt

½ teaspoon pepper
2 tablespoons fresh lemon juice

Wash and dry lettuce and tear into bite-sized pieces. Combine with scallion and dill in a large bowl. Just before serving, mix all ingredients for dressing and pour over salad. Toss. Toss again with grated cheese, if you are using it.

SUMMER SALAD
Kalokerini Salata

YIELD: 4 TO 6 SERVINGS

3 tomatoes, cut in wedges
1 cucumber, sliced
1 onion, sliced
2 green peppers, cut into
   rings
¼ cup minced flat-leaf
   parsley
6 tablespoons olive oil

2 tablespoons wine vinegar
salt and pepper to taste
½ pound feta cheese, cut
   into small chunks
12 Kalamata olives
½ teaspoon torn fresh
   oregano leaves

Place tomatoes, cucumber, onion, peppers, and parsley in large salad bowl. Combine olive oil, vinegar, salt, and pepper and pour over salad. Sprinkle feta and olives over salad, add oregano, and toss.

TOMATO SALAD
Domatosalata

YIELD: 8 SERVINGS

2 medium onions
1 tablespoon salt
5 to 6 tomatoes

2 teaspoons torn fresh
   oregano leaves
¼ cup olive oil
salt to taste

Cut onions in half and slice thin lengthwise. Sprinkle slices with 1 tablespoon salt, cover with cold water, and soak for 5 minutes. Drain.
    Cut tomatoes into small pieces. Add onion slices, oregano, olive oil, and salt. Toss lightly. Let salad marinate at least 1 hour before serving.

AVGOLEMONO SAUCE
Saltsa Avgolemono

YIELD: 2 CUPS

Avgolemono (meaning egg-lemon) is the favorite sauce of Greek cookery. It is used in soups and stews and over meats and vegetables.

3 eggs
½ teaspoon salt (optional)

6 tablespoons fresh lemon
juice
1 cup boiling chicken stock

In a saucepan, beat eggs until frothy. Gradually add lemon juice and hot liquid, stirring constantly. Add salt and simmer over very low heat, stirring constantly, until mixture has thickened. Do not allow mixture to come to a boil.

Blender or food processor method

Add eggs to container and blend on high speed until frothy, at least 2 minutes. Add salt and lemon juice, and blend 1 minute longer. With motor running, slowly add hot liquid. When all liquid is blended, return to pot and simmer on low heat, stirring constantly, until thickened.

Note: If thicker sauce is desired, stir in 1 tablespoon cornstarch while beating eggs.

BÉCHAMEL SAUCE

YIELD: 4 CUPS

1 stick (¼ pound) butter
10 tablespoons flour
4 cups hot milk

2 eggs, lightly beaten
salt and pepper to taste

Melt butter in a saucepan and over low heat slowly add flour, blending well. Add hot milk, stirring rapidly; continue stirring until sauce thickens. Remove from heat and add eggs, salt, and pepper. Stir to blend.

Note: Sauce can be kept in refrigerator for 1 day. To reheat, place sauce in a double boiler, stirring constantly. It can also be reheated in a microwave oven. Cover with plastic wrap, vent, and heat on medium power. Cooking time varies depending on wattage and amount to be reheated. Check every 2 minutes.

EGGPLANT-TOMATO SAUCE
Saltsa me Melitzana

YIELD: 2 CUPS

4 tablespoons butter
2 teaspoons chopped garlic
½ cup chopped onions
2 cups skinned, chopped
  eggplant

1 cup tomato sauce
½ teaspoon dried oregano
¼ teaspoon salt
1 teaspoon sugar
½ cup water

Melt butter in a medium-size saucepan. Sauté garlic, onions, and eggplant for 5 minutes, or until tender. Add tomato sauce, oregano, salt, sugar, and water. Simmer, uncovered, for 20 minutes, stirring frequently. Add more water if sauce is too thick.

GARLIC SAUCE
Skordalia

YIELD: 2 CUPS

Skordalia is a sauce made with garlic and thickened with potatoes, nuts, or bread. Garlic is indispensable to skordalia, and skordalia is indispensable to a variety of fried foods—fish, squash, eggplant, and many other foods.

3 tablespoons minced garlic	1 cup olive oil
3 or 4 boiled potatoes, mashed, or 6 slices white bread, crusts removed, soaked in ½ cup cold water, and squeezed dry	⅓ cup white wine vinegar salt and pepper to taste

Hand method

Combine garlic with mashed potatoes or bread in a mortar. Blend to form a soft paste. Add olive oil and vinegar alternately in very small amounts, stirring briskly. Add salt and pepper. Continue to whisk until sauce is thick.

Blender or food processor method

Place garlic and potatoes or bread in bowl and blend. Add olive oil and vinegar and continue to blend. If too thick, add ¼ cup cold water. Add salt and pepper. Blend until creamy and thick.

GARLIC SAUCE WITH WALNUTS
Skordalia me Karidia

Serve this with fried or broiled fish, fried eggplant, squash, or boiled beets.

3 tablespoons minced garlic
½ teaspoon salt
¾ cup walnuts
10 slices white bread,
   trimmed and soaked in ½
   cup cold water, then
   squeezed dry

1 cup olive oil
½ cup white wine vinegar
1 cup warm water

Hand method

Combine garlic, salt, and walnuts in mortar. Add moist bread and pound until well mashed. Add olive oil and vinegar alternately, beating thoroughly after each addition. Add warm water; blend well. If a thinner sauce is preferred, add a little more warm water. Correct seasoning with salt to taste.

Blender or food processor method

Place garlic in bowl, add salt, walnuts, and ½ cup water. Blend 1 minute. Add moist bread, olive oil, and vinegar, alternately. Add remaining ½ cup water. If thinner sauce is preferred, add more water. Correct seasoning with salt.

Note: When you are finished with the preparations, be sure to clean mortar with vinegar or lemon juice, to remove the garlic smell.

MEAT SAUCE FOR MACARONI
Makaronada

YIELD: 4 TO 6 SERVINGS

½ cup minced onion
2 teaspoons minced garlic
3 tablespoons butter
1 pound ground beef
1 teaspoon salt
½ teaspoon pepper
1 cup tomato sauce
½ cup water

½ teaspoon ground
  cinnamon
dash of ground cloves or
  allspice
½ cup dry red wine
1 pound cooked macaroni
grated kefalotiri cheese

Sauté onion and garlic in butter. Add meat and brown, seasoning with salt and pepper. Blend tomato sauce and water, add to mixture, and bring to a boil. Add spices and simmer for 45 minutes. Add wine and simmer for 15 minutes. Serve over macaroni, with grated kefalotiri cheese.

TOMATO SAUCE
Saltsa Domates

YIELD: 1 CUP

4 tablespoons minced onion
2 tablespoons olive oil
2 cups tomato puree or
  sauce
3 tablespoons dry red wine

1 teaspoon salt
½ teaspoon pepper
¼ teaspoon ground
  cinnamon
¼ teaspoon ground cloves

Sauté onion in oil until soft. Add remaining ingredients in order listed and heat to boiling point. Simmer 15 minutes. Serve with any meat, poultry, or fish that has been broiled, fried, or barbecued, or over pasta.

MARINADE
Marinata

YIELD: 2½ CUPS

Marinata is the term for marinade or barbecue sauce.

1 cup fresh lemon juice
1 cup red wine
½ cup olive oil
1 teaspoon dried oregano

1 tablespoon minced garlic
½ cup minced onion
salt and pepper to taste

Combine all ingredients and pour over meat or poultry. Refrigerate overnight and use to brush meat or poultry.

OLIVE OIL AND LEMON SAUCE
Ladolemono

YIELD: ½ CUP

3 tablespoons olive oil
3 tablespoons fresh lemon
  juice

1 teaspoon torn fresh
  oregano leaves
salt and pepper to taste

Beat olive oil and lemon juice until creamy. Beat in oregano, salt, and pepper. Use over shellfish, fish, chicken, or lamb chops.

ROSEMARY SAUCE
Saltsa Savoro

YIELD: 1½ CUPS

Rosemary sauce is an excellent accompaniment for fried fish or sautéed liver.

½ cup olive oil
3 tablespoons all-purpose
    flour
⅓ cup white vinegar
1 tablespoon tomato paste

2 cups water
1 teaspoon minced garlic
½ teaspoon dried rosemary
1 bay leaf
salt and pepper to taste

Heat olive oil. Add flour and then vinegar and continue to stir. Dilute tomato paste in water and add to pan with garlic, rosemary, bay leaf, salt, and pepper. Cook over medium heat, stirring, until sauce thickens. Remove bay leaf and refrigerate for several hours. Serve at room temperature.

YOGURT SALAD DRESSING
Saltsa me Yaourti

YIELD: 1½ CUPS DRESSING

3 tablespoons olive oil
2 tablespoons fresh lemon
   juice
¼ cup mayonnaise
½ teaspoon salt

1 teaspoon minced garlic
⅛ teaspoon ground cumin
1 tablespoon minced fresh
   dill
1 cup plain yogurt

Mix oil, lemon juice, and mayonnaise in a bowl. Add salt, garlic, cumin, and dill. Very gently, fold in yogurt. Chill.

HOMEMADE MAYONNAISE
Spitikia Mayoneza

YIELD: 2 CUPS

1 tablespoon powdered
   mustard
¼ teaspoon sugar
dash of white pepper
1 teaspoon salt

2 teaspoons white vinegar
2 egg yolks
1⅔ cups olive oil
3 tablespoons fresh lemon
   juice

Combine mustard, sugar, pepper, and salt. Add vinegar and egg yolks and beat together with whisk until well combined. Add oil one drop at a time, beating constantly. When mayonnaise starts to thicken, thin with lemon juice and continue beating, alternately adding lemon juice and oil.

FETA DRESSING
Saltsa me Feta

YIELD: 1 QUART

2 cups mayonnaise
  (preferably Homemade
  Mayonnaise, see p. 182)
1 tablespoon minced garlic

½ cup red wine vinegar
1 teaspoon dried oregano
3 tablespoons olive oil
2 cups crumbled feta cheese

Combine all ingredients except feta in a bowl and blend well. Crumble feta and add to mixture. Refrigerate in a covered jar.

Note: All ingredients except feta can be placed in a blender or food processor and creamed until smooth. Add feta and refrigerate.

VEGETABLES

ARTICHOKES A LA POLITIKA	Anginares a la Politika
BOILED GREEN VEGETABLES WITH LEMON DRESSING	Horta Vrasta me Ladolemono
BRAISED VEGETABLES	Horta Yahni
IMAM BAILDI (L)	
EGGPLANT PHYLLO PIE	Melitzanopita
LEEK PHYLLO PIE	Prasopita
FAVA (L)	
MOLDED SPINACH PHYLLO PIE	Spanakopita se Forma
SPINACH AND RICE (L)	Spanakorizo
SQUASH PHYLLO PIE	Kolokithopita
STUFFED TOMATOES WITH RICE (L)	Yemistes Domates Laderes me Rizi

In a land where the private vegetable and herb garden is a common sight, it is no surprise that the vegetable dishes hold a place of pride on the Greek menu. Although eggplant and artichokes are probably the vegetables most associated with Greece, cabbage, squash, cauliflower, fresh peas, string beans, and tomatoes are also standard fare (it is almost redundant to say "fresh" peas, since processed foods have made few inroads in Greece). In the legume family, lentils, chick-peas, fava beans, and white beans are commonly, and inventively, used throughout Greece.

Perhaps one of the reasons for the importance of vegetables in the Greek diet is the strict observance of Lent among the majority of Greeks. During the forty-day period of abstinence from meat and animal protein, religious Greeks must rely (without too much hardship, mind you) on Stuffed Tomatoes with Rice, Fava, and Spinach and Rice, to name only a few. These and other Lenten recipes are designated (L).

ARTICHOKES A LA POLITIKA
Anginares a la Politika

The Complete Book of
GREEK COOKING

YIELD: 6 SERVINGS

Artichokes are a favorite vegetable of the Greeks. Care must be taken in preparing artichokes so that they do not darken. Frozen artichoke hearts, defrosted, can be substituted in this recipe.

4 cups cold water
6 tablespoons fresh lemon juice
4 tablespoons flour
6 large artichokes (see "How to Prepare Fresh Artichokes," p. 309) or three 10-ounce packages artichoke hearts, thawed

1 lemon, halved
½ cup finely chopped onion
1½ cups olive oil
12 small whole white onions
salt to taste
¼ teaspoon sugar
½ cup finely chopped dill

In large saucepan sauté chopped onion in ½ cup olive oil until soft. Add whole white onions, 3 tablespoons lemon juice, remaining olive oil, salt, sugar, and water to cover. Bring mixture to a boil and add prepared artichokes and chopped dill. Cook slowly for 30 to 45 minutes. (If frozen artichokes are used, reduce cooking time to 20 minutes.) Let cool in sauce and serve cold.

Variation: 1 pound cleaned fresh fava beans can be added. Combine with artichokes and cook slowly for 30 minutes.

188

BOILED GREEN VEGETABLES WITH LEMON DRESSING

Horta Vrasta me Ladolemono

YIELD: 2 TO 4 SERVINGS

2 pounds chicory or
2 pounds dandelion greens
or

2 pounds endive or
2 pounds escarole

LEMON DRESSING

½ cup olive oil
1½ tablespoons fresh
lemon juice

salt and pepper to taste

Any of the above vegetables can be boiled in salted water until tender, about 10 minutes. Drain well. Cut vegetables while warm. Add olive oil, lemon juice, salt, and pepper. Serve hot or cold.

BRAISED VEGETABLES
Horta Yahni

YIELD: 4 TO 6 SERVINGS

4 cups minced onion
¾ cup olive oil
1 pound fresh tomatoes,
    sliced thin
¼ cup chopped flat-leaf
    parsley

salt and pepper to taste
vegetables (see below; a
    total of 6 cups of
    vegetables can be
    combined)
1 cup water

Sauté onion in olive oil until wilted. Add tomatoes, parsley, salt, pepper, and vegetables and sauté over medium heat for 3 minutes. Add water and continue to simmer, covered, according to directions for individual vegetables.

The following vegetables can be used:

Cauliflower—4-pound head. Break into florets and sprinkle with lemon juice. Add to onion sauce mixture and cook for 20 minutes, or until tender.

Fava beans—3 pounds fresh or three 10-ounce packages frozen fava beans, thawed. Add fava beans and ¼ cup chopped dill to onion sauce mixture. Cover and simmer for 35 minutes, or until beans are cooked.

Okra—2 pounds fresh or two 10-ounce packages frozen okra, thawed. If using fresh okra, wash and trim by removing cone-shaped portions at top. Place okra in bowl, sprinkle with ½ cup vinegar, and let stand for 1 to 2 hours. Rinse thoroughly in cold water. Combine with onion sauce mixture and cook for 30 minutes, or until tender.

Green beans—2 pounds, with ends snapped off. Add beans and water to cover to onion sauce mixture. Cover and cook until beans are tender, about 20 minutes.

IMAM BAILDI

YIELD: 6 SERVINGS

Imam Baildi is a delicious dish made with eggplant, tomatoes, onions, garlic, parsley, and olive oil. Although this dish has a Turkish name, the Asia Minor Greeks *(mikrasiates)*, who lived in Turkey for hundreds of years, are credited with creating it. There is an amusing story about the name of this dish, which means "The priest (imam) fainted." A Turkish imam was very fond of eggplant. His wife was always thinking up new ways to serve it to him. One day she prepared this recipe, and the imam found it so good that he fainted in ecstasy. (Two other versions are that the imam fainted over the great amount of oil required to make the dish, and that he fainted because the dish was so rich.)

12 small baby eggplants,
   about 2 pounds
1¼ cups olive oil
salt to taste
4 cups sliced onion
2 tablespoons minced garlic
½ cup chopped parsley

3 large tomatoes, peeled,
   seeded, and chopped, or 2
   cups crushed tomatoes
½ cup water
½ teaspoon salt
¼ teaspoon pepper

Preheat oven to 350 degrees.

Cut two lengthwise slits along each eggplant. Brush on all sides with ¼ cup olive oil and salt lightly; place in a baking dish. Bake for 20 minutes, or until soft.

While eggplants are baking, prepare sauce

Sauté onions and garlic in remaining cup of olive oil until wilted. Add parsley, tomatoes, ½ cup water, salt, and pepper. Bring to a boil and simmer for 15 minutes. Carefully spoon some sauce into the incisions in the eggplants. Pour remaining sauce over eggplants and continue to bake for 10 minutes. Serve at room temperature.

EGGPLANT PHYLLO PIE
Melitzanopita

YIELD: 20 PIECES

1 large or 2 medium
    eggplants (2 pounds
    total)
salt
½ cup olive oil
½ cup chopped onions
1 cup minced green peppers
3 tablespoons butter, plus
    1 stick (¼ pound) butter,
    melted, for brushing
    phyllo

one 1-pound can crushed
    tomatoes
salt and pepper to taste
1 cup Béchamel Sauce (see
    p. 176)
1 pound feta cheese,
    crumbled
4 eggs, beaten
½ pound phyllo pastry

Preheat broiler.

Cut eggplant into ¼-inch round slices. Sprinkle with salt and place in a colander to drain.

Lightly brush each side of eggplant slices with oil, and place on a large baking sheet. Place under preheated broiler until lightly browned on each side.

Preheat oven to 350 degrees.

In a large saucepan, sauté onions and green peppers in 3 table-spoons butter until wilted. Add tomatoes, salt, and pepper. Simmer for 20 to 25 minutes.

While this is simmering, prepare Béchamel Sauce and cool. Add half of feta and beaten eggs to Béchamel Sauce.

Brush a sheet of phyllo with melted butter and place in a 9 x 12-inch baking pan (keep remaining phyllo covered with plastic wrap). Repeat with 7 additional sheets, lining pan. (See "How to Work with Phyllo," p. 312.) Spread half of eggplant slices over phyllo. Sprinkle with remaining feta and spread with half of Béchamel Sauce. Top with half of onion-tomato sauce. Add remaining eggplant slices and top with remaining Béchamel Sauce and onion-tomato sauce. Cover with remaining phyllo sheets, each brushed with butter. Score top lightly with a sharp pointed knife into serving pieces. Bake for 30 to 35 minutes, or until golden. Let sit for 15 minutes before serving.

Optional: Eggplant can be peeled if you prefer.

Variation: Zucchini (or a mixture of zucchini and eggplant) can be substituted. Slice zucchini in ¼-inch rounds and sauté in olive oil until lightly browned. Proceed as above.

Vegetables

Note: This recipe can be prepared ahead of time, up to two days before baking. In addition, it can be frozen, unbaked. When ready to use, place, unthawed, in a 375-degree oven, and bake 45 to 50 minutes, or until golden.

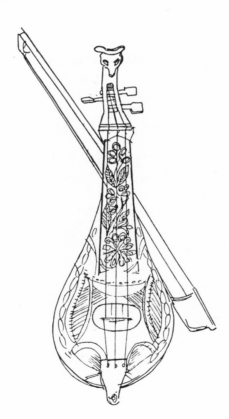

LEEK PHYLLO PIE
Prasopita

YIELD: 24 PIECES

10 medium-sized leeks
1 stick butter, plus 1 stick butter, melted, for brushing phyllo (½ pound)
1 tablespoon minced fresh dill

salt and pepper to taste
2 cups crushed tomatoes
¼ cup white wine
4 eggs
1 pound fresh mizithra or ricotta cheese
20 sheets phyllo pastry

Preheat oven to 375 degrees.

Prepare leeks by cutting off roots and coarse tops; wash well to remove grit and peel off any yellowed or bruised outer layers. Cut into 1-inch-thick slices; you should have 3 cups.

In a large frying pan, melt 1 stick butter, add leeks, dill, salt, and pepper, and sauté lightly. Add tomatoes and wine and simmer until all liquid has evaporated.

Beat eggs and add cheese, mixing well. Add cooled leeks.

Line a 9 x 13 x 2-inch pan with 8 individually buttered sheets of phyllo. (See "How to Work with Phyllo," p. 312). Add leek mixture and cover with 12 buttered sheets of phyllo. With a sharp knife score the top layers of phyllo into 24 squares and bake for 30 to 40 minutes, or until golden. When pie cools, cut all the way through the squares. To serve, reheat at 350 degrees for 20 to 30 minutes; serve warm.

Note: Mizithra is a soft, unsalted cheese very popular in Greece. It is similar to ricotta and is available in Greek specialty food stores.

FAVA

Vegetables

YIELD: 4 TO 6 SERVINGS

1 cup yellow split peas
½ cup minced onions
1 teaspoon minced garlic
1 fresh tomato, peeled,
   seeded and chopped, or
   ½ cup crushed canned
   tomatoes

1 teaspoon salt
1 teaspoon dried or
   1 tablespoon fresh
   chopped mint (optional)
1 tablespoon chopped
   parsley
1 tablespoon olive oil

Wash peas, cover with water, and bring to a boil; skim. Add onions, garlic, tomato, salt, and mint. Simmer, covered, until water is absorbed (about 30 minutes). Stir occasionally. Before serving, sprinkle with parsley and olive oil. Serve hot or cold.

Note: Fava has a very thick, smooth consistency. Olive oil is dribbled over each serving to suit the individual taste.

MOLDED SPINACH PHYLLO PIE
Spanakopita se Forma

YIELD: 12 TO 16 PIECES

½ cup chopped scallions
2 tablespoons butter, plus 2 sticks (½ pound) butter, melted, for brushing phyllo
2 pounds fresh spinach, picked over, washed, and drained, or four 10-ounce packages frozen chopped spinach, thawed and drained

6 eggs, lightly beaten
½ pound feta cheese, crumbled
8 ounces cottage cheese
2 tablespoons farina
½ cup minced flat-leaf parsley
½ cup fresh chopped dill, or 1 tablespoon dried dill
salt and pepper to taste
1 pound phyllo pastry

Preheat oven to 350 degrees.

Sauté scallions in 2 tablespoons butter until tender. Chop spinach and place in a large saucepan. Cover and cook until wilted, about 15 minutes. Drain, pressing out as much liquid as possible. (If frozen spinach is used, thaw and drain thoroughly.) Mix together scallion, eggs, feta, cottage cheese, farina, parsley, dill, and spinach. Season lightly with salt and pepper.

Butter a 2-quart decorated ring mold. Unfold phyllo and place under plastic wrap to keep it from drying out. (See "How to Work with Phyllo," p. 312.) Remove one sheet of pastry at a time, brush with melted butter, and begin lining mold (1½ inches of pastry should hang over outer edge of mold). Continue fitting phyllo sheets into mold, turning it as you go in order to make even layers. (The sheets will overlap in center hole of mold.) Use about 20 sheets of phyllo. Fill mold with spinach mixture. Draw overhanging outer edges of phyllo over filling. Arrange remaining sheets of phyllo, buttered, one at a time, to completely cover filling; cut out and discard the pastry over center hole of mold.

Place mold on a cookie sheet to catch butter drippings. Bake for 1¼ hours, or until golden brown and puffed. Let stand in mold 5 to 15 minutes before unmolding onto a warm platter.

Note: If when unmolded the crust is not crisp and golden, return to oven to brown top.

Note: This dish can be frozen, unbaked. To serve, bake without prior thawing for about 1¾ hours, or until golden and puffed. It can also be baked ahead, unmolded, and reheated at 350 degrees for 20 to 30 minutes before serving.

[LENTEN]

SPINACH AND RICE
Spanakorizo

YIELD: 4 TO 6 SERVINGS

Spanakorizo is a delicious combination of spinach and rice, equally good warm or cold. It is served often during Lent.

2 cups minced onions
½ cup olive oil
1 tablespoon tomato paste
2 pounds cleaned chopped
  spinach or four 10-ounce
  packages frozen chopped
  spinach, thawed

1 cup raw converted rice
2 sprigs fresh mint or 1
  tablespoon chopped
  fresh dill
salt and pepper to taste
2½ cups hot water

Sauté onions in oil until wilted, about 5 minutes. Add tomato paste, spinach, and rice and sauté. Add mint (or dill), salt, pepper, and hot water, cover, and simmer until rice is cooked and liquid has been absorbed. Do not stir.

Variation: 2 pounds chopped Swiss chard can be substituted for spinach.

SQUASH PHYLLO PIE
Kolokithopita

YIELD: 20 PIECES

3 pounds small zucchini
salt to taste
1 tablespoon vegetable oil
2 tablespoons butter, plus 1
  stick (¼ pound) butter,
  melted, for brushing
  phyllo
salt and pepper to taste

5 eggs
¾ pound feta cheese
2 tablespoons minced
  flat-leaf parsley
2 tablespoons minced dill
½ cup toasted breadcrumbs
½ cup milk
¾ pound phyllo pastry

Preheat oven to 350 degrees.

Clean and scrape zucchini, grate coarsely, and put in a colander; sprinkle with salt and let drain for 1 hour. Heat oil and 2 tablespoons butter in a large pot. Add squash and sauté; toss a few times, but do not brown. Add salt and pepper and remove from heat.

Beat eggs in a bowl. Cut or crumble cheese into pieces about the size of peas, and add to eggs along with parsley, dill, breadcrumbs, and milk. Season with salt and pepper and mix well. Pour into pot with squash and mix again.

Butter a 9 x 12 x 2-inch baking pan. Brush half the phyllo with melted butter, one sheet at a time (cover remainder in plastic wrap to keep from drying out), and overlap in baking pan so that bottom and sides are completely covered and 2 inches of pastry extend beyond rim of pan all around. (See "How to Work with Phyllo," p. 312.) Pour squash mixture into pan and spread evenly. Fold overhanging phyllo up over the squash and brush well with melted butter. Lay remaining phyllo sheets on top, again brushing with melted butter one sheet at a time. Butter the top well. Score top layers of phyllo, and bake for 1 hour, or until golden. Cool and cut into serving pieces.

Note: If you have a food processor, slice zucchini into thin pieces, using the thinnest blade. You can also use the food processor grating blade for a finer cut.

Note: This recipe can be baked in a deep-dish pie pan or 12-inch quiche pan. It can be prepared and frozen, unbaked. When ready to use, place unthawed in a preheated 375-degree oven and bake for 1 hour 15 minutes, or until golden.

vegetables

[LENTEN]

STUFFED TOMATOES WITH RICE

Yemistes Domates Laderes me Rizi

YIELD: 12 SERVINGS

12 large tomatoes	½ cup chopped fresh dill
salt to taste	½ cup raisins or currants
1 teaspoon sugar	½ cup pine nuts
3 cups minced onions	1 cup raw converted rice
1½ cups olive oil	salt and pepper to taste
½ cup chopped flat-leaf parsley	½ cup water

Wash tomatoes, slice off caps, and reserve; scoop out pulp, chop, and reserve. Sprinkle inside of tomatoes with salt and sugar. Sauté onions in ¼ cup of the olive oil until soft.

Preheat oven to 350 degrees.

Mix onion, parsley, dill, raisins or currants, pine nuts, rice, chopped tomato pulp, and 1 cup olive oil. Sauté for 3 minutes. Season to taste with salt and pepper. Fill tomatoes with this mixture. Cover with tomato caps and place in casserole with remaining ¼ cup olive oil and water. Cover with aluminum foil. Bake for 30 to 40 minutes, or until tops are golden and rice is cooked, basting occasionally. Remove from heat and cool. Serve at room temperature.

Note: Tomatoes can be cooked on the stove top. Cover with aluminum foil and simmer for about 30 minutes, basting occasionally.

BREAD

EASTER TWIST	*Tsoureki*
CHRISTMAS BREAD	*Christopsomo*
NEW YEAR'S CAKE	*Vasilopeta*
ISLANDER CORN BREAD	*Bobota*
LATTICE TARTS	*Gyristaria*
OLIVE MUFFINS	*Eliopsomakia*
ORANGE SESAME SEED ROLLS	*Psomakia me Portokali*
SESAME SALT STICKS	*Bastounakia*
SESAME TEA ROLLS	*Psomakia me Prozimi*
SWEET BREAD RINGS	*Kouloures*
WHOLE WHEAT BISCUITS (L)	*Paximadia me Sitarenio Alevri*
ENVELOPE BREAD (L)	*Peta*

read is the staff of life in Greece, as elsewhere, but it also takes on an almost religious significance, especially during the Christmas and Easter seasons. (Breads suitable for Lenten use are designated L.) No holiday is complete without a festive bread, rich in eggs, sweet butter, and sesame seeds. But in a country where bread is still routinely baked at home, unique, marvelously flavored breads are common the year round. In this latter category, we include Olive Muffins, Sesame Tea Rolls, and the marvelous Sweet Bread Rings sold by street vendors as a midday snack.

Note: The following recipes have been tested with all-purpose flour.

EASTER TWIST
Tsoureki

YIELD: ABOUT 5 TO 6 LARGE TWISTS

Tsoureki is an Easter cake sprinkled with sesame seeds and decorated with red eggs.

4 to 5 packages (4 to 5 tablespoons) active dry yeast
¾ cup warm water
½ cup all-purpose flour, plus 5 pounds sifted flour, or more as needed
1 tablespoon plus 3 cups sugar
¼ teaspoon plus 1 tablespoon salt
12 eggs, plus 1 or 2 eggs, beaten, for topping

2 cups milk, scalded and cooled
5 sticks (1¼ pounds) unsalted butter, melted
1 tablespoon ground masticha flavoring or 1 teaspoon ground mahlepi flavoring (see note) or 1 tablespoon vanilla extract
sesame seeds for topping
red-dyed hard-boiled eggs for decoration (see "All About Easter Eggs," p. 309)

Mix yeast with water. Add ½ cup flour, 1 tablespoon sugar, and ¼ teaspoon salt. Stir, and let rise in a warm place until mixture bubbles and foams, about 10 minutes.

In a very large bowl beat 12 eggs. Add 3 cups sugar, cooled milk, melted butter, and 1 tablespoon salt. Stir in yeast mixture. Blend masticha (or mahlepi or vanilla extract) with sifted flour and add to liquid to make a stiff and elastic dough. Knead well on a floured board for about 5 minutes. Place dough in a greased bowl; cover with a damp towel and let rise until double in bulk. Punch down and turn over in bowl. Cover with plastic wrap and a damp towel and let rise again until almost double in bulk. (The second rising should not take as long as the first.)

Preheat oven to 350 degrees.

Shape dough into fifteen to eighteen 14-inch-long ropes, braid 3 at a time, and place on greased round bread pans or cookie sheets to rise; cover. When they have doubled in bulk, brush with beaten eggs and sprinkle with sesame seeds. Arrange 3 or 4 red eggs on each braid in the shape of a cross. If long braids are made, put 1 red egg at the top.

Bake for 30 to 40 minutes, or until golden.

Note: This recipe can be used for New Year's bread, omitting the red eggs. Garnish with slivered almonds, writing the year with the almonds.

Note: Mahlepi is made from the seeds of the fruit of the mahlepi bush.

Bread

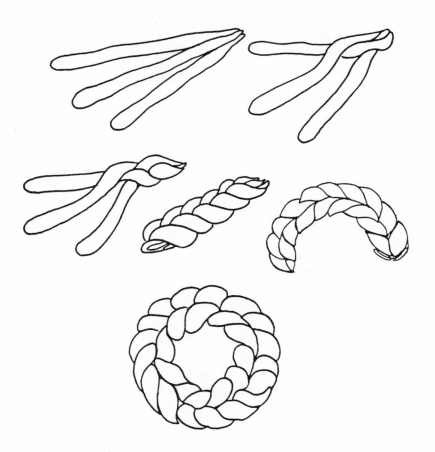

CHRISTMAS BREAD
Christopsomo

YIELD: 2 LARGE BRAIDS

This is the traditional bread baked for the Christmas holiday in various parts of Greece.

3 packages (3 tablespoons) active dry yeast
½ cup warm water
1 teaspoon plus 1½ cups sugar
2 tablespoons plus 7 to 8 cups all-purpose flour
1¼ teaspoons salt
5 eggs
1½ cups milk, scalded and cooled

1 teaspoon ground masticha flavoring (see note) or 1 teaspoon vanilla extract
2 sticks (½ pound) unsalted butter, melted
1 cup slivered blanched almonds
½ cup white raisins
1 teaspoon grated lemon peel

Combine yeast, warm water, 1 teaspoon sugar, 2 tablespoons flour, and ¼ teaspoon salt in a bowl. Let stand in a warm place until mixture bubbles and foams, about 10 minutes.

In a large bowl, beat together 4 eggs, 1½ cups sugar, 1 teaspoon salt, cooled milk, and yeast mixture. Add 3 cups of flour and masticha or vanilla extract. Add melted butter, almonds, raisins, and lemon peel. Continue to add flour and knead well about 5 minutes, or until dough is quite stiff but elastic. Place in greased bowl. Cover first with plastic wrap and then with a damp towel. Let dough rise in a warm place until double in bulk. Punch down and turn over in bowl.

Cover and let rise for 30 minutes more. Shape dough into 6 ropes and braid 3 at a time. Place braids on a lightly greased cookie sheet and let rise for 40 minutes.

Preheat oven to 350 degrees.

Beat remaining egg and brush each braid with it. Bake for 30 minutes, or until golden brown.

Variation: 1 cup mixed candied fruit can be added with the almonds.

Note: Masticha is a flavoring made from the sap of the *masticho-dendro* bush, which grows only on the island of Chios.

Bread

NEW YEAR'S CAKE
Vasilopeta

YIELD: ONE 10-INCH CAKE; 10 TO 12 SERVINGS

Vasilopeta is a cake made in honor of Saint Basil, whose feast day is January 1. Cakes differ in the various regions of Greece: some are a type of bread, others a type of rich yeast cake, others are flat, made of cookie dough. The cakes may differ, but all include the customary hidden silver coin. It symbolizes good luck to the person who finds the coin in his piece of cake. The head of the family cuts slices in a very precise order. The first piece goes to Saint Basil (Vasili = vasilopeta = Basil's bread), for the cake is made in his honor. The second piece goes to Christ. The third piece is for the oldest member of the family, and on down to the youngest. The following recipe is the most traditional version. See Easter Twist (p. 204) for a variation.

2 sticks (½ pound) unsalted butter, at room temperature
2 cups sugar
3 cups all-purpose flour
6 eggs
2 teaspoons double-acting baking powder

1 cup lukewarm milk
½ teaspoon baking soda
1½ tablespoons fresh lemon juice
½ cup chopped nuts (walnuts, almonds, or pistachios)
¼ cup sugar

Preheat oven to 350 degrees.

Cream butter and sugar together until light. Add flour and stir until mixture resembles coarse meal. Add eggs, one at a time, beating well after each addition. Stir baking powder into milk and stir into egg mixture. Mix baking soda and lemon juice and stir in. Mix well.

Pour into a greased round layer cake pan 10 inches in diameter and 2 inches deep. Bake for 20 minutes. Sprinkle with nuts and sugar and bake 20 to 30 minutes longer, or until cake tests done. Cool 10 minutes in pan and invert onto serving plate. Serve right side up.

Islander Corn Bread
Bobota

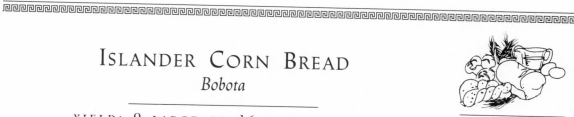

Bread

YIELD: 9 LARGE OR 16 SMALL PIECES

This is a modified and far more palatable version of a Greek wartime staple made only of cornmeal, honey, and water. Though today's Bobota has come a long way from its humble origins, it is not popular everywhere in Greece because of its association with war and poverty.

1 cup cornmeal
1 cup sifted all-purpose
    flour
1 teaspoon double-acting
    baking powder
¼ teaspoon baking soda
¼ teaspoon salt
¼ cup sugar

3 tablespoons honey
⅓ cup orange juice
¾ cup warm water
3 tablespoons vegetable oil,
    warmed
1 teaspoon grated orange
    peel
½ cup currants

SYRUP

½ cup sugar
½ cup water
2 teaspoons fresh lemon
    juice

1 stick cinnamon
1 tablespoon honey
confectioner's sugar
    (optional)

Combine sugar, water, lemon juice, and cinnamon in a medium-sized saucepan, and bring to a boil. Simmer for 20 minutes. Remove from heat and add honey. Return syrup to low heat and simmer for 2 minutes. Remove from heat.

Preheat oven to 375 degrees.

Sift all dry ingredients into a large bowl. Combine the honey, orange juice, warm water, and warm oil. Stir into dry mixture, beating until smooth. Fold in orange peel and currants. Pour batter into a well-greased 7 x 7 x 2-inch square pan and bake for 25 minutes, or until golden. Leave in pan to cool, then pour warm Basic Sweet Syrup over it or sprinkle with confectioners' sugar. Cut into squares and serve immediately.

Note: Syrup can be stored in the refrigerator for 1 month. To use, bring to room temperature.

LATTICE TARTS
Gyristaria

YIELD: 12 TO 15 TARTS

This tart is a specialty from Cyprus.

2 packages (2 tablespoons)
  active dry yeast
½ teaspoon plus 1
  tablespoon sugar
2½ cups warm water
6 to 6½ cups all-purpose
  flour
2 teaspoons salt

1 teaspoon ground masticha
  flavoring or 1 teaspoon
  vanilla extract
1 teaspoon ground
  cinnamon
1 egg, beaten
sesame seeds for topping

Combine yeast, ½ teaspoon sugar, 1½ cups warm water, and 2 cups of flour in a medium-sized bowl. Cover and let rest in a warm place until mixture bubbles and foams, about 10 minutes. Punch down and combine in a large mixing bowl with salt, masticha or vanilla extract, remaining sugar, cinnamon, and 1 cup warm water. Gradually add only enough of remaining 4 to 4½ cups flour to make a soft dough. Knead for 10 to 15 minutes, until smooth and elastic. Place in a floured bowl, cover, and let rise in a warm place until double in bulk.

Preheat oven to 350 degrees.

Punch down dough and break off 12 pieces about the size of a small orange. Roll each piece into a 6-inch-long rope and seal ends to form circles. Break off pieces of remaining dough to form 6 pencil-thin strips for each dough ring. Create a lattice effect by crisscrossing strips over dough rings. If any dough remains, continue adding and crisscrossing strips to make a tighter lattice. Place on a buttered baking sheet, brush with egg and sprinkle with sesame seeds.

Cover and let rise for 30 minutes. Bake for 25 minutes or until golden. Cool on racks.

OLIVE MUFFINS
Eliopsomakia

YIELD: 2 DOZEN MUFFINS OR 2 LOAVES

This is a specialty from the island of Cyprus.

2 cups (1¼ pounds) chopped pitted black olives

4 cups all-purpose flour

1 cup grated onion

1½ cups olive oil, plus additional oil to brush muffin tins

3 tablespoons chopped fresh mint, or 2 teaspoons crushed dried mint

2 tablespoons sugar

2 heaping tablespoons double-acting baking powder

Preheat oven to 350 degrees.

Rinse olives and drain. Dry on paper towels.

Combine all ingredients, adding baking powder last. Brush muffin cups with oil and dust with flour. (Do not use paper baking cups.) Bake for 40 to 45 minutes, or until golden. Serve warm.

Variation: Recipe can be baked in 9 x 5-inch loaf pans. Increase baking time by 15 minutes.

ORANGE SESAME SEED ROLLS
Psomakia me Portokali

YIELD: 2 DOZEN ROLLS

⅓ cup lukewarm water
1 tablespoon flour
½ teaspoon sugar
2 packages (2 tablespoons)
   active dry yeast
2 cups milk
⅓ cup melted unsalted
   butter

4 tablespoons sugar
1 teaspoon salt
2 eggs, well beaten
2 tablespoons orange juice
2 tablespoons grated orange
   rind
6 cups all-purpose flour

TOPPING

¼ cup light cream
½ teaspoon sugar

1 cup sesame seeds

In a small bowl, place ⅓ cup lukewarm water, 1 teaspoon flour, and ½ teaspoon sugar. Sprinkle yeast over mixture, stir, and set aside for 10 minutes.)

Scald 1 cup milk and let cool. Combine cooled milk with butter, 4 tablespoons sugar, salt, eggs, orange juice, and orange rind and beat with electric mixer for 5 minutes. Heat remaining milk until lukewarm and dissolve yeast in it. Add this to mixture and blend thoroughly. Add flour and mix by hand. Put dough on a floured board and knead until smooth, about 5 minutes. Put mixture in a large, well-greased bowl, and turn to grease dough completely. Cover with a damp cloth and let rise in a warm place for 1½ to 2 hours, or until double in bulk. Turn dough out on a floured board and knead a few times. Cut off pieces the size of a lemon, roll between palms of hands into 8-inch-long ropes, and tie in a knot.

Prepare the topping

Mix cream and sugar together and brush on knotted rolls. Dip rolls in sesame seeds and place on a greased cookie sheet 3 inches apart. Cover with a cloth and put in a warm place until double in bulk, about 1½ to 2 hours. Preheat oven to 350 degrees.

Bake for 25 to 30 minutes.

Sesame Salt Sticks
Bastounakia

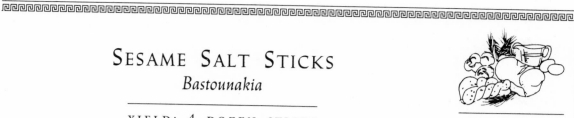

YIELD: 4 DOZEN STICKS

2 packages (2 tablespoons)
  active dry yeast
2 cups warm water
1 tablespoon sugar
1 tablespoon salt

5 cups all-purpose flour
  (approximately)
½ cup cornmeal
coarse salt for topping
sesame seeds for topping

In a large bowl, mix yeast, warm water, sugar, and salt and let stand until bubbly, approximately 5 to 10 minutes.

Gradually add flour, kneading about 5 minutes, or until dough is stiff. Put in a greased bowl. Cover first with plastic wrap and then with a damp towel. Let rise in a warm place until double in bulk, about 1½ to 2 hours. Punch dough down, turn over, cover with plastic wrap and damp towel and let rise for another 15 minutes. Pinch off pieces of dough, roll out into sticks, and place on cookie sheets that have been sprinkled with cornmeal. Let sticks rise until double in bulk, about 1 to 1½ hours.

Preheat oven to 400 degrees.

Dampen tops of sticks with water and sprinkle with coarse salt and sesame seeds. Bake for 10 minutes, or until brown.

Variation: Coarsely ground pepper or whole caraway seeds can be substituted for sesame seeds.

SESAME TEA ROLLS
Psomakia me Prozimi

YIELD: ABOUT 4 DOZEN ROLLS

2 packages (2 tablespoons) active dry yeast
⅓ cup warm water
3 tablespoons plus 7 to 7½ cups all-purpose flour
½ teaspoon plus 1 cup sugar
2½ teaspoons salt
2 cups milk, scalded and cooled

3 eggs, beaten, plus 1 egg, beaten, for topping
1 teaspoon ground masticha flavoring or 1 teaspoon vanilla extract
1 stick (¼ pound) unsalted butter, melted and cooled
sesame seeds for topping

In a medium-sized bowl, combine yeast, warm water, 3 tablespoons flour, ½ teaspoon sugar, and ½ teaspoon salt. Set aside in a warm place until mixture bubbles and foams, about 10 to 15 minutes.

Combine milk, 1 cup sugar, 2 teaspoons salt, 3 eggs, and masticha or vanilla extract; add to yeast mixture. Sift 3½ cups flour into yeast mixture and beat well with a spoon. Add cooled butter. Gradually add remaining flour (as much as necessary) and knead until dough is smooth and elastic, about 5 minutes. Place in a greased bowl, cover with plastic wrap and a damp towel, and let rise in a warm place until double in bulk, about 1½ hours.

Punch down, turn over in bowl, cover with plastic wrap and a damp towel, and let rise again until almost double in bulk, about 1 hour. Pinch off walnut-sized pieces of dough and roll into thin ropes. Tie these into knots or twists. Place on a greased cookie sheet, cover with plastic wrap and a damp towel, and let rise again, about 30 minutes to 1 hour.

Preheat oven to 350 degrees.

Brush with beaten egg and sprinkle with sesame seeds. Bake until golden brown, about 12 to 20 minutes, depending on size.

SWEET BREAD RINGS
Kouloures

YIELD: 4 DOZEN RINGS

7 cups sifted all-purpose
  flour
¼ cup warm water
½ cup warm milk
2 yeast cakes or 2 packages
  (2 tablespoons) active dry
  yeast
1 teaspoon salt

1 stick (¼ pound) butter,
  melted
3 eggs, lightly beaten
⅓ cup cold milk
¾ cup sugar
1 tablespoon vanilla extract
2 tablespoons brandy
1 cup light cream

Sift 2 cups flour into a large bowl. In a small bowl, combine warm water and milk. Dissolve yeast in this liquid and add to flour. Mix thoroughly to make a loose dough. Cover with plastic wrap and a damp towel, let rise in a warm place for about 1½ hours. After first rising, sift together remaining flour and salt. Add melted butter and mix until evenly distributed. In another bowl combine eggs, cold milk, sugar, vanilla, and brandy and mix well. Add to the risen dough, mixing with a heavy spoon until smooth. Add flour and butter mixture and knead together for 10 minutes, or until very smooth.

Cut off pieces of dough about the size of a large walnut and roll between the hands to form 3-inch-long ropes. Seal ends of ropes to form circles and place 2 inches apart on greased cookie sheet. Brush tops with cream and let rise, covered with a damp towel, for 1½ hours.

Preheat oven to 350 degrees.

Bake rings for 15 to 20 minutes, or until golden.

[LENTEN]

WHOLE WHEAT BISCUITS

Paximadia me Sitarenio Alevri

YIELD: 9 DOZEN BISCUITS

These are very hard biscuits that should be dipped in coffee, tea, or water before eating. For breakfast, they are traditionally sprinkled with a little olive oil and eaten with cheese.

3 packages (3 tablespoons) active dry yeast
½ teaspoon sugar
1 cup warm water

5 pounds whole wheat flour
2 tablespoons salt
5 cups lukewarm water

In a bowl dissolve the yeast and sugar in warm water. Cover and put in a warm place until quite foamy, about 5 minutes. Put flour in another bowl. Make a well in flour and pour yeast mixture into well, adding flour from sides of bowl. Let rest for 3 minutes. Dissolve salt in 5 cups lukewarm water and add slowly into flour while kneading. Continue kneading until dough is smooth but firm, about 10 minutes (add more water if dough becomes unworkable). Divide dough into seven balls and shape into loaves. Mark loaves into 1-inch diagonal slices, cutting halfway down. Cover with plastic wrap and a damp towel and let rise in a warm place until double in bulk, about 1½ to 2 hours.

Preheat oven to 375 degrees.

Place loaves on oiled cookie sheets and bake for 40 minutes, or until golden. Remove from oven and cool; slice all the way through. Place slices on cookie sheets and return to oven. Lower oven temperature to 250 degrees and bake for 3 hours, or until biscuits are hard.

Note: Biscuits can be used as croutons in salads: Lightly sprinkle biscuits with cold water and cut into bite-size pieces.

[LENTEN]
ENVELOPE BREAD
Peta

YIELD: 12 PIECES

The ubiquitous bread of Greece has hundreds of uses.

1 package (1 tablespoon)
   active dry yeast
3½ cups all-purpose flour
1¼ cups warm water

2 tablespoons olive oil
1 teaspoon salt
¼ teaspoon sugar

In a mixing bowl, combine yeast with 1½ cups of flour. Combine water, oil, salt, and sugar and add to yeast mixture. Beat for ½ minute with an electric mixer at low speed; then beat for 3 minutes at high speed. Work in remaining flour by hand to form a smooth and elastic dough. Put in a greased bowl in a warm spot, cover, and let rise for 45 minutes. Punch dough down, divide into 12 pieces, and roll each into a ball. Let rest for 10 minutes.

Flatten each ball into a 5-inch circle. Place on a greased baking sheet; cover and let rest for 20 to 30 minutes.

Preheat oven to 400 degrees.

Bake for 9 or 10 minutes, until puffed and lightly browned on bottom. Immediately wrap in foil and cool.

DESSERTS

CAKES

CHESTNUT CAKE WITH WHIPPED CREAM	*Tourta me Kastana*
GOLD AND WALNUT CAKE	*Karidato Kozanis*
APRICOT CHOCOLATE CUSTARD CAKE	*Pantespani me Krema Tsokolatas*
APRICOT SAUCE CAKE	*Tourta me Verikoko*
ORANGE CAKE	*Pantespani Portokali*
SAINT FANOURIOS CAKE	*Fanouropita*
PUMPKIN CAKE	*Keik Kolokithas*
NUT CAKE	*Karidopeta*
TAHINI CAKE (L)	*Tahinopita Nistisimi*
CORINTHIAN RAISIN CAKE	*Tourta me Stafides Korinthou*
GOLDEN NUT-MERINGUE CAKE	*Melachrino Xantho*
WALNUT CAKE	*Karidopeta Horis Siropi*
FARINA CAKE	*Ravani*
YOGURT CAKE	*Yiaourtopita*
LENTEN NUT CAKE (L)	*Karidopeta Nistisimi*
CINNAMON NUT RING	*Tourta me Kanela*
RUM TORTE	*Tourta Methismeni*
WALNUT TORTE	*Tourta me Karidia*
CHOCOLATE REFRIGERATOR TORTE	*Tourta Tsokolatas Psigiou*
NOUGAT TORTE	*Tourta Nougatina*

CREAM TORTE	*Tourta me Krema*
APRICOT TART	*Pasta Flora*
HONEY PIE	*Melopeta*
OVEN-BAKED HALVA	*Halva Fournou*
HALVA (STOVE-TOP STYLE)	*Halvas tis Katsarolas*

COOKIES

ALMOND COOKIES	*Pastoules*
BUTTER COOKIES	*Koulourakia*
ANISE AND SESAME SEED COOKIES	*Koulourakia me Glikaniso*
ALMOND ROUNDS	*Amygthalota*
FLAOUNES	
KOURABIEDES	
ICED KOURABIEDES	*Zaharomeni Kourabiedes*
FENIKIA WITH WINE	*Fenikia Krassata*
SKALTSOUNIA COOKIES	*Skaltsounia*
SKALTSOUNIA WITH RAISINS (L)	*Skaltsounia me Stafides*
YO-YO	*Yioyio*
WINE COOKIES	*Tsourekakia*
PINE NUT CRESCENTS	*Misofengara me Koukounaria*
SWEET BISCUITS	*Paximadakia*

PHYLLO DESSERTS

BAKLAVA	
ALMOND TRIANGLES	*Trigona*
ALMOND AND WALNUT TRIANGLES	*Trigona me Amigdala ke Karidia*
ALMOND PHYLLO SQUARES	*Amigdalopeta*
SARAGLI	

ALMOND ROLLS	Roula me Amigdala
BAKLAVA ROLLS	Sourota
COPENHAGEN	
BOUGATSA	
NUT ROLL	Baklava Rolo
KATEMERIA	
BIRDS' NESTS	Folitses
MERINGUE WRAPPED IN PHYLLO	Marenga Rolo
ORANGE GALATOBOUREKO	Galatoboureko me Portokali
ROLLED GALATOBOUREKA	Roula Galatoboureka
CUSTARD FLUTES	Floyeres
KADAIFE EKMEK	
KADAIFE ROLLS	Kadaife Roula
FLAT KADAIFE	Kadaife Tapsiou
CUSTARD KADAIFE	Kadaife me Krema

OTHER DESSERTS

BATTER PUFFS	Svinghi
SWEET FRITTERS	Loukoumades
HONEY ROLLS	Diples
QUICK SWEET FRITTERS	Loukoumades Horis Mayia
MELON WITH OUZO	Peponi me Ouzo

PUDDINGS

CARAMEL CUSTARD	Krema Karamela
GRAPE PUDDING	Moustalevria
YOGURT	Yiaourti
RICE PUDDING	Rizogalo

It is a well-known fact that the Greeks have a sweet tooth. For proof, just peer into a typical *zaharoplastion,* or pastry shop, and observe the enormous array of calorie-laden delights. In this chapter we will take you on a tour of that pastry shop and present the highlights of the Greek baker's art—from a rich Chestnut Cake with Whipped Cream and a delectable Pumpkin Cake to Nougat Torte and Baklava Rolls, a variation of the ever-popular Baklava; from cookies in an array of sizes and shapes to Honey Pie and the nonpareil Greek Halva. Home dessert makers will have fun preparing and eating these delectable goodies.

Name days, weddings, and feast days are some of the occasions for serving certain specific sweets and pastries. Christmas is synonymous with Kourabiedes; New Year's Day is celebrated with the traditional sweet bread New Year's Cake (see p. 208) and Easter brings forth Wine Cookies and Butter Cookies. A baptism or a wedding means that there will be Baklava. It's best to summarize the chapter by saying: "Calorie watchers beware."

Note: The following recipes have been tested with all-purpose flour.

CAKES

꙰꙰꙰꙰꙰꙰꙰꙰꙰꙰

CHESTNUT CAKE WITH WHIPPED CREAM
Tourta me Kastana

YIELD: 10 TO 12 SERVINGS

Chestnuts are plentiful in Greece. This is a simplified version of a very popular—and delicious—Greek dessert.

6 eggs, separated	**1 teaspoon vanilla extract**
1¼ cups sugar	**⅛ teaspoon salt**
1 cup canned unsweetened chestnut puree	**1½ cups heavy cream, whipped**
½ cup chopped almonds, lightly toasted	**one 10-ounce can glacé chestnuts**

Preheat oven to 325 degrees.

In a bowl beat egg yolks and sugar with electric mixer or a whisk until mixture forms ribbons when beater is lifted. Add chestnut puree, chopped almonds, and vanilla extract. In a separate bowl, beat egg whites with salt until stiff. Fold one fourth of the whites into yolk mixture and combine well. Gently fold remaining whites into yolk mixture. Pour batter into two buttered and floured 9-inch cake pans and bake for 35 minutes, or until cake tester comes out clean. Let layers cool in the pans for 15 minutes, then turn onto racks and cool completely. Fill and frost layers with whipped heavy cream. Cut glacé chestnuts in half horizontally and garnish cake.

GOLD AND WALNUT CAKE
Karidato Kozanis

YIELD: 36 TO 40 SERVINGS

This cake comes from the area of Greece called Kozani, in the northern part of the country. It is unusual because it consists of two layers that are baked one on top of the other in the same pan.

FIRST LAYER

4 eggs
1 cup sugar
3 cups cake flour (not self-rising)

3 teaspoons double-acting baking powder
2 sticks (½ pound) unsalted butter, melted and cooled

SECOND LAYER

10 eggs
4 cups sugar
6 cups chopped walnuts
2 cups zwieback crumbs
1 teaspoon ground cinnamon

½ teaspoon ground cloves
¼ cup water
2 cups heavy cream, whipped (optional)

Preheat oven to 350 degrees.

Prepare first layer

Beat eggs, and gradually add sugar, beating all the while. Sift flour with baking powder and add slowly to the mixture. Add half the melted, cooled butter to the batter. Pour remaining butter into a 10 x 15 x 3-inch baking pan. Pour batter into pan and bake for 15 to 20 minutes, or until cake tester comes out clean.

Prepare second layer

Beat second batch of eggs until creamy. Add sugar slowly. Add chopped nuts, zwieback crumbs, cinnamon, cloves, and water and beat until smooth. Remove first layer from oven, pour batter for second layer on top, and continue to bake for 25 minutes, or until tester comes out clean (do not overbake). Cool in pan. When cool, cut in diamonds and serve with whipped cream, if desired.

APRICOT CHOCOLATE CUSTARD CAKE
Pantespani me Krema Tsokolatas

YIELD: 10 TO 12 SERVINGS

Pantespani is the Greek word for sponge cake.

5 eggs
1 cup sugar
½ teaspoon salt

1 teaspoon vanilla extract
1¼ cups all-purpose flour,
    sifted

CHOCOLATE CUSTARD

¾ cup sugar
2 tablespoons cornstarch
3 eggs
1½ cups milk
1 teaspoon vanilla extract

1 ounce unsweetened
    chocolate, shaved
1 stick (¼ pound) unsalted
    butter, at room
    temperature

one 16-ounce jar apricot
    preserves

chocolate sprinkles or finely
    shaved chocolate for
    topping

Preheat oven to 350 degrees.

Grease two 9-inch layer cake pans, line with wax paper, and grease again. Beat eggs until light. Gradually beat in sugar, salt, and vanilla and continue to beat until batter is thick and takes some time to level out when beater is withdrawn. Use an electric beater for this if possible. Carefully fold in flour, 2 tablespoons at a time, mixing until blended after each addition. Pour batter into cake pans and bake for 25 minutes, or until cake tester comes out clean. Cool 10 minutes; remove from pan. When completely cool, split layers horizontally.

While cake is baking, prepare chocolate custard

Combine sugar and cornstarch in a saucepan and add eggs, blending well. Stir in milk and cook over low heat, stirring constantly, until thick, about 10 minutes. Remove from heat and stir in vanilla extract and shaved chocolate. Cover and cool. Cream butter until soft, and add to cooled chocolate mixture. Blend well and cool.

Spread chocolate custard between cake layers. Spread top and sides of cake with apricot preserves and cover sides with chocolate sprinkles or finely shaved chocolate. Chill in refrigerator until ready to serve.

Note: This is a very rich cake; cut thin pieces.

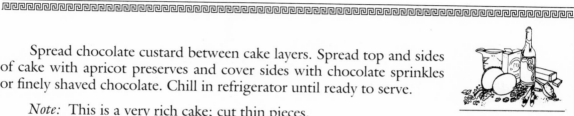

Desserts

APRICOT SAUCE CAKE
Tourta me Verikoko

YIELD: 10 TO 12 SERVINGS

¾ cup chopped dried
  apricots
1 cup water
2 cups sugar
10 tablespoons unsalted
  butter, at room
  temperature
1 teaspoon vanilla extract

1 teaspoon grated lemon
  peel
2 eggs
½ teaspoon salt
2 teaspoons double-acting
  baking powder
2 cups all-purpose flour
1 cup milk

In a small pan, combine apricots, water, and ½ cup sugar; bring to a boil. Cover and simmer gently for 20 minutes. Puree mixture in blender or food processor, or press through a food mill. There should be 1½ cups of puree. If quantity is not correct, either boil, stirring constantly, to reduce, or add water to bring to the exact measure. Blend in 2 tablespoons of butter. Set aside to cool.

Preheat oven to 350 degrees.

In a large mixing bowl, beat together remaining 8 tablespoons butter and 1½ cups sugar until blended. Add vanilla and lemon peel and beat in eggs one at a time. In another bowl, sift together salt, baking powder, and flour. Add flour mixture to butter mixture alternately with milk, beating well after each addition.

Pour batter into a greased and floured 9-inch square pan. Spoon apricot sauce evenly over batter. Bake for 50 to 55 minutes, or until cake tester comes out clean and cake begins to pull away from sides of pan. Serve warm.

ORANGE CAKE
Pantespani Portokali

YIELD: 16 SERVINGS

1 cup sugar
5 eggs, separated
2 sticks (½ pound) unsalted
  butter, melted
4 tablespoons fresh orange
  juice

1 tablespoon grated orange
  peel
1 cup all-purpose flour
3½ teaspoons double-acting
  baking powder

SYRUP

2 cups water
1 cup sugar

2 teaspoons orange extract
  or 2 teaspoons curaçao or
  Grand Marnier liqueur

Preheat oven to 375 degrees.

Mix sugar and egg yolks well. Stir in melted butter, orange juice, peel, flour, and baking powder. Beat egg whites until stiff but not dry. Carefully fold egg whites into orange mixture. Butter an 8 x 10-inch or 9 x 9-inch baking pan. Pour batter into prepared pan and bake for 10 minutes. Lower oven temperature to 350 degrees, and bake for 30 minutes longer, or until cake tests done.

While cake is baking, prepare syrup

Combine water and sugar, bring to a boil, and simmer for 10 minutes. Add orange extract or liqueur, stir, and remove from heat.

When cake has cooled, pour hot syrup over it. Cut into square- or diamond-shaped serving pieces.

SAINT FANOURIOS CAKE
Fanouropita

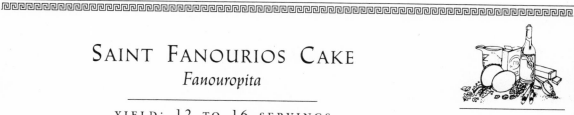

YIELD: 12 TO 16 SERVINGS

Saint Fanourios is the patron saint of the "lost and found." According to tradition, whenever a treasured possession is lost, the owner pledges to bake a fruit cake for Saint Fanourios in the hope of finding it. When the article is found the owner makes good his vow and presents the cake to his neighborhood church for blessing. Afterward, it is distributed to the poor.

1 cup orange juice
½ cup brandy
2 tablespoons unsalted
  butter
2 cups golden raisins
¾ cup sugar
½ cup honey
½ teaspoon salt
1 tablespoon ground
  cinnamon

¼ teaspoon ground cloves
2 cups all-purpose flour
2 teaspoons double-acting
  baking powder
½ teaspoon baking soda
2 tablespoons grated orange
  peel
½ cup sesame seeds
  (optional)
¼ cup brandy

Preheat oven to 325 degrees.

Combine orange juice, brandy, butter, raisins, sugar, honey, salt, cinnamon, and cloves in a large heavy-bottomed saucepan. Bring to a boil, reduce heat, and simmer for 10 minutes, or until thick and syrupy. Set pot in cold water to cool mixture completely.

Sift flour, baking powder, and baking soda into cooled syrup. Beat vigorously for 8 to 10 minutes, or until batter is smooth and bubbly. Stir in grated peel.

Turn into well-buttered 7-inch fluted tube pan or 8-inch loaf pan. Sprinkle with sesame seeds. Bake for 1 to 1½ hours, or until a knife inserted in the center comes out clean. Sprinkle with brandy and cool cake in pan.

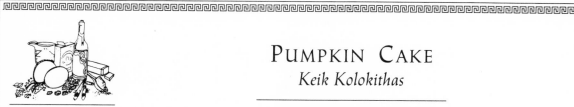

PUMPKIN CAKE
Keik Kolokithas

YIELD: 10 TO 12 SERVINGS

3 cups all-purpose flour
2 cups sugar
2 teaspoons double-acting
  baking powder
1 teaspoon baking soda
1 teaspoon salt
1 teaspoon ground
  cinnamon
1 cup finely chopped
  walnuts
1½ cups vegetable oil
4 eggs, well beaten

2 cups fresh pumpkin,
  cooked and pureed or
  1 pound (2 cups) canned
  unsweetened pumpkin
  puree
1 square (1 ounce)
  unsweetened chocolate,
  melted and cooled
1 cup chopped raisins,
  soaked in ½ cup warm
  water, then drained

Preheat oven to 350 degrees.

Combine flour, sugar, baking powder, baking soda, salt, cinnamon, and walnuts in a large bowl and mix well. Make a well in center of dry ingredients and add oil, eggs, and pumpkin puree mixed with chocolate. Mix until ingredients are well blended. Fold in raisins. Spread in a greased 9-inch round tube pan and bake for 60 to 70 minutes, or until knife inserted in center comes out clean. Cool in pan. Wrap and store at room temperature for 24 hours before serving. (Cake can be refrigerated or frozen.)

Note: To puree pumpkin, peel and cut pumpkin into small cubes. Place in a pot with ½ cup water. Steam until tender, about 10 minutes. Drain and puree by hand or in a food processor. Leftover pumpkin can be frozen.

NUT CAKE
Karidopeta

Desserts

YIELD: 48 SERVINGS

12 eggs, separated
1½ cups sugar
1 teaspoon vanilla extract
3 cups finely chopped
   walnuts
3 cups finely chopped
   blanched almonds

16 pieces zwieback, crushed
   fine
1 tablespoon grated orange
   peel

RUM SYRUP

2 cups sugar
4½ cups water
1 cinnamon stick

1 lemon slice
½ cup light rum

Preheat oven to 350 degrees.

In a large bowl, beat egg whites until stiff. In another bowl, beat yolks with sugar until thick and pale in color. Beat in vanilla extract. In another bowl, mix together nuts, zwieback, and orange peel. Gradually fold beaten egg whites into yolk mixture and fold in nut mixture. Pour batter into a greased 16 x 13 x 3-inch pan and bake for 1 hour, or until cake tester comes out clean.

While cake is baking, make the syrup

In a saucepan, combine sugar, water, cinnamon, and lemon. Bring to a boil, and simmer until sugar is dissolved, about 5 minutes. Remove from heat and stir in rum.

Immediately pour hot syrup over hot cake. Cover with aluminum foil. After cake has cooled completely, cut into diamond-shaped pieces.

Note: Cake can be frozen, once it has been cut. Serve at room temperature.

Note: This recipe can be halved and baked in a 13 x 9 x 2-inch pan.

Variation: Use all walnuts or all almonds, if desired.

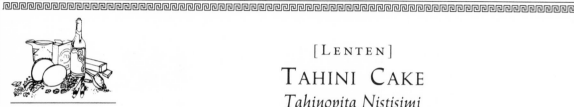

[LENTEN]

TAHINI CAKE

Tahinopita Nistisimi

YIELD: 36 SERVINGS

This is one of the few cakes that can be prepared during Lent because there is no butter in it.

1 cup tahini (sesame seed paste, available in Greek or Middle Eastern specialty shops)
1 cup sugar
2 tablespoons cognac
1 teaspoon baking soda
1½ to 2 cups all-purpose flour

2 teaspoons ground cinnamon
1 cup chopped walnuts
½ cup golden raisins
½ cup glacé fruit
1 cup orange juice

confectioners' sugar for topping

Preheat oven to 350 degrees.

If tahini has separated, stir to blend. Beat tahini in a large bowl with an electric mixer and gradually add sugar. Combine cognac and baking soda and add to mixture.

Sift together 1½ cups of flour with cinnamon and combine with walnuts, raisins, and glacé fruit.

Add flour mixture and orange juice alternately to tahini batter, mixing thoroughly after each addition. (At this point beat by hand if you have been using an electric mixer.) Add water or more flour only if necessary to attain proper consistency—batter should be thicker than an average cake batter.

Butter a 9 x 12 x 2-inch baking pan and line the bottom with buttered wax paper. Pour in batter and spread evenly. Bake for 45 minutes, or until cake is a deep chestnut color. Cool in pan. Dust with confectioners' sugar while cake is still warm. When cake is completely cool, cut into bars or diamond shapes.

Variation: 1 cup walnuts and 1 cup raisins, or 2 cups walnuts can be used instead of the mixture indicated.

CORINTHIAN RAISIN CAKE
Tourta me Stafides Korinthou

YIELD: 10 TO 12 SERVINGS

This cake is served at breakfast. Many hotels in Greece offer it with their continental breakfast.

1½ sticks (6 ounces) unsalted butter, at room temperature
1¾ cups sugar
4 eggs
2 cups milk
3 teaspoons ground cinnamon
½ teaspoon ground cloves
1 teaspoon grated lemon peel
1 teaspoon grated orange peel
3½ cups all-purpose flour
½ cup raisins or currants
3 teaspoons double-acting baking powder
½ cup confectioners' sugar

Preheat oven to 350 degrees.

In a large bowl, cream butter and sugar for 5 minutes. Add eggs, milk, 1 teaspoon cinnamon, ground cloves, lemon and orange peels, and half the flour. Combine raisins, baking powder, and remaining flour and blend with egg mixture until smooth. Pour into a greased 5 x 9-inch loaf pan (which should be three-quarters full). Bake for 40 minutes, or until cake tester comes out clean. Cool in pan and turn cake onto a plate. Combine confectioners' sugar with remaining cinnamon and dust top of cake.

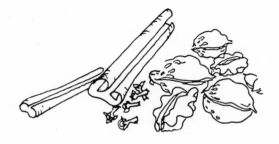

GOLDEN NUT-MERINGUE CAKE
Melachrino Xantho

YIELD: 30 TO 35 SERVINGS

2 sticks (½ pound) unsalted
    butter, at room
    temperature
1½ cups sugar
4 eggs
6 egg yolks (use whites for
    meringue, below)

1 tablespoon grated lemon
    peel
1½ cups all-purpose flour
2½ teaspoons double-acting
    baking powder
1 tablespoon cognac
¼ cup milk

MERINGUE

6 egg whites
1 cup sugar
2 teaspoons fresh lemon
    juice

4 cups chopped walnuts

SYRUP

½ cup sugar

1 cup water

Preheat oven to 350 degrees.

Cream butter until light and gradually beat in sugar. Beat eggs and egg yolks until light; gradually beat into creamed mixture. Stir in grated lemon peel. Sift together flour and baking powder and stir into egg mixture alternately with cognac and milk. Butter a 10 x 14 x 2-inch pan; pour batter into pan and bake about 40 minutes, or until cake tests done. Remove from oven and cool in pan. Lower oven temperature to 300 degrees.

While cake is cooling, prepare meringue

Beat egg whites until they stand in soft peaks. Gradually beat in sugar, continuing to beat until meringue is glossy. Add lemon juice, and fold in chopped nuts.

Spread meringue-nut mixture over cooled cake. Return to oven, and bake for 15 to 20 minutes, or until meringue is browned. Cool cake.

While cake is cooling, prepare syrup

Combine sugar and water in a saucepan. Bring to a boil, and simmer 10 minutes.

When cake is cool, pour hot syrup over it, cover with aluminum foil, and let stand until cool. Cut into 2-inch squares to serve.

Note: This cake is best if made 3 or 4 days in advance of serving. Cover with plastic wrap or aluminum foil and refrigerate. Remove three hours before serving and bring to room temperature.

WALNUT CAKE
Karidopeta Horis Siropi

YIELD: 24 SERVINGS

The traditional Karidopeta is served with a syrup; this delicious version is so rich that it is served without one.

8 eggs
3½ cups sugar
1 stick (¼ pound) unsalted butter, melted
4 cups chopped nuts (walnuts or almonds)
1 cup ground zwieback
½ teaspoon baking soda
1 teaspoon ground cinnamon

1 teaspoon ground nutmeg
2 teaspoons double-acting baking powder
2 tablespoons brandy
1½ tablespoons fresh lemon juice
1 cup heavy cream, whipped (optional)

Preheat oven to 350 degrees.

In a large mixing bowl, beat eggs with sugar. Add butter and, when well blended, add remaining ingredients except cream.

Grease well an 11 x 14-inch rectangular cake pan. Pour mixture into pan and bake for 35 minutes, or until cake tester comes out clean. Cool completely in pan. Cut into squares. Can be served with whipped cream.

The Complete Book of
GREEK COOKING

FARINA CAKE
Ravani

YIELD: 48 SERVINGS

4 sticks (1 pound) unsalted
    butter, at room
    temperature
2 cups sugar
12 eggs
2 cups sifted all-purpose
    flour

2 tablespoons double-acting
    baking powder
1½ cups regular uncooked
    farina

SYRUP

4 cups sugar
4 cups water

1 tablespoon vanilla extract

1 cup heavy cream, whipped
    (optional)

½ cup toasted chopped nuts
    (optional)

Preheat oven to 350 degrees.

In a large bowl, beat butter with an electric mixer until fluffy. Slowly add sugar, continuing to beat. At low speed, add eggs, one at a time, beating well after each addition. Sift flour and baking powder together, then add to mixture. Add farina and mix well until batter is fairly thick. Spread batter evenly in a greased 11 x 17-inch cake pan. Bake for 40 to 45 minutes, or until cake tester comes out clean.

While cake is baking, prepare syrup

In saucepan, combine sugar, water, and vanilla extract. Bring to a boil and simmer for 40 minutes. Once cake is done, ladle hot syrup over hot cake (keep cake in baking pan). Cover with aluminum foil and let cool. When cake is completely cool, cut into 1½-inch squares.

If you wish, put a dollop of whipped cream on each square and top with toasted chopped nuts.

Note: Recipe can be successfully halved. This cake freezes well.

YOGURT CAKE
Yiaourtopita

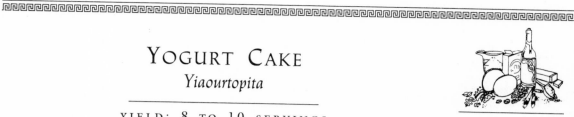

YIELD: 8 TO 10 SERVINGS

2 cups yogurt, undrained
3½ cups farina
1 teaspoon baking soda
2 teaspoons double-acting
   baking powder

2¼ cups sugar
1 cup chopped blanched
   almonds
2 tablespoons grated orange
   peel

SYRUP

3 cups water
3½ cups sugar

1 tablespoon grated lemon
   peel

Preheat oven to 350 degrees.

Place yogurt in a bowl and stir with a fork. In another bowl, combine farina with baking soda and baking powder, add to yogurt. Add sugar, almonds, and orange peel to the yogurt mixture and mix well for 2 or 3 minutes. Pour batter into a well-greased 9-inch square baking pan and bake for 30 to 40 minutes, or until cake tester comes out clean.

While cake is baking, prepare the syrup

Place water and sugar in a saucepan and bring to a boil. Add lemon peel. Simmer for 10 minutes.

Pour hot syrup over hot cake. Let cool. Cut into 8 to 10 pieces.

[LENTEN]

LENTEN NUT CAKE
Karidopeta Nistisimi

YIELD: 24 SERVINGS

This cake is prepared during the Lenten period because there is no butter in it.

4 cups all-purpose flour
1 tablespoon ground cloves
3 teaspoons double-acting
  baking powder
1 cup raisins
1 cup vegetable oil
1½ cups sugar
2 cups water
1 teaspoon baking soda

½ cup cognac
1 tablespoon grated lemon
  peel
1½ cups chopped walnuts
confectioners' sugar for
  topping
ground cinnamon for
  topping

Preheat oven to 350 degrees.

Sift flour into a bowl with cloves and baking powder. Sprinkle a little of the flour mixture over raisins. Add oil to flour and blend well. Make a well in the center of flour-oil mixture. Add sugar, 2 cups water, and baking soda dissolved in cognac. Mix lightly. Add lemon peel, raisins, and nuts. Mix well. Grease a 9 x 12-inch pan and pour in batter. Bake for about 1 hour, or until cake tester comes out clear. Cool in pan, remove, and sprinkle with confectioners' sugar and cinnamon. Cut into squares and serve cold.

CINNAMON NUT RING
Tourta me Kanela

YIELD: 12 TO 14 SERVINGS

This is commonly referred to as the "one, two, three" cake because it has 1 cup butter, 2 cups sugar, and 3 cups flour. It is a very basic pound cake made in a tube pan.

2 sticks (½ pound) unsalted butter or margarine, at room temperature
2 cups sugar
4 eggs
2 teaspoons double-acting baking powder

1 cup warm milk
3 cups all-purpose flour
2 teaspoons ground cinnamon
½ cup chopped almonds
½ cup chopped walnuts

Preheat oven to 350 degrees.

Grease a 10-inch tube pan and dust with flour.

Blend butter and sugar in a mixing bowl. Add eggs and beat until well blended. Combine baking powder with warm milk and stir into batter. Add flour and beat until batter is creamy and smooth. Add cinnamon, almonds, and walnuts. Pour batter into pan and bake for 50 minutes, or until cake tester comes out clean. Cool 15 minutes before removing from pan.

Variation: Other nuts (pecans, for instance) can be used instead of almonds and walnuts.

RUM TORTE
Tourta Methismeni

YIELD: 12 SERVINGS

1 stick (¼ pound) unsalted butter, at room temperature
1 cup sugar
2 eggs, separated
1 teaspoon grated orange peel
2 cups sifted all-purpose flour

2 teaspoons double-acting baking powder
¼ teaspoon salt
¼ teaspoon baking soda
½ cup orange juice
3 tablespoons light rum
¼ teaspoon almond extract
½ teaspoon vanilla extract

WHIPPED CREAM FILLING

2 teaspoons unflavored gelatin
2 tablespoons water

2 cups heavy cream
½ cup confectioners' sugar
⅓ cup light rum

CHOCOLATE FROSTING

4 squares (4 ounces) unsweetened chocolate
1 cup confectioners' sugar
2 tablespoons hot water

2 eggs
6 tablespoons unsalted butter, softened

TOPPING

6 tablespoons light rum

1½ cups chopped walnuts

Preheat oven to 350 degrees.

Cream butter with ¾ cup of sugar until soft and fluffy. Beat in egg yolks, one at a time. Add orange peel. Sift together flour, baking powder, salt, and baking soda.

Combine orange juice with rum and almond and vanilla extracts. Add liquids to butter-sugar mixture alternately with sifted dry ingredients, blending well.

In a separate bowl, beat egg whites until they form soft peaks, gradually adding ¼ cup sugar. Fold batter into egg whites. Pour into two greased 9-inch layer cake pans. Bake for 25 minutes, or until cake tester comes out clean. Cool in pan.

Prepare filling

Sprinkle gelatin over water in a small saucepan. Warm over low heat until gelatin dissolves. Let cool until gelatin resembles the consistency of egg whites, about 5 to 10 minutes.

Whip heavy cream with sugar until thick. Gradually add rum. Beat in gelatin until just stiff enough to hold its shape.

Prepare frosting

Place the chocolate in top of a double boiler over simmering water; stir until melted. Remove from heat and add sugar and water. Beat in eggs one at a time. Add butter and beat until smooth and light.

To assemble, cut each cake layer in half horizontally to make four layers. Sprinkle one layer with 2 tablespoons rum, then spread one third of cream filling over it. Top with a second layer; sprinkle it with rum and a third of cream filling; repeat process with third layer. When fourth layer is in place, frost top and sides of cake with chocolate frosting. Press walnuts into sides of cake. Refrigerate overnight.

WALNUT TORTE
Tourta me Karidia

YIELD: 10 TO 12 SERVINGS

9 eggs, separated
1 cup sugar
3 cups ground walnuts
½ cup dry breadcrumbs
1 tablespoon grated orange peel
2 teaspoons grated lemon peel

1 teaspoon ground cinnamon
½ teaspoon ground cloves
½ teaspoon salt
2 teaspoons double-acting baking powder
1 teaspoon vanilla extract
½ cup water

BRANDY BUTTER CREAM

1 stick (¼ pound) unsalted butter, at room temperature
2 cups confectioners' sugar (1 pound)

⅛ teaspoon salt
1 egg
1 teaspoon vanilla extract
2 tablespoons brandy

⅔ cup coarsely broken walnuts

Preheat oven to 350 degrees.

Line the bottoms of three 8-inch layer cake pans with wax paper and lightly butter pans.

In a medium-sized bowl, beat egg yolks with sugar at high speed until very thick and lemon-colored. In a large bowl, stir together ground walnuts, breadcrumbs, orange peel, lemon peel, cinnamon, cloves, salt, and baking powder. Mix vanilla extract and water with egg yolks, then stir into walnut mixture.

In another large bowl, beat egg whites until stiff but not dry. Fold gently into walnut batter until thoroughly combined. Pour into prepared pans.

Bake for 30 minutes, or until cake tester comes out clean. Invert pans on racks, loosen each cake around the edges, and turn out of pan. Remove wax paper and let cool.

Prepare the brandy butter cream filling

Beat butter in a small bowl until creamy. Add sugar and salt and blend well. Beat in egg, vanilla extract, and brandy.

Fill and frost the three layers. Lightly press broken walnuts into frosting on top of the torte.

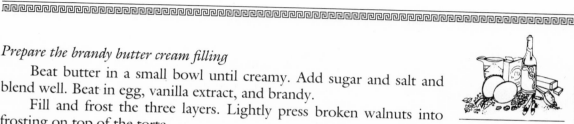

CHOCOLATE REFRIGERATOR TORTE
Tourta Tsokolatas Psigiou

YIELD: 10 TO 12 SERVINGS

Store-bought tea biscuits are used extensively in Greece. Here they are part of an interesting combination.

8 ounces social tea biscuits
½ cup milk
1 ounce brandy
2 sticks (½ pound) unsalted butter, at room temperature

1 cup confectioners' sugar
3 eggs, separated
2 teaspoons vanilla extract
¼ cup unsweetened cocoa
½ cup almonds, blanched and toasted

Break biscuits in half and soak in milk and brandy. Beat butter with sugar for about 5 minutes. Add yolks to the butter-sugar mixture. Mix in vanilla extract, cocoa, and nuts. Beat egg whites until stiff and fold into mixture. Blend in moistened biscuits and pour into a well-buttered loaf pan lined with buttered wax paper. Put in freezer until hard, about 4 hours. Remove from freezer ½ hour before serving, and keep in refrigerator until ready to serve.

Nougat Torte
Tourta Nougatina

YIELD: 10 TO 12 SERVINGS

CRUST

3 cups finely chopped
blanched almonds, or
3 cups finely chopped
walnuts
1¼ cups sugar

1 tablespoon ground
cinnamon
8 egg whites, at room
temperature
flour for dusting cake pans

FILLING

3 tablespoons all-purpose
flour
3 tablespoons cornstarch
½ cup sugar

8 egg yolks
3 cups milk
1 teaspoon vanilla extract

TOPPING

3 tablespoons apricot
preserves
2 cups heavy cream,
whipped

½ cup chopped toasted
almonds
candied cherries, sliced, for
decoration

Preheat oven to 300 degrees.

Prepare the crust

In a mixing bowl, combine chopped nuts, sugar, and cinnamon. In a large bowl, beat egg whites until stiff. Fold egg whites into nut mixture. Line the bottoms of three 8-inch round baking pans with wax paper, and butter and flour them lightly. Pour one third of the mixture into each pan and flatten to form crusts. Bake for 15 minutes, or until cake tester comes out clean. Cool in pan.

While crust is in the oven, prepare the filling

Combine flour, cornstarch, sugar, egg yolks, and 1 cup milk in top of a double boiler. Mix well with a whisk. Set over simmering water, add remaining milk, and cook until mixture thickens. Add vanilla extract. Remove from heat and cool in the refrigerator.

To assemble, place one layer on a serving plate and cover well with half the filling. Top with a second layer and the remaining filling. Spread preserves over the third layer and place on top of filling. Cover top and sides with whipped cream. Sprinkle with toasted almonds and decorate with sliced cherries.

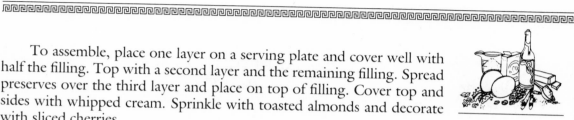

CREAM TORTE
Tourta me Krema

YIELD: 15 SERVINGS

Tourta is the Greek word for butter cake. Zwieback, in Greece called paximathi, is a dry, toastlike cookie.

one 6-ounce box zwieback, ground
1 stick (¼ pound) unsalted butter, melted
½ cup sugar
1 teaspoon ground cinnamon

5 cups milk
5 teaspoons cornstarch
5 tablespoons sugar
6 eggs, separated
¼ teaspoon salt
1 teaspoon vanilla extract

Combine zwieback crumbs, melted butter, sugar, and cinnamon in a bowl. Reserve 1 cup of this crumb mixture and press remaining crumbs onto bottom and sides of a 9 x 11 x 2-inch cake pan.

Preheat oven to 350 degrees.

Heat 4 cups milk in a small saucepan and set aside. In another saucepan, combine cornstarch, sugar, egg yolks, salt, and remaining cup of milk. Gradually stir in hot milk. Cook over low heat, stirring constantly, for about 8 minutes, or until custard thickens. Add vanilla extract. Pour custard mixture into prepared pan. Beat egg whites until stiff and spread evenly over custard. Sprinkle with reserved crumb mixture, and bake for 40 to 45 minutes, or until cake tester comes out clean. Cool and cut into 2-inch squares.

APRICOT TART
Pasta Flora

YIELD: 30 TO 40 PIECES

Pasta Flora means "flower tart." The filling is usually made with apricot preserves, but quince or cherry are popular alternatives.

2 sticks (½ pound) unsalted butter, at room temperature
½ cup sugar
3 egg yolks, beaten
1 teaspoon vanilla extract
½ teaspoon double-acting baking powder

¼ cup milk
2 tablespoons brandy
4 cups all-purpose flour
1 pound apricot preserves
1 egg white, lightly beaten

Preheat oven to 350 degrees.

In a large bowl, cream butter and sugar together. Add egg yolks and vanilla extract and mix well. Mix baking powder with the milk, and stir in with the brandy. Stir in enough flour to make a soft dough. Roll out thin two thirds of the dough on a floured board and with it line a buttered shallow 10 x 14-inch pan, or pat dough thin into pan. Cover dough with apricot preserves. Roll out thin remaining dough and cut into long strips. Cover preserves with the strips, making a lattice pattern. Brush with egg white and bake 30 minutes, or until cake tester comes out clean. Cut into squares and remove from pan while warm.

Variation: 2 cups grated quince preserves or 1-pound jar cherry preserves can be used instead of apricot preserves.

HONEY PIE
Melopeta

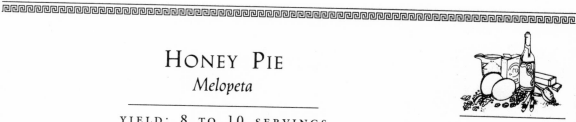

Desserts

YIELD: 8 TO 10 SERVINGS

This is an Easter treat on the island of Sifnos. The pie is made from a soft unsalted ewe's milk cheese called mizithra. Since mizithra is not easily obtainable outside Greece, fresh ricotta cheese, which it closely resembles, can be substituted.

PIE SHELL

2 cups all-purpose flour
½ cup sugar
5½ tablespoons unsalted butter, at room temperature

1 egg plus 1 egg yolk
2 tablespoons cognac

FILLING

1 pound soft mizithra or ricotta cheese
3 eggs
½ cup honey
1 tablespoon grated lemon peel

3 tablespoons all-purpose flour
⅓ cup sugar

ground cinnamon for topping

Preheat oven to 350 degrees.

Prepare pie shell

Mix flour, sugar, and butter together in a small mixing bowl. Add egg, egg yolk, and cognac and blend well. Press half of the mixture evenly in a 9-inch pie plate. (Freeze the other half for another time or use as a crust for a second pie.)

Combine all filling ingredients and pour into unbaked pie shell. Sprinkle with cinnamon and bake for 1 hour, or until firm. Serve at room temperature.

OVEN-BAKED HALVA
Halva Fournou

YIELD: 24 SERVINGS

5 eggs
2 cups sugar
2 sticks (½ pound) unsalted
  butter, melted and cooled
2 cups milk
1 teaspoon vanilla extract
one 14-ounce box uncooked
  regular farina

2 teaspoons double-acting
  baking powder
1¼ teaspoons baking soda
1 teaspoon ground
  cinnamon
1 cup chopped walnuts or
  slivered almonds

SYRUP

2 cups sugar
2½ cups water

1½ tablespoons fresh lemon
  juice

Preheat oven to 325 degrees.

Beat eggs in a medium-sized mixing bowl. Gradually add sugar, butter, milk, vanilla extract, and dry ingredients and mix well. Add nuts. Pour into a greased 10 x 14 x 2-inch baking pan. Bake for 40 to 45 minutes, or until cake tester comes out clean.

In the meantime, prepare syrup

Combine sugar, water, and lemon juice, bring to a boil, and simmer for 15 minutes.

Pour hot syrup over hot halva. Cut in squares.

Halva (Stove-Top Style)
Halva tis Katsarolas

YIELD: 12 SERVINGS

Most non-Greeks associate the word *halva* with a very sweet sesame candy. In Greece, however, the term also applies to a popular dessert made with farina. Fast and easy to make, Greek halva is an excellent last-minute dessert for unexpected guests.

1 stick (¼ pound) unsalted butter
1 cup regular uncooked farina
⅛ cup pine nuts, toasted (optional)

1 cup sugar
1 cup milk
1 cup water
ground cinnamon for topping

Melt butter in a heavy skillet. Stir in farina and nuts and brown over low heat for about 15 minutes, stirring constantly.

While farina is browning, combine sugar, milk, and water in a saucepan. Bring to a boil and boil for 10 minutes.

When farina is browned, slowly stir hot syrup into it. Remove from heat, cover skillet with a dish towel to absorb steam, cover with lid, and let stand for 30 minutes.

Serve warm in bowls, sprinkled with cinnamon. Or spread halva onto a shallow platter to cool. Cut into diamond-shaped pieces and serve cold sprinkled with cinnamon.

COOKIES

ALMOND COOKIES
Pastoules

YIELD: 45 TO 50 COOKIES

3 sticks (¾ pound) unsalted
   butter, at room
   temperature
1 cup sugar
1 teaspoon double-acting
   baking powder
4 eggs, separated and at
   room temperature

3¼ cups all-purpose flour
12 ounces shelled almonds,
   chopped
confectioners' sugar for
   dipping
1 cup orange marmalade or
   raspberry preserves

Preheat oven to 350 degrees.

Cream butter and sugar in a large bowl. Add baking powder and egg yolks, one at a time. When yolks are blended, add flour, 1 cup at a time, blending to form a soft dough.

In another bowl, beat egg whites until fluffy but not stiff.

Shape dough into round, flattened balls 1 inch in diameter. Dip each cookie into beaten egg whites and then roll in chopped almonds. Make a groove in the center of each cookie and place on an ungreased cookie sheet about 1 inch apart. Bake for 20 to 25 minutes, or until lightly golden. Let cool on the sheet and then dip in confectioners' sugar. Place ¼ teaspoon preserves in the center of each cookie.

BUTTER COOKIES
Koulourakia

YIELD: 8 TO 10 DOZEN SMALL COOKIES

Desserts

Koulourakia are butter cookies made in various shapes—little circles, small braids, tiny coils, figure eights, etc. The recipe makes a large amount, but the cookies keep well (if you have a good hiding place).

4 sticks (1 pound) unsalted
   butter, at room
   temperature
2 cups sugar
6 eggs
2 teaspoons vanilla extract

8 to 9 cups all-purpose flour
2 tablespoons double-acting
   baking powder
1 egg beaten with
1 tablespoon water

Preheat oven to 375 degrees.

Cream butter and gradually beat in sugar. Beat eggs until light; add to butter mixture and beat thoroughly. Add vanilla extract. Sift together flour and baking powder. Carefully blend into butter-egg mixture to make a soft dough. Shape dough with lightly floured hands into desired shapes and arrange on ungreased cookie sheets (see diagram below). Brush with beaten egg and water. Bake for 20 minutes, or until golden brown. Cool on racks.

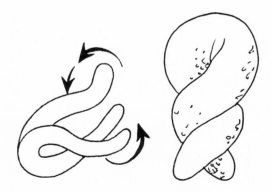

ANISE AND SESAME SEED COOKIES
Koulourakia me Glikaniso

YIELD: 8 DOZEN COOKIES

¾ cup olive oil
1 tablespoon aniseed
1 tablespoon sesame seeds
1 cup sugar
½ cup fresh lemon juice
1 teaspoon grated lemon
  peel
1 teaspoon grated orange
  peel

4½ cups sifted all-purpose
  flour
1 tablespoon ground
  cinnamon
sliced blanched almonds for
  topping
cinnamon sugar for topping
  (see note)

Preheat oven to 375 degrees.

Heat olive oil, aniseed, and sesame seeds over medium heat for 5 minutes. Cool. Add sugar, lemon juice, lemon peel, and orange peel.

Combine flour and cinnamon. Stir flour, one cup at a time, into oil mixture. Work dough with hands until smooth. Cover and let stand for 30 minutes.

Roll out dough on a lightly floured board to a thickness of ¼ inch. Cut with a 2-inch round cookie cutter and place on an ungreased cookie sheet. Decorate with almond slices, pressing so they adhere. Bake for 12 to 15 minutes, or until light brown. Sprinkle with cinnamon sugar and cool on racks.

Note: To make cinnamon sugar, combine 1 tablespoon cinnamon with 2 tablespoons sugar. Mix thoroughly.

Note: This recipe can be cut in half.

ALMOND ROUNDS
Amygthalota

YIELD: APPROXIMATELY 24 COOKIES

Amygthalota are sweet cookies similar to marzipan, made of ground almonds and sugar, and dipped in rose water.

1 pound (4 cups) blanched almonds
1 cup sugar
1 teaspoon vanilla extract
3 egg whites, lightly beaten
⅓ cup soft breadcrumbs, made from day-old white bread, edges trimmed
1 cup orange-flavor water or rose water (available at Greek specialty shops)
confectioners' sugar for dusting

Preheat oven to 350 degrees.

In a food processor or by hand, grind almonds with 2 tablespoons sugar until very fine. Add remaining sugar, vanilla extract, egg whites, and breadcrumbs. Knead to form a dough. Break off pieces of dough about the size of a walnut. Shape into 1½-inch rounds. Arrange on buttered cookie sheet and bake for 15 minutes, or until golden. Cool on sheet.

Dip each cookie into orange-flavor water or rose water and dust generously with confectioners' sugar. Store in an airtight container.

FLAOUNES

YIELD: 24 TO 30 COOKIES

These are the traditional Easter cookies of Cyprus.

¾ cup corn oil
2 eggs
4 teaspoons sugar
3 pieces masticha flavoring
   (optional; see glossary in
   Appendix) or ½ teaspoon
   aniseed

¼ cup milk, warmed
2½ cups all-purpose flour
1 teaspoon double-acting
   baking powder
¼ teaspoon salt

FILLING

2 cups ricotta cheese or soft
   fresh mizithra
1 cup grated kefalotiri (or
   romano) and kasseri
   cheese, mixed

2 eggs
2 tablespoons uncooked
   semolina or farina
2 tablespoons finely
   chopped fresh mint leaves

sesame seeds for topping

In a mixing bowl, beat corn oil with 1 egg until thick. Add 3 teaspoons sugar and beat. Pound masticha or aniseed with remaining teaspoon of sugar and add to batter. Add warm milk. Blend well. In another bowl, sift flour with baking powder and salt. Gradually add to batter, mixing by hand when dough becomes thick. Knead for 6 to 10 minutes, or until elastic and smooth. Cover and let rest for a few hours before rolling.

In the meantime, prepare filling

Combine ricotta or mizithra, grated cheeses, eggs, semolina or farina, and mint. The filling should be thick and flavorful.

Preheat oven to 350 degrees.

Break off sections of dough and roll out as thin as possible. Using a round plate or pastry cutter, cut out 6-inch circles. Fill center of each with 2 heaping tablespoons of filling. Fold up sides of circle to form squares or triangles, or some of each, leaving cheese filling exposed in center. Put on greased cookie sheets. Beat remaining egg and use to brush dough edges. Sprinkle the Flaounes with sesame seeds and bake for 20 to 25 minutes, or until dough is crisp and a golden chestnut color and filling is firm. Serve warm.

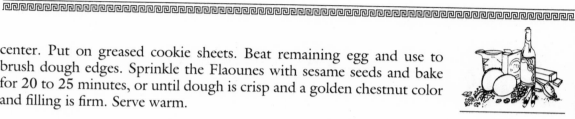

Variation: 1 teaspoon cinnamon can be substituted for mint, and ½ cup raisins can be added along with cheese. Cottage or farmer cheese can be used instead of ricotta if you are counting calories. Also, instead of making the dough from scratch, you might want to use refrigerated butterflake dinner rolls. Separate and flatten the pieces and proceed as described above.

KOURABIEDES

YIELD: 75 COOKIES

Kourabiedes are the favorite cookie of the Greeks—a rich, short cookie covered with powdered sugar. They are made for all festive occasions.

1 pound whipped sweet butter, at room temperature
¾ cup confectioners' sugar
2 teaspoons vanilla extract

2 tablespoons brandy
4½ cups all-purpose flour confectioners' sugar for dusting

Preheat oven to 350 degrees.

Whip butter until white. Slowly add confectioners' sugar, vanilla extract, and brandy. Gradually add flour, 1 cup at a time. Shape into small crescents and place on ungreased cookie sheets. Bake for 20 minutes, or until cookies are sand-colored.

Sift confectioners' sugar onto a large sheet of wax paper. Upon removing cookies from oven, carefully place on sugar and sift additional sugar over tops and sides. Cool thoroughly on racks before storing.

Variation: Add one cup finely chopped blanched almonds to the soft dough and proceed as above.

ICED KOURABIEDES
Zaharomeni Kourabiedes

YIELD: 2 DOZEN COOKIES

½ pound whipped sweet
  butter, at room
  temperature
½ cup confectioners' sugar

1 egg yolk
1½ tablespoons cognac
2½ cups all-purpose flour
  (approximately)

ICING

2 cups sifted confectioners'
  sugar

2 tablespoons hot milk
½ teaspoon almond extract

Preheat oven to 325 degrees.

In a mixing bowl, beat butter with electric mixer for about 5 minutes at medium speed. Gradually add sugar and beat 3 minutes more. Add egg yolk and beat another 3 minutes. Add cognac and beat another minute. Gradually add 2 cups flour and mix well at low speed until dough is soft and slightly sticky (add up to ½ cup flour if dough is too sticky). Shape dough by hand into any cookie shape desired; cookies should be about ½ inch thick. Place on an ungreased cookie sheet and bake for 15 minutes, or until pale golden. Cool on racks.

Make the icing

Blend sugar, milk, and almond extract well. Spread over cooled Kourabiedes.

Fenikia with Wine
Fenikia Krassata

YIELD: 10 DOZEN COOKIES

Fenikia are honey-dipped cookies, sometimes called Melomakarona. The recipe is said to have originated with the Venetians, hence the name.

3 cups corn oil
2 sticks (½ pound) unsalted butter, at room temperature
1 cup sugar
1 teaspoon double-acting baking powder
1 cup dry white wine

3 tablespoons whiskey
9 to 10 cups all-purpose flour
4 to 4½ cups walnuts, chopped fine
1 teaspoon ground cinnamon

SYRUP

2 cups water
2 cups honey

2 cups sugar

Preheat oven to 350 degrees.

Combine oil, butter, and sugar in a mixing bowl; blend well. Dilute baking powder in wine and add to batter. Add whiskey and flour, 1 cup at a time, to form a soft dough. Shape dough 1 tablespoonful at a time into oblong, sausage-shaped cookies about 2 inches long. Place on an ungreased cookie sheet. Bake for 20 to 25 minutes, or until golden. Remove and cool on racks.

In a small bowl, combine chopped walnuts with cinnamon and set aside.

When cookies are cool, prepare syrup

Combine water, honey, and sugar in a heavy saucepan and boil for 10 minutes. Reduce heat to low and dip each cookie in warm syrup, then roll in walnut-cinnamon mixture.

Note: Cookies can be baked and stored in an airtight container. When ready to use, dip in hot syrup and roll in chopped walnuts. Syrup can be stored in refrigerator and reheated and reused as needed.

Skaltsounia Cookies
Skaltsounia

YIELD: APPROXIMATELY 40 CRESCENTS

These turnovers filled with nuts or cheese and either fried or baked are favorites on the Greek islands.

FILLING

1 cup chopped walnuts
1 cup chopped unblanched almonds
½ cup sesame seeds, toasted and pounded in a mortar
¼ cup sugar
3 tablespoons cognac

1 teaspoon grated nutmeg
½ teaspoon ground cinnamon
grated peel and juice of 2 tangerines or 1 large orange

DOUGH

1 stick (¼ pound) butter, at room temperature
⅓ cup sugar
⅓ cup vegetable oil
⅓ cup fresh orange juice
½ teaspoon ground cinnamon

¼ teaspoon baking soda
1½ tablespoons brandy
½ teaspoon double-acting baking powder
2 to 3 cups all-purpose flour

confectioners' sugar for dusting

Make the filling

In a small bowl, mix the nuts, sesame seeds, sugar, cognac, nutmeg, cinnamon, tangerine peel, and juice. Set aside.

Make the dough

Cream butter until light. Gradually add sugar and oil; continue beating for about 5 minutes. Add orange juice, cinnamon, and baking soda diluted in brandy. Sift baking powder with 1 cup flour and add to mixture. Slowly add enough flour to form a soft dough, and knead for about 2 minutes.

Preheat oven to 350 degrees.

Roll out dough, one rounded tablespoonful at a time, into 4- or 5-inch circles. Place a teaspoon of the filling on one half of each circle. Fold the other half down to form a crescent. Press with the fingers to seal the edges or use a pastry crimp. Place on ungreased cookie sheet and bake for 15 to 20 minutes, or until a very light rosy color. Immediately dust with confectioners' sugar and cool in pans.

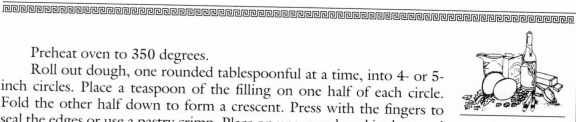

Desserts

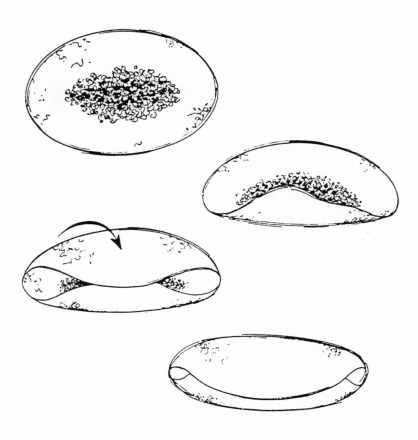

[LENTEN]

SKALTSOUNIA WITH RAISINS

Skaltsounia me Stafides

YIELD: 24 TO 26 COOKIES

DOUGH

3 cups all-purpose flour
1 teaspoon double-acting
  baking powder
1 cup tahini (sesame seed
  paste available in Greek
  specialty shops)

½ cup warm water
2 tablespoons honey

FILLING

½ cup chopped walnuts
½ cup chopped unblanched
  almonds

½ cup seedless raisins
½ cup orange marmalade
2 tablespoons honey

rose water for sprinkling

1½ cups confectioners'
  sugar

Preheat oven to 350 degrees.

Make dough

Sift flour and baking powder together. Add tahini and blend with fingers. Add water and honey. Roll dough out to a thickness of ⅓ inch and cut into 5-inch rounds.

Prepare filling

Combine nuts, raisins, marmalade, and honey. Place 1 tablespoon of filling on each round of dough. Fold dough to form a half circle, brush with a little water to seal, and press edges together. Put on ungreased cookie sheets and bake 30 minutes, or until golden. Sprinkle with rose water while hot and dust with confectioners' sugar. Cool on sheets.

Note: This dough makes a good Lenten *(nistisimo)* pie crust for any purpose.

Yo-Yo
Yioyio

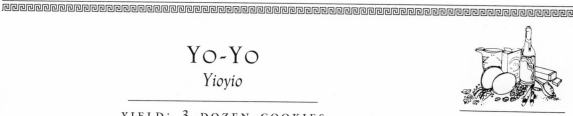

YIELD: 3 DOZEN COOKIES

4 sticks (1 pound) unsalted
  butter, at room
  temperature
½ cup confectioners' sugar
1 egg, beaten
1 cup finely chopped
  blanched almonds
5 tablespoons brandy
⅓ cup orange juice

1 teaspoon double-acting
  baking powder
4½ to 5 cups sifted all-
  purpose flour
2 cups apricot or raspberry
  preserves
confectioners' sugar for
  dusting

Preheat oven to 350 degrees.

Cream butter until very light. Add sugar, egg, almonds, brandy, and orange juice and beat for 2 minutes. Sift baking powder with flour and carefully blend into butter mixture. Shape into small round cookies the size of a quarter and about ¼ inch thick, or roll dough out to a thickness of ¼ inch and cut with a round cookie cutter. Bake on ungreased cookie sheet for 15 minutes, or until lightly golden. Cool on racks.

Spread preserves over half the cookies and top with remaining half to form "sandwiches." Sprinkle a piece of wax paper with confectioners' sugar and place cookies on it. Sprinkle more confectioners' sugar on top to cover completely. Cool thoroughly on wax paper before storing.

WINE COOKIES
Tsourekakia

YIELD: 75 COOKIES

The traditional Tsourekakia cookies are made at Eastertime by taking three 3-inch-long strips of dough, laying them next to each other, and pinching them together at the ends, like three fingers. These represent the symbolic trinity of Easter.

1¼ cups sugar
3 sticks (¾ pound) unsalted butter, at room temperature
½ cup vegetable oil
⅛ cup cognac

1 teaspoon double-acting baking powder
½ cup dry white wine
6 to 7 cups all-purpose flour
1 egg, lightly beaten with 1 tablespoon water

Preheat oven to 350 degrees.

Cream sugar and butter until well blended. Add oil and beat well. Add cognac. Dilute baking powder in ¼ cup wine and add to batter. When well blended, add remaining ¼ cup of wine. Slowly add flour, 1 cup at a time. Work flour to form a soft dough, using your hands as mixture thickens. To facilitate handling, divide dough into chunks, knead each chunk several minutes, and roll out to a thickness of ¼ inch.

Shape dough into various forms

To make trinity cookies, roll dough into 3 strips, ¼ inch thick and 2 inches long. Place three strips next to each other, and pinch the edges

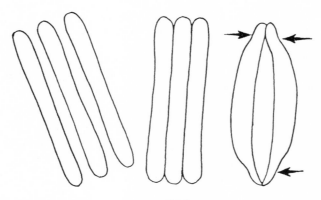

together at the top and bottom of the cookie. To make crescents, roll dough ¼ inch thick and 3 inches long; form into a crescent. To make twists, roll dough ¼ inch thick and 4 inches long. Fold in half and twist. The rolled dough can also be cut with any type of cookie cutter.

Place on an ungreased cookie sheet. Using a pastry brush, brush each cookie with a little egg wash. Bake for 30 minutes, or until golden brown. Cool completely on racks. Store in airtight containers.

Note: Recipe can be doubled successfully.

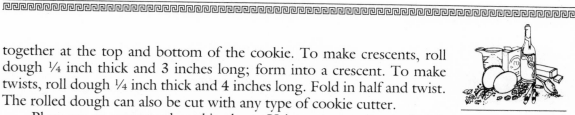

Desserts

PINE NUT CRESCENTS
Misofengara me Koukounaria

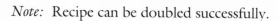

YIELD: 42 COOKIES

2 sticks (½ pound) unsalted butter, at room temperature
⅔ cup sugar
3 egg yolks
1 teaspoon grated orange peel

½ teaspoon vanilla extract
2¾ cups all-purpose flour
⅓ cup pine nuts
3 tablespoons honey

Preheat oven to 325 degrees.

In a bowl beat together butter and sugar until creamy. Beat in egg yolks, one at a time. Add orange peel and vanilla extract. Stir in flour and blend well.

Measure about 1 tablespoon of dough for each cookie and roll between lightly floured palms into ropes about 2½ inches long. Place cookies 2 inches apart on a greased cookie sheet. Shape each into a crescent.

Press pine nuts firmly into cookies to anchor. Heat honey over low heat until it liquefies and brush it liberally over cookies. Bake for 15 minutes, or until golden. Cool cookies on a rack. Store in airtight container.

The Complete Book of
GREEK COOKING

SWEET BISCUITS
Paximadakia

YIELD: 10 TO 12 DOZEN BISCUITS

Paximadakia are sweet biscuit-type cookies, excellent with coffee or tea.

3 sticks (¾ pound) unsalted
  butter, at room
  temperature
1 cup corn oil
2 cups sugar
2 teaspoons vanilla extract
2 eggs
¼ teaspoon baking soda

1 cup warm milk
10 to 12 cups all-purpose
  flour
2 teaspoons double-acting
  baking powder
1 egg, lightly beaten with 1
  tablespoon water
½ cup sesame seeds

Preheat oven to 350 degrees.

Cream butter and corn oil until light and fluffy. Gradually add sugar and vanilla extract. Beat in eggs one at a time and continue mixing. Dissolve baking soda in warm milk and add to mixture. Mix 1 cup flour with baking powder and add to batter. Continue adding flour until you have a soft dough.

Divide dough into six parts. Pat into narrow loaves about 1 inch high and 12 inches long. Place on an ungreased cookie sheet. Score loaves into ½-inch slices. Brush with egg wash and sprinkle with sesame seeds. Bake for 20 to 25 minutes, or until lightly brown. Remove from oven and slice through while hot. Turn slices on their sides and return to oven. Bake for 10 to 15 minutes, or until golden brown. Cool on racks and store in airtight containers.

PHYLLO DESSERTS

ᴨᴨᴨᴨᴨᴨᴨᴨᴨᴨᴨᴨ

Despite the wide array of cakes, pies, and cookies that appear on the preceding pages, to most people Greek desserts mean phyllo-based pastries. This extremely versatile paper-thin dough appears in the appetizer and entrée sections of this book, but it is as a dessert that phyllo truly comes into its own. Who can resist that layered edifice of nuts, fruits, and melt-in-the-mouth dough known as Baklava or that shredded version of phyllo known as kadaife? Diets are quickly forgotten in the presence of such delectable delights as Baklava Rolls and Galatoboureko. Although phyllo is not difficult to work with, it does take a certain amount of practice. We strongly recommend that you read "How to Work with Phyllo" (p. 312) before undertaking any of the following recipes.

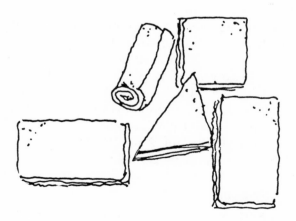

BAKLAVA

YIELD: 30 TO 36 PIECES

Baklava, the most famous Greek dessert, is made with nuts, spices, butter, and phyllo pastry.

1 pound (4 cups) blanched
    almonds or walnuts or a
    combination of both,
    finely chopped
¾ cup sugar
1 tablespoon ground
    cinnamon

1 pound phyllo pastry
3 sticks (¾ pound) unsalted
    butter, melted, for
    brushing phyllo

SYRUP

2 cups water
¾ cup sugar
1 tablespoon fresh lemon
    juice

one 2-inch strip of lemon
    rind
¾ cup honey

Preheat oven to 300 degrees.

Combine nuts, sugar, and cinnamon. Keeping unused sheets covered with plastic wrap, place 8 sheets of phyllo pastry, one at a time, in bottom of an 8 x 14 x 2-inch pan, brushing each sheet with melted butter (see "How to Work with Phyllo," p. 312). Sprinkle top sheet generously with ¼ cup nut mixture and cover with 2 buttered phyllo sheets. Sprinkle with ¼ cup nut mixture. Continue adding buttered phyllo sheets, sprinkling every second sheet with nut mixture, until all nut mixture is used. Place remaining phyllo sheets on top, buttering each sheet.

Cut Baklava into small diamond-shaped pieces with a sharp knife. Place a pan of water on the lowest shelf in oven. Place Baklava on middle shelf above the water and bake for 2 to 2½ hours, or until golden, making sure that the water pan is always full.

While Baklava is in the oven, prepare syrup

Combine in a saucepan water with all ingredients except honey.

Bring to a boil, and simmer for 15 minutes. Add honey, and simmer 5 minutes more. Remove lemon peel and cool.

Remove Baklava from oven and pour cool syrup over hot pastry.

Note: Can be prepared and frozen, unbaked. When ready to use, bake, unthawed, in a 300-degree oven 3 to 3½ hours, or until golden.

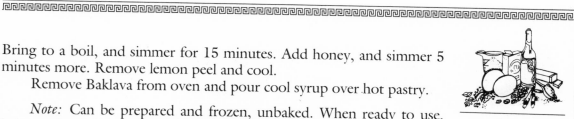

Desserts

Optional: The top of each Baklava piece can be studded with a single clove for decoration and flavor. (You do not eat the clove.)

ALMOND TRIANGLES
Trigona

YIELD: 75 PIECES

3 cups ground blanched
  almonds
2 cups sugar
1 cup water
3 tablespoons rose water or
  1 tablespoon vanilla
  extract

1 tablespoon lemon juice
1 pound phyllo pastry
3 sticks (¾ pound) unsalted
  butter, melted, for
  brushing phyllo
confectioners' sugar for
  topping

Preheat oven to 350 degrees.

Combine almonds, sugar, water, rose water or vanilla extract, and lemon juice. Cook over low heat, stirring constantly, until mixture becomes thick and pasty.

Cut phyllo sheets into thirds. Cover two-thirds with plastic wrap. Prepare triangles according to directions and diagrams in "How to Work with Phyllo" (p. 312). Use 1 teaspoon filling for each triangle. Brush triangles with butter and place on an ungreased baking sheet. Bake for 30 minutes, or until golden. Remove from sheet to cool. When slightly cool, sprinkle with confectioners' sugar.

Note: Triangles can be frozen, unbaked. When ready to use, place unthawed in a preheated 350-degree oven. Bake for 45 minutes, or until golden.

ALMOND AND WALNUT TRIANGLES
Trigona me Amigdala ke Karidia

YIELD: 100 PIECES

¾ pound (3 cups) blanched
   almonds, coarsely
   chopped
¾ pound (3 cups) walnuts,
   coarsely chopped
5 eggs
2 cups sugar

1½ pounds phyllo pastry
4 sticks (1 pound) unsalted
   butter, melted, for
   brushing phyllo
confectioners' sugar for
   topping

Preheat oven to 350 degrees.

Combine almonds and walnuts in a small bowl and set aside.

Beat eggs with sugar until thick and lemon-colored. Add nuts. Cut phyllo sheets into thirds lengthwise. Brush pastry strips with melted butter, one at a time. (Keep remaining strips covered with plastic wrap.) Place a teaspoon of filling on the bottom of each strip and fold into a triangular shape (see "How to Work with Phyllo," p. 312). Place on an ungreased baking sheet; brush tops with melted butter. Bake for 30 minutes, or until golden. Remove from sheets to cool; sprinkle with confectioners' sugar.

Note: Triangles can be frozen, unbaked. When ready to use place unthawed in a preheated 350-degree oven. Bake 45 minutes, or until golden.

ALMOND PHYLLO SQUARES
Amigdalopeta

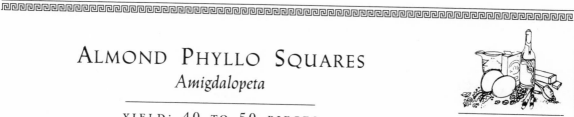

YIELD: 40 TO 50 PIECES

6 eggs, separated
½ cup sugar
1 teaspoon double-acting
   baking powder
1 cup ground zwieback
2 cups ground unblanched
   almonds

¼ teaspoon salt
1 pound phyllo pastry
1½ sticks (6 ounces)
   unsalted butter, melted,
   for brushing phyllo

SYRUP

2 cups sugar
1 cup water

1 teaspoon fresh lemon
   juice

Preheat oven to 350 degrees.

Beat egg yolks with sugar until thick. Add baking powder, zwieback crumbs, almonds, and salt and set aside. In another bowl, beat egg whites until stiff but not dry. Fold into almond mixture. Grease a 9 x 13-inch pan. Brush half the phyllo sheets with melted butter, one at a time, and overlap in the greased pan so as to cover the entire bottom and sides, with some overhang on all edges. (Keep unused sheets covered with plastic wrap; see "How to Work with Phyllo," p. 312.) Pour almond mixture over phyllo sheets. Fold over overhanging phyllo and place remaining sheets, brushed one at a time with butter, over the filling. After all the sheets have been used, score (but do not cut all the way through) the top layers of pastry sheets with a sharp knife to make 2-inch squares. Bake for 35 to 45 minutes, or until golden. Remove from oven and cool.

While pastry is baking, prepare syrup

Combine sugar, water, and lemon juice in a saucepan. Bring to a boil and simmer for 15 minutes. Pour hot syrup over cooled pastry.

SARAGLI

YIELD: 50 PIECES

Saragli is a nut-filled phyllo pastry shaped in long narrow rolls, shirred together, and covered with syrup after baking.

1½ pounds (6 cups) walnuts or almonds, chopped, or a combination of both
3 teaspoons ground cinnamon
1 teaspoon ground cloves

½ cup sugar
1 pound phyllo pastry
4 sticks (1 pound) unsalted butter, melted, for brushing phyllo

SYRUP

2 cups water
4 cups sugar
1 cup honey

2 teaspoons fresh lemon juice
1 cinnamon stick

Preheat oven to 350 degreees.

Combine nuts, cinnamon, cloves, and sugar. Place 1 sheet of phyllo before you, with the widest side closest to you; keep unused sheets covered with plastic wrap; see "How to Work with Phyllo," p. 312). Brush with melted butter; place a second sheet over the first and butter it; place a third sheet over the second and sprinkle with ¼ cup nuts. Place a fourth sheet over nut mixture-phyllo stack, butter it, and sprinkle with ¼ cup nuts. Fold in side edges. Starting from bottom edge closest to you, roll up the phyllo like a jelly roll. It will look like a cylinder, about 2 inches high. Using a spatula, place the Saragli roll seam side down on an ungreased baking sheet. Continue in this manner, rolling tightly. Place as many Saragli close to each other as baking sheet will hold. Slice each roll halfway through into 1-inch pieces. Brush with melted butter. Bake for 30 minutes, or until golden. Cut completely through. Stand each piece upright, and return to the baking sheet; bake an additional 10 minutes.

While Saragli are in the oven, prepare the syrup

Combine all ingredients in a large saucepan, and bring to a boil. Simmer for 20 minutes, removing any scum as it rises. Set aside to cool.

While still hot, dip each piece into cold syrup. Drain on wire racks.

Note: Dipped, cooled Saragli can be frozen. To serve, bring to room temperature; they should be thawed within 1 hour.

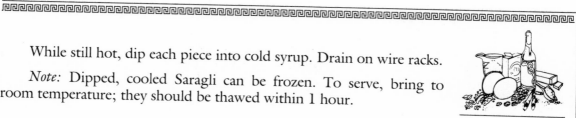

ALMOND ROLLS
Roula me Amigdala

YIELD: 75 PIECES

1½ cups sugar
½ cup water
1 teaspoon fresh lemon
    juice
1 pound (4 cups) blanched
    almonds, finely chopped
½ teaspoon vanilla extract

1 egg white
1 pound phyllo pastry
4 sticks (1 pound) unsalted
    butter, melted, for
    brushing phyllo
confectioners' sugar for
    topping

Preheat oven to 350 degrees.

Place sugar in a large saucepan. Add ½ cup water and lemon juice and bring to a boil to make a syrup. When mixture begins to thicken, immediately add chopped almonds and vanilla extract and stir vigorously. When mixture is very thick remove from heat and let cool. Beat egg white until soft peaks form; add to cooled mixture, and stir well.

Cut phyllo into thirds lengthwise, keeping unused sheets covered with plastic wrap. Brush each strip with melted butter, one at a time. Place 1 teaspoon of the filling at the bottom of each strip and roll up (see "How to Work with Phyllo," p. 312). Place rolls, seam side down, on an ungreased baking pan and brush with melted butter. Bake for 25 to 30 minutes, or until golden. Remove from pan and cool on racks. Serve sprinkled with confectioners' sugar.

Note: These rolls can be prepared and frozen unbaked. When ready to use, place unthawed in a preheated 350-degree oven and bake 40 to 45 minutes, or until golden.

BAKLAVA ROLLS
Sourota

YIELD: 75 PIECES

SYRUP

2 cups sugar
2 cups water
1 tablespoon fresh lemon
   juice

1 stick cinnamon
⅓ cup honey

FILLING

½ pound (2 cups) walnuts,
   chopped
½ cup finely chopped
   zwieback
1 teaspoon ground
   cinnamon
¼ cup sugar

1 pound phyllo pastry
3 sticks (¾ pound) unsalted
   butter, melted, for
   brushing phyllo
1 dowel or pencil, about ½
   inch in diameter and 10
   inches long

Prepare syrup

Combine sugar, water, lemon juice, and cinnamon in a saucepan. Bring to a boil, and simmer for 40 minutes. Remove from heat and stir in honey. Set aside to cool.

Preheat oven to 350 degrees.

Combine walnuts, zwieback, cinnamon, and sugar. Cut phyllo sheets into thirds; cover with plastic wrap until ready to use (see "How to Work with Phyllo," p. 312). Using one sheet of phyllo at a time, brush with butter and place 1 teaspoon filling along lower bottom edge of phyllo. Fold in side edges; then fold bottom up over the filling. Place a dowel or pencil on bottom edge of phyllo (see diagram) and use to roll pastry into a cylinder. Push in rolled phyllo from both sides, toward center, to gather. Hold pastry with left hand and pull out dowel with right hand. Place on an ungreased cookie sheet. Repeat procedure until phyllo and nut mixture are used up. Butter top of each Sourota well. Remove from sheet. Bake about 15 minutes, until golden.

Dip hot pastry in cold syrup; place on dish. Do not cover.

Note: Baked and dipped Sourota can be frozen. To serve, thaw at room temperature for about 1 hour. These can also be frozen, unbaked. When ready to use, place in preheated 350-degree oven, unthawed. Bake for 30 minutes, or until golden. Proceed as explained above.

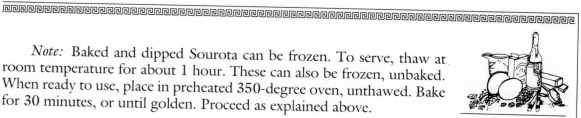

Desserts

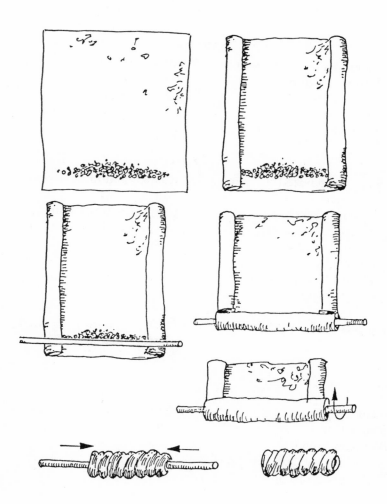

COPENHAGEN

YIELD: 5 DOZEN

Copenhagen is an elegant dessert first made in honor of King George I, the prince of Denmark who was elected king of Greece in 1863.

PASTRY

4 sticks (1 pound) unsalted butter, at room temperature

1 cup sugar

3 egg yolks

1 tablespoon grated orange peel

1 tablespoon cognac

3½ to 4 cups all-purpose flour

FILLING

15 eggs, separated

1 cup sugar

1½ pounds (6 cups) blanched almonds, toasted and finely chopped

½ pound (2 cups) walnuts, finely chopped

2 teaspoons double-acting baking powder

2 teaspoons cinnamon

2 teaspoons almond extract

1 tablespoon cognac

8 sheets phyllo pastry

1 stick (¼ pound) unsalted butter, melted, for brushing phyllo

SYRUP

6 cups sugar

3 cups water

8 ounces honey

1½ tablespoons fresh lemon juice

Preheat oven to 350 degrees.

Make the pastry

Cream butter with sugar until light and fluffy. Add egg yolks, one at a time, and beat for 2 minutes after each addition. Add grated orange peel and cognac. Gradually add flour to form a soft dough.

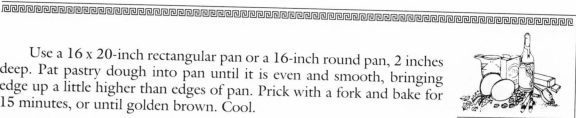

Use a 16 x 20-inch rectangular pan or a 16-inch round pan, 2 inches deep. Pat pastry dough into pan until it is even and smooth, bringing edge up a little higher than edges of pan. Prick with a fork and bake for 15 minutes, or until golden brown. Cool.

Prepare the filling

Beat egg yolks until light. Gradually add sugar and continue to beat until mixture is thick and pale in color. Fold in almonds, walnuts, baking powder, cinnamon, almond extract, and cognac.

In a separate bowl, beat egg whites until stiff but not dry and fold carefully into egg yolk mixture. The mixture is difficult to handle, so use a large spatula to fold. Turn mixture into the cool baked crust.

Keeping unused sheets covered with plastic wrap, place one sheet of phyllo at a time over egg mixture, brushing each sheet with melted butter. Score top of dessert (see "How to Work with Phyllo" for cutting instructions, p. 312). Bake for about 1 hour, or until a knife inserted into the filling comes out clean. Remove from oven and cut in diamond-shaped or square serving pieces.

While cake is baking, prepare syrup

Combine sugar, water, honey, and lemon juice. Bring to a boil and simmer for 15 minutes. Cool.

Pour the syrup over the hot dessert. Serve at room temperature.

Note: This dessert freezes well. Prepare dessert, bake, score, and pour syrup over hot dessert. When cool, cover with foil and freeze. Remove from freezer at least 8 hours before serving.

BOUGATSA

The Complete Book of
GREEK COOKING

Slices of Bougatsa are sold in street stands throughout Greece as a quick snack. It is served warm, sprinkled with confectioners' sugar.

6 cups milk
1 cup sugar
2 eggs, beaten
1 cup regular uncooked
  farina
3 sticks (¾ pound) unsalted
  butter, melted, for
  brushing phyllo

1 pound phyllo pastry
ground cinnamon for
  topping
confectioners' sugar for
  topping

Preheat oven to 350 degrees.

Combine milk, sugar, eggs, and farina in a saucepan and bring to a boil over medium heat, stirring constantly to prevent mixture from burning and lumping. When mixture bubbles and thickens, remove from heat immediately.

Butter two 14 x 18-inch pans with a little of the melted butter. Keeping unused sheets covered with plastic wrap, butter ¼ of the phyllo sheets, one at a time (see "How to Work with Phyllo," p. 312). Overlap them in one pan so as to cover the entire bottom and sides, with some overhang on all edges. Repeat procedure with second pan, using ¼ of the phyllo and buttering and overlapping each sheet. Pour half the farina mixture over the phyllo in each pan. Cover each with remaining phyllo sheets, buttering each sheet and overlapping them. Fold over overhanging phyllo from bottom crust and seal with the top. Prick top with a fork in several places. Bake for 25 minutes, or until brown. Remove from oven and let cool. For best results, refrigerate several hours or overnight. Before serving, cut into squares, place on an ungreased baking sheet and reheat in a preheated 300-degree oven for 10 minutes. Sprinkle with cinnamon and confectioners' sugar before serving.

Note: This dessert keeps, refrigerated, for a few days. It can also be baked, cooled, and frozen for later use. When ready to use, place unthawed in 300-degree oven for about 20 minutes, until defrosted and warm.

Nut Roll
Baklava Rolo

YIELD: 5 DOZEN

3 cups finely chopped nuts:
  almonds, walnuts,
  pistachios, or any
  combination,
¼ cup sugar
½ teaspoon ground cloves

¼ teaspoon ground
  cinnamon
1 pound phyllo pastry
4 sticks (1 pound) unsalted
  butter, melted, for
  brushing phyllo

SYRUP

1 cup water
1 cup honey

1 teaspoon fresh lemon
  juice

Preheat oven to 350 degrees.

Combine nuts, sugar, cloves, and cinnamon and set aside. Brush 2 sheets of phyllo (one at a time) with melted butter and arrange one sheet atop the other (keep remainder covered in plastic wrap; see "How to Work with Phyllo," p. 312). Sprinkle with 2 tablespoons of the mixture. Repeat this procedure until there are three layers of phyllo with nuts (six sheets). Roll lengthwise, jelly roll-style, and place on an ungreased cookie sheet, seam side down. Slice each roll into 1-inch pieces on a diagonal (do not cut all the way through). Prepare four more rolls in the same fashion. Brush nut rolls generously with butter. Bake for 20 minutes, or until golden.

While pastry bakes, bring water to a boil, then add honey and lemon juice. Simmer for 10 minutes. Stir to blend, remove from heat, and cool. Using a pastry brush, brush cooled syrup on hot pastry rolls. Cut slices through; remove from sheets and cool on racks.

Note: Rolls can be prepared and frozen, unbaked. When ready to use, place unthawed in a preheated 350-degree oven and increase baking time about 15 minutes.

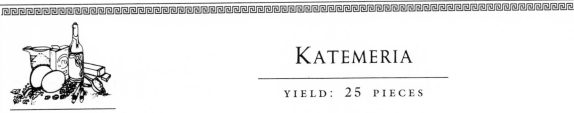
KATEMERIA

YIELD: 25 PIECES

This is an ideal brunch or late evening dessert.

6 eggs
1 teaspoon double-acting
  baking powder
1 pound large curd cottage
  cheese
1 pound phyllo pastry
3 sticks (¾ pound) unsalted
  butter, melted, for
  brushing phyllo

confectioners' sugar for
  topping
ground cinnamon for
  topping

Preheat oven to 350 degrees.

Combine eggs with baking powder and cottage cheese. Mixture will be lumpy. Butter one sheet of phyllo (keep unused phyllo covered with plastic wrap; see "How to Work with Phyllo," p. 312). Spread a large tablespoon of filling across one of the narrow edges of the sheet, covering about one third of the phyllo. Fold in each of the long edges, then fold up narrow edges, envelope-style. Place on an ungreased baking

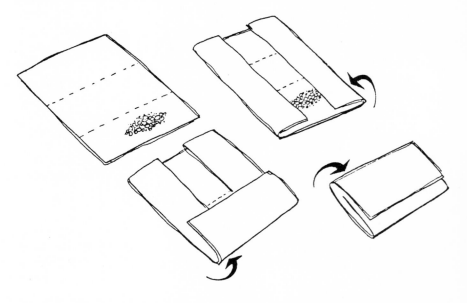

pan. (To simplify lifting each envelope, use a flat metal spatula; lift and place on pan.) Brush tops with melted butter. Bake for 20 to 30 minutes, or until puffed and golden. Serve at once, sprinkled with confectioners' sugar and cinnamon.

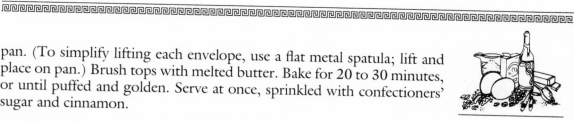

Note: Katemeria can be frozen unbaked. Place unthawed in a preheated 350-degree oven 35 to 45 minutes, or until puffed and golden. Katemeria can be prepared the night before, refrigerated, and baked in the morning.

Meringue Wrapped in Phyllo
Marenga Rolo

YIELD: 36 TO 40 PIECES

SYRUP

1½ cups sugar
1 lemon slice

1 cup water

FILLING

6 eggs, separated
1 cup confectioners' sugar
1 pound (4 cups) almonds, ground

1 cup citrus fruit, peeled and cut into small pieces
1 teaspoon vanilla extract

1 pound phyllo pastry

2 sticks (½ pound) unsalted butter, melted, for brushing phyllo

Prepare the syrup

Combine all ingredients in a saucepan. Bring to a boil and simmer for 15 minutes. Cool.

Prepare the filling

Beat egg yolks with confectioners' sugar in an electric mixer until lemon-colored. In a separate bowl, beat egg whites until thick and

(continued)

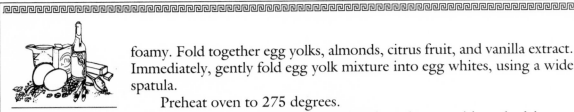

foamy. Fold together egg yolks, almonds, citrus fruit, and vanilla extract. Immediately, gently fold egg yolk mixture into egg whites, using a wide spatula.

Preheat oven to 275 degrees.

Take 6 pieces of phyllo and brush each one with melted butter, laying one on top of the other (keep unused phyllo covered with plastic wrap; see "How to Work with Phyllo, p. 312). Lay the sheets directly on an ungreased cookie sheet. Spread a quarter of the filling at bottom of phyllo layers on the wide end and roll it up like a jelly roll, folding in the ends so filling doesn't come out. Make 3 more rolls. Prick rolls with a fork and butter tops. Bake for 1 hour, or until golden. Remove from oven, let stand a few minutes, and pour cool syrup over the rolls, slowly. When ready to serve, cut into slices. Serve at room temperature.

ORANGE GALATOBOUREKO
Galatoboureko me Portokali

YIELD: 2 DOZEN

4 cups milk
4 tablespoons unsalted butter, plus 1 stick (¼ pound unsalted butter, melted, for brushing phyllo
⅓ cup sugar

½ cup uncooked regular farina
4 eggs
3 tablespoons orange juice concentrate, undiluted
1 teaspoon vanilla extract
½ pound phyllo pastry

ORANGE SYRUP

1 cup water
1½ cups sugar
1 cinnamon stick

2 whole cloves
2 teaspoons grated orange peel

Scald milk in a large saucepan; stir in 4 tablespoons butter and sugar. Gradually add farina, stirring constantly, and bring mixture slowly to a boil. Remove from heat.

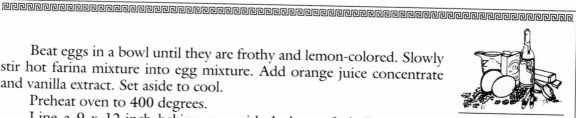
Beat eggs in a bowl until they are frothy and lemon-colored. Slowly stir hot farina mixture into egg mixture. Add orange juice concentrate and vanilla extract. Set aside to cool.

Preheat oven to 400 degrees.

Line a 9 x 12-inch baking pan with 1 sheet of phyllo (some of which should hang over the pan) and brush with butter (keep unused phyllo covered with plastic wrap; see "How to Work with Phyllo," p. 312). Layer 5 more sheets of buttered phyllo in the pan so that bottom and sides are completely covered, with some overhang on all edges. Pour in cooled custard. Cover with 1 sheet of phyllo; brush with butter. Layer 5 more individually buttered sheets of phyllo on top, and fold in overhang. With a sharp knife, slice through top layers of phyllo, marking off 2¼-inch squares or diamond shapes. Bake for 10 minutes; reduce oven temperature to 350 degrees and bake for 45 minutes, or until golden.

While pastry bakes, prepare the syrup

Place ingredients in a large saucepan, bring to a boil, and simmer for 10 minutes. Let cool. Place pastry pan on a rack and cool for 5 minutes. Pour cooled orange syrup over galatoboureko. Cut all the way through and serve at room temperature.

ROLLED GALATOBOUREKA
Roula Galatoboureka

YIELD: 75 PIECES

6 eggs
2 cups sugar
1 quart milk
½ cup regular uncooked
   farina
1 teaspoon grated lemon
   peel

1 pound phyllo pastry
3 sticks (¾ pound) unsalted
   butter, melted, for
   brushing phyllo
confectioners' sugar for
   topping

Combine eggs and sugar and blend well. Put milk in a saucepan, add eggs, and heat gently to just below the boiling point (otherwise eggs will set). Add farina, and cook, stirring continuously to avoid burning, until mixture barely boils. When mixture thickens, immediately remove from heat, add lemon peel, and cool.

Preheat oven to 350 degrees.

Cut each phyllo sheet in thirds and brush with melted butter, one at a time (keep unused phyllo covered with plastic wrap; see "How to Work with Phyllo," p. 312). Place 1 teaspoon of filling about ¼ inch from the edge of a narrow end of a strip; fold in sides. Roll up and place seam side down on ungreased baking sheets. Brush with melted butter. Bake for 25 to 30 minutes, or until golden. Rolls can be served at room temperature or reheated for a few minutes until they become lukewarm. Sprinkle with confectioners' sugar.

Note: Rolls can be frozen, unbaked. When ready to use, bake, unthawed, in a preheated 350-degree oven for 40 to 45 minutes, or until golden. Remove from sheet and cool on racks.

CUSTARD FLUTES
Floyeres

YIELD: 2 DOZEN

6 egg yolks
1 cup sugar
1 cup regular uncooked
 farina
6 cups scalded milk
1 tablespoon grated lemon
 peel or 1 teaspoon vanilla
 extract

12 phyllo sheets
2 sticks (½ pound) unsalted
 butter, melted, for
 brushing phyllo

SYRUP

4 cups sugar
1 tablespoon fresh lemon
 juice

2 cups water

Preheat oven to 350 degrees.

In a large bowl, beat egg yolks with sugar. Add farina and mix well. Slowly stir in scalded milk and lemon peel or vanilla extract. Return mixture to pot and cook, stirring constantly, until mixture thickens, about 15 minutes. Cool.

Cut sheets of phyllo pastry in half, keeping pastry not in use carefully covered with plastic wrap (see "How to Work with Phyllo," p. 312). Brush each piece evenly with melted butter and fold in half. Place 1 tablespoon of filling at one end and fold edges toward middle. Butter and roll up each piece. Place on an ungreased baking pan; brush with melted butter. Bake for 25 to 30 minutes, or until golden.

While custard flutes are baking, prepare syrup

Combine all ingredients in a saucepan. Bring to a boil, and simmer for 15 minutes. Cool.

Pour cool syrup over hot custard flutes.

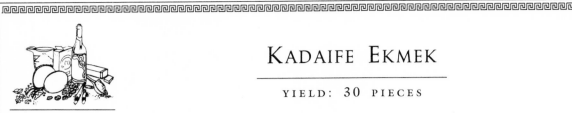

KADAIFE EKMEK

YIELD: **30 PIECES**

The Complete Book of
GREEK COOKING

The Greeks who lived in Asia Minor were called *mikrasiates,* and were considered to be great cooks. For political reasons, they were forced to make a mass exodus from Asia Minor in 1922. Most returned to Greece. This particular recipe is one that they brought with them. It is a very rich dessert that consists of two baked layers of kadaife filled with a rich custard cream and topped with a syrup.

SYRUP

2 cups water
3 cups sugar

2 teaspoons fresh lemon
   juice

2 pounds kadaife
6 sticks (1½ pounds)
   unsalted butter, melted

1 cup warm milk

FILLING

2 quarts heavy cream
5 tablespoons cornstarch

2 tablespoons sugar

Prepare the syrup

    Combine all ingredients in a saucepan and bring to a boil. Simmer for 15 minutes. Set aside.
    Preheat oven to 350 degrees.
    Prepare kadaife (see "How to Work with Kadaife," p. 311). Open kadaife and separate the strands. Divide it equally and spread on two 11 x 15-inch pans. Brush half the melted butter over the pastry in each pan and bake for 20 minutes, or until pastry is golden. Remove from oven and sprinkle pastry in each pan with warm milk. Pour half the cold syrup over the pastry in each pan, cover pans with towels to keep pastry moist, and let cool.

Prepare the filling

    Dilute cornstarch with 1 cup heavy cream. Blend well, and set aside. Heat remaining heavy cream until it almost comes to a boil. Stir in cornstarch mixture and 2 tablespoons sugar slowly, and cook, stirring constantly, until cream is thick and no longer tastes of starch. Cool and chill.

Spread filling over pastry in one pan. Invert pastry from other pan on top. Cut into squares and turn pieces upside down on serving dish.

Desserts

KADAIFE ROLLS
Kadaife Roula

YIELD: 24 PIECES

SYRUP

2½ cups water
4 cups sugar
2 teaspoons fresh lemon
  juice

1 teaspoon grated lemon
  peel
1 cinnamon stick

FILLING

2 cups walnuts, chopped, or
  a combination of chopped
  almonds and walnuts
¼ cup ground zwieback
¼ cup sugar

1 teaspoon ground
  cinnamon
⅛ teaspoon ground cloves
2 tablespoons cognac

1 pound kadaife

3 sticks (¾ pound) unsalted
  butter, melted

Prepare the syrup

Combine all ingredients in a saucepan and bring to a boil. Simmer for 20 minutes, then set aside to cool.

Preheat oven to 350 degrees.

(continued)

The Complete Book of
GREEK COOKING

Prepare the filling

Combine walnuts, zwieback, sugar, cinnamon, cloves, and cognac.

Separate the strands of kadaife and shape into 24 rectangular sections 10 to 12 inches long and 3 inches wide (see "How to Work with Kadaife," p. 311). Place 1 heaping tablespoon of filling at one narrow end of the kadaife. Roll, jelly roll fashion, squeeze to make the roll tight, and place on an ungreased baking pan. Continue until all the kadaife is used. Brush 1 tablespoon melted butter over each roll. Bake until golden, about 25 to 30 minutes.

Pour cold syrup over hot kadaife. Cover and let stand until all the syrup is absorbed.

Note: These rolls can be baked and frozen. When ready to serve, thaw at room temperature for about 1 hour.

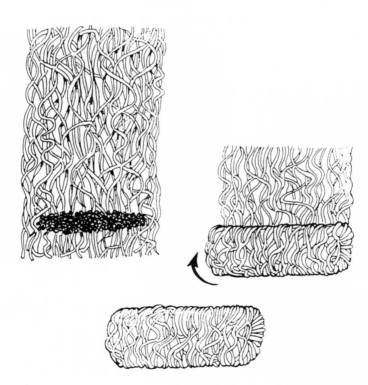

FLAT KADAIFE
Kadaife Tapsiou

Desserts

YIELD: 28 TO 36 PIECES

SYRUP

6 cups water
4 cups sugar
1 stick cinnamon

2 teaspoons fresh lemon
juice
rind of 1 lemon

FILLING

2 cups chopped walnuts
2 cups chopped unblanched
almonds

¼ cup sugar
1 tablespoon ground
cinnamon

1 pound kadaife

3 sticks (¾ pound) unsalted
butter, melted

Prepare the syrup

Place all ingredients in a large saucepan; bring to a boil and simmer for 20 minutes. Set aside to cool.

Preheat oven to 350 degrees.

Prepare the filling

Combine walnuts, almonds, sugar, and cinnamon and mix well.

Open the kadaife and air (see "How to Work with Kadaife," p. 311). Arrange half the kadaife in a greased 9 x 13 x 2-inch pan. Brush half the melted butter over it. Sprinkle the nut mixture over the kadaife. Arrange remaining kadaife over the mixture and brush remaining melted butter over all. Bake for 30 to 40 minutes, or until golden. Remove kadaife from oven and immediately pour cool syrup over it. Cover with a towel; let stand until cool. Cut into 2-inch squares.

Note: This recipe can be frozen with the syrup. To serve, thaw several hours at room temperature.

CUSTARD KADAIFE
Kadaife me Krema

YIELD: 36 TO 40 PIECES

4 cups milk
1 cup regular uncooked
  farina
3 tablespoons unsalted
  butter, plus 4 sticks (1
  pound) unsalted butter,
  melted

1½ cups sugar
1 tablespoon vanilla extract
8 eggs
1 tablespoon grated orange
  or lemon peel
1 pound kadaife

SYRUP

3 cups water
4 cups sugar
2 tablespoons fresh lemon
  juice

5 cloves
1 cinnamon stick

Preheat oven to 350 degrees.

Bring milk to a boil in a large saucepan, add farina and 3 tablespoons butter, stir thoroughly, and remove from heat.

Combine sugar, vanilla extract, eggs, and grated peel. Blend thoroughly. Add to milk and farina mixture; return to heat. Cook over medium heat, stirring constantly, until thickened and smooth. Remove from heat and cool.

Spread half the kadaife in a 12 x 15 x 3 inch pan. (see "How to Work with Kadaife," p. 311). Brush half the melted butter over it. Spread the milk mixture evenly over the kadaife. Add the rest of the kadaife and the remaining melted butter. Bake for about 1 hour, or until golden.

While pastry bakes, make the syrup

Combine all the ingredients in a saucepan along with the other syrup ingredients; bring to a boil and simmer for 15 minutes. Set aside to cool.

Pour cool syrup over hot kadaife; cover with a towel and let cool before serving. Cut into 2-inch squares.

BIRDS' NESTS
Folitses

YIELD: 80 PIECES

1 pound (4 cups) walnuts,
  finely chopped
4 tablespoons sugar
½ teaspoon ground
  cinnamon

1 pound phyllo pastry
4 sticks (1 pound) unsalted
  butter, melted, for
  brushing phyllo

SYRUP

2 cups water
4 cups sugar
2 lemon slices

1 cinnamon stick
1 teaspoon almond extract

TOPPING

¼ pound (1 cup) pistachio
  nuts, finely chopped

1 cup apricot preserves

Preheat oven to 350 degrees.

Combine walnuts, sugar, and cinnamon. Cut phyllo pastry sheets into 4 equal strips. Brush each strip with melted butter, working with one strip at a time and keeping remainder covered with plastic wrap (see "How to Work with Phyllo," p. 312). Spread 1 heaping teaspoon of walnut mixture over each phyllo strip, leaving a 1-inch margin all around. Fold all edges in toward the middle. Press down firmly on one end of the strip with forefinger of one hand and with the other keep wrapping the strip around forefinger to form a "bird's nest." Tuck the last inch of pastry strip under the nest. Brush top of each roll with melted butter. Place on ungreased baking sheet and bake for 15 minutes, or until golden. Cool nests slightly on sheet before dipping in syrup.

Prepare syrup

Combine all ingredients in a saucepan. Bring to a boil and simmer for 15 minutes. Keep over low heat. Dip nests gently in syrup, letting excess drain back into saucepan. Sprinkle with chopped pistachio nuts and decorate each center with a scant teaspoon of apricot preserves.

OTHER DESSERTS

᭍᭍᭍᭍᭍᭍᭍᭍᭍᭍᭍

BATTER PUFFS
Svinghi

YIELD: 28 TO 30 3-INCH PUFFS

Sometimes referred to as Greek doughnuts, Svinghi are similar to Sweet Fritters (see page 291).

1 cup boiling water
4 tablespoons butter or
  margarine
¼ teaspoon salt
1 tablespoon sugar
½ teaspoon grated orange
  peel

1 cup all-purpose flour
1 teaspoon double-acting
  baking powder
4 eggs

SYRUP

2 cups sugar
1 cup water

2 teaspoons fresh lemon
  juice

2 cups vegetable oil for
  frying

ground cinnamon for
  topping

In a medium-size saucepan, combine boiling water, butter, salt, sugar, and orange peel and bring to a boil. Sift together flour and baking powder. Add dry ingredients all at once to hot mixture in saucepan, whisking briskly over medium heat until the mixture forms a compact mass and leaves the sides of the pan. Remove from heat and let cool 1 minute. Add eggs, one at a time, beating hard after each addition. The mixture should be smooth, glossy, and thick. Let rest for 10 minutes.

Desserts

Prepare the syrup

Combine ingredients in a medium-size saucepan. Bring to a boil, and simmer for 15 minutes. Set aside and keep warm.

In a deep pan, heat the oil to 360 degrees.

Drop tablespoonfuls of batter into the oil without crowding. The batter will at first sink, then rise as it puffs. When puffs rise, turn to fry on all sides, using tongs. When puffs are completely golden, remove from oil and let drain on paper towels. Place on a warm platter. Dribble warm syrup over the puffs, and sprinkle with cinnamon. Serve warm.

Variation: Instead of syrup, warm a 16-ounce jar of honey, uncovered, in hot water. Spoon over puffs.

SWEET FRITTERS
Loukoumades

YIELD: 4 DOZEN FRITTERS

Loukoumades, a well-loved dessert, are sweet fritters fried in hot oil until golden brown and served warm with honey syrup and cinnamon.

2 tablespoons active dry yeast, softened in ½ cup warm water	2 cups milk
	3 cups all-purpose flour
	1 egg
1 tablespoon sugar	

SYRUP

1 cup honey	2 cups sugar
1 cup water	

vegetable oil for frying, approximately 2 cups	ground cinnamon for topping

Combine the yeast-water mixture with sugar, milk, flour, and egg to make a very thick, sticky batter. Cover with plastic wrap and a damp towel; let rise for 1 hour.

(continued)

Prepare the syrup

Combine all ingredients in a large saucepan. Bring to a boil, and simmer for 15 minutes. (Syrup should be warm when dribbled over the fritters.)

In a deep-frying pan, heat 3 inches of oil to 360 degrees.

Drop tablespoonfuls of batter into oil and fry until golden on all sides. Remove fritters from oil and drain on absorbent paper. Dribble warm syrup over them. Place on racks to drain and sprinkle with cinnamon. Serve immediately.

Variation: Instead of syrup, warmed honey can be used as a topping. Place one 16-ounce jar of honey, uncovered, in hot water. Simmer until warm. Dribble warmed honey over the puffs.

HONEY ROLLS
Diples

YIELD: APPROXIMATELY 5 DOZEN ROLLS

Diples are a favorite teatime treat. The dough is rolled very thin, cut into small pieces, and fried in hot oil. As one's hand becomes more practiced, the diples can be tied in bow knots or rolled in fancy shapes. Diples are served with syrup, cinnamon, and finely chopped nuts.

3 egg yolks
3 whole eggs
2 tablespoons fresh orange juice
2 teaspoons double-acting baking powder

3 to 3½ cups all-purpose flour
hot vegetable oil for frying, approximately 2 cups

SYRUP

2 cups (1 pound) honey

½ cup water

ground cinnamon for sprinkling

2 cups chopped walnuts

Beat egg yolks and eggs lightly. Add orange juice. Sift baking powder into 1 cup flour, add to mixture. Stir enough remaining flour into the eggs to make a soft dough. Turn dough out onto lightly floured board and knead with floured hands until smooth. Dough will be a little sticky. Keep kneading until dough blisters and forms bubbles when sliced with a knife, at least 10 minutes.

Take a quarter of the dough at a time and roll out paper-thin on a heavily floured board. Cut into 4 x 6-inch strips. Fill a deep-frying pan with 2 inches oil; heat to 360 degrees. Drop strips, one at a time, into hot oil; turn immediately, using two forks, and roll up into a cylinder. Remove from oil when golden. Drain on paper towels and cool.

Desserts

Prepare the syrup

Combine honey and water in a large saucepan. Bring to a boil, and simmer 15 minutes. Skim off the froth. Keep warm.

Dip cool rolls into hot syrup. Place on cake racks to drain, and sprinkle with cinnamon and chopped nuts.

Note: Store undipped honey rolls in an airtight container and refrigerate. Store unused syrup in refrigerator, too. Dip honey rolls in heated syrup as needed, and sprinkle with cinnamon and nuts.

Quick Sweet Fritters
Loukoumades Horis Mayia

YIELD: 2½ DOZEN FRITTERS

These sweet fritters are especially easy because they are made with self-rising cake flour instead of yeast.

SYRUP

½ cup honey
1 cup sugar

½ cup water

BATTER

1 cup milk

1¼ cups self-rising cake
   flour

vegetable oil for frying,
   approximately 2 cups

ground cinnamon for
   topping

1 cup chopped walnuts

Prepare the syrup

Combine all ingredients in a saucepan. Bring to a boil, and simmer for 15 minutes. Set aside.

Prepare the batter

Combine milk and flour and beat until batter is thick and bubbly. Let rest for 15 minutes.

In a heavy saucepan heat 2 inches of oil to 360 degrees. Drop tablespoonfuls of batter into hot oil. Fry only a few at a time and turn as soon as the loukoumades are golden brown. When brown all over, drain on absorbent paper, place on serving platter, and sprinkle with syrup, cinnamon, and chopped nuts. Serve warm.

Variation: Instead of syrup, warmed honey can be used. Place one 16-ounce jar of honey, uncovered, in hot water. Simmer until warm. Dribble over the puffs, and sprinkle with cinnamon and nuts.

Variation: 1 cup yogurt or ½ cup milk and ½ cup yogurt can be used in place of 1 cup milk listed above. These fritters will have a mildly sour taste.

MELON WITH OUZO
Peponi me Ouzo

YIELD: 6 TO 8 SERVINGS

Ouzo is a clear, aromatic spirit distilled from grapes and flavored with aniseed. When diluted with ice or water, ouzo becomes cloudy and white.

1 large cantaloupe or 2 small ones, about 3 pounds	**½ cup sugar** **½ cup ouzo** **peel of 1 lime (optional)**

Cut cantaloupe in half; remove seeds and filaments. Either remove pulp with a melon ball cutter or peel halves and slice. Put melon in a glass bowl. Combine sugar and ouzo in a pitcher and pour over melon. Let stand for at least 3 hours, turning fruit occasionally. Grate lime peel over fruit, if desired.

PUDDINGS

CARAMEL CUSTARD
Krema Karamela

YIELD: 8 TO 10 SERVINGS

1½ cups sugar
1 quart milk
6 eggs
¼ teaspoon salt

2 teaspoons vanilla extract
½ cup slivered blanched
   almonds (optional)

Preheat oven to 350 degrees.

Caramelize 1 cup sugar in a heavy skillet over low heat, stirring constantly. (Do not brown or sugar will become bitter.) Prepare an 8-quart ovenproof mold, or an 8 x 11-inch pan, by heating it in the oven for a few minutes. (This prevents the sugar syrup from cracking.) Pour caramelized sugar into the mold or pan, coating all sides. Set aside.

In a large pot, scald milk and cool slightly.

In a medium-sized bowl, beat eggs, add remaining ½ cup sugar, salt, and vanilla extract, and beat well. Slowly stir in milk. Pour mixture into coated mold.

Place mold in a pan containing 1 inch hot water and bake for about 1 hour, or until a knife inserted near center comes out clean. Remove from oven, cool, and refrigerate several hours before serving. Invert on a chilled platter and unmold, spooning syrup over custard. Sprinkle almonds on top.

GRAPE PUDDING
Moustalevria

YIELD: 16 TO 20 SERVINGS

This unusual pudding is served throughout Greece at grape harvest time. Fresh grapes are squeezed either by hand or in a juice extractor to collect the mousto, or grape juice, that is the main ingredient of the pudding.

10 cups grape juice (mousto made from 10 to 12 pounds seedless white grapes, squeezed)
1 slice white bread
½ cup cornstarch

1 cup all-purpose flour
ground cinnamon for topping
1 cup sesame seeds
1 cup chopped walnuts

Place grapes in a food processor or juice extractor, a few at a time, and pulverize. Strain. Place strained juice in a large pot, break up bread, add to liquids. Boil mousto for 5 minutes. Cool and strain through a cheesecloth, being sure to strain all the bread particles from the liquids.

Measure 8 cups of clear grape liquid. Mix 2 cups liquid with cornstarch and flour. Bring the rest to the boiling point. Add flour mixture a little at a time, stirring constantly until the mixture thickens. Pour into small dishes and immediately sprinkle with cinnamon, sesame seeds, and nuts. Serve cold.

Note: Bottled grape juice cannot be substituted for the fresh grape liquids.

YOGURT
Yiaourti

YIELD: SIXTEEN 4-OUNCE SERVINGS

Yiaourti (yogurt) is a type of soured milk made by adding a culture (fermented milk that is curdled to a custardlike consistency by lactic-acid-producing microorganisms) to fresh milk. The Greeks claim many benefits from yogurt, including cure for stomach ailments and dyspepsia as well as longevity.

2 quarts whole milk   **4 tablespoons prepared
                            plain yogurt**

Bring milk to a boil, stirring so mixture does not stick to bottom of saucepan. Cook for about 30 minutes over medium heat. Stir occasionally. Remove from heat and allow to cool until your little finger can remain in the milk for about 20 seconds. Thin yogurt in a cup with a little of the milk and pour back into the milk. Stir until well blended. Pour into a large heavy bowl or into individual thick glass containers. Cover well and keep in a warm place for 6 to 8 hours or overnight, until yogurt is set. Cover with a double thickness of paper towels to absorb excess liquid. Refrigerate. Serve chilled. If thicker yogurt is preferred, empty the yogurt into a muslin bag and suspend to allow excess liquid to drain out.

Yogurt can be served as a sauce over vegetables or rice, or as desired.

Note: This recipe can be divided successfully.

RICE PUDDING
Rizogalo

YIELD: 8 SERVINGS

2 cups water
½ cup long-grain rice
1 quart milk
2 egg yolks

1 cup sugar
½ teaspoon salt
ground cinnamon

Bring water to a boil and add rice. Simmer, covered, for 15 to 20 minutes. Add milk (be careful milk does not boil over) and continue to cook, stirring often, for about 30 minutes, or until rice is soft and mixture is thick.

Beat egg yolks and sugar until thick and pale in color. Gradually stir in rice mixture, mix well, and return to saucepan. Add salt and cook over low heat for about 2 minutes, stirring constantly to prevent curdling. Pour into pudding dishes and sprinkle with cinnamon. Serve warm, or cool to room temperature and then refrigerate; serve cold.

Preserves

᚛᚛᚛᚛᚛᚛᚛᚛᚛᚛᚛

SOUR CHERRY PRESERVES	*Vissino Glyko*
GRAPEFRUIT MARMALADE	*Frapa Marmelada*
QUINCE PRESERVE	*Kythoni Glyko*

In Greece, it is the custom that when a guest comes to visit, he is offered a sweet, called *glyko*. The sweet is placed in a large bowl, set on a tray that also contains a small dish, a glass of water, and a spoon. When the guest is offered this sweet, he is expected to take a spoonful of glyko, place it on the small dish, take small bites, drink some of the water, and wish the hostess good health.

Today, this custom may be falling by the wayside, but the popularity of eating preserves still remains.

SOUR CHERRY PRESERVES
Vissino Glyko

YIELD: FOUR 8-OUNCE JARS

1 pound fresh black or red
    sour cherries
1 cup water

2 cups sugar
1½ tablespoons fresh lemon
    juice

Wash and pit cherries, reserving pits in a small bowl. Add water to the pits and set aside.

Put 1 cup sugar in a medium-sized saucepan. Place a layer of cherries on top, and then ½ cup sugar, another layer of cherries, and remaining sugar.

Strain water from cherry pits, and add to the cherries. Let mixture stand for 1 hour, then bring to a boil and simmer for 30 minutes, or until syrup thickens to consistency of honey. Stir gently at intervals while cooking and skim off any scum that rises to top. Add lemon juice at end of cooking time to prevent syrup from crystallizing. Spoon into sterilized jars, cool, and refrigerate.

GRAPEFRUIT MARMALADE
Frapa Marmelada

YIELD: EIGHT 8-OUNCE JARS

4 medium grapefruits,
    about 2 pounds total
water

approximately 4 cups sugar
3 tablespoons fresh lemon
    juice

To make grapefruit marmalade, you only use the grapefruit skin (rind). Wash and dry grapefruits thoroughly.

(continued)

Remove pulp from grapefruit shells, slice rinds into strips, then slice strips thin. Place rind in saucepan and cover with water. Soak overnight. (It is important to soak overnight so that the bitterness in the grapefruit is eliminated.) Next day, place saucepan with water and rind over moderate heat; bring to a boil. Reduce heat and simmer until rind is transparent, about 1 hour, adding more water if needed. Measure cooked rind with its liquid (it should be about 4 cups). Add an equal amount of sugar (about 4 cups). Simmer until the jelly stage is reached (jelly sticks to spoon when tilted). Add lemon juice and simmer for another 5 minutes. Pour into sterilized jars and seal tightly.

Note: The grapefruit skin can be grated in the food processor. Proceed as above, soaking in water overnight.

QUINCE PRESERVES
Kythoni Glyko

YIELD: FOUR 8-OUNCE JARS

1 pound quince
2 cups sugar
¾ cup water
2 cinnamon sticks

2 whole cloves
1 tablespoon fresh lemon
   juice

Peel and core the quince. Reserve the seeds and place them in a cheesecloth bag. Tie securely and set aside.

Grate quince flesh on a coarse grater or in a food processor. Place grated quince in saucepan with sugar, water, cinnamon sticks, and cloves. Add cheesecloth bag. Simmer for about 1 hour, or until syrup thickens to the consistency of honey. Stir at intervals and skim off scum that rises to top while cooking. Add lemon juice at the end of cooking time to prevent syrup from crystallizing. Continue to simmer until glassy and jellylike. Discard cheesecloth bag of seeds, cinnamon sticks, and cloves. Spoon into sterilized jars, cool, and refrigerate.

Note: Preserves can be used in a tart such as Apricot Tart (see p. 246).

Appendix

A Word on Greek Coffee
The Popular Teas of Greece
All About Easter Eggs
How to Prepare Fresh Artichokes
How to Clean Fresh Mussels
How to Prepare Fresh Squid
How to Use and Freeze Fresh Grape Leaves
How to Work with Kadaife
How to Work with Phyllo
Some Common Greek Cooking Terms and Ingredients
The Cheeses of Greece
What Are Kolyva?
What About Greek Wines?

A Word on Greek Coffee

Greek coffee comes from beans that are roasted and pulverized into a fine powder. The brewed coffee is thick, strong, and aromatic. Greek coffee is unique because it is served with a foam on top, called *kaimaki*. It is traditionally brewed in a long-handled cylindrical pot known as a *briki* (though a small, deep saucepan will do as well). *Briki* pots come in 2-, 4- or 6-demitasse sizes and are available in Greek specialty shops. Greek coffee cannot be made in larger quantities because the kaimaki comes to the top of the coffee pot and it loses its proper consistency if made with larger amounts of coffee and water. Without the kaimaki, or foam, the unusual coffee flavor is lost.

Greek coffee is usually served plain, moderately sweet, or very sweet; below is a general recipe that will serve for all three levels of sweetness. Reaching a consensus on how to brew kafedaki, however, was no mean feat, since every Greek has his or her own way of doing it.

PLAIN (Sketo)	MEDIUM (Metrio)	SWEET (Glyko)
2 DEMITASSE CUPS		
½ cup water 1 tablespoon Greek coffee	1 teaspoon sugar ½ cup water 1 tablespoon Greek coffee	2 teaspoons sugar ½ cup water 1 tablespoon Greek coffee

Place the sugar (if used) and water in the *briki* or saucepan and stir until sugar dissolves. Bring to a boil. Remove pot from the heat and add the coffee; stir well. Return pot to low heat. As soon as the coffee has risen almost to the rim of the coffee pot, remove the pot from the heat and let the coffee subside (about 15 seconds). Return pot to heat, and heat again, almost to the boiling point; remove from heat and let coffee subside again, about 15 seconds. Return the pot to heat a third time, and as soon as the coffee starts to rise to the rim, remove from heat and

pour a little coffee into each demitasse cup to distribute the kaimaki. (Having the coffee rise three times is what gives the kaimaki the correct consistency.)

Pour the remaining coffee into each cup, being careful not to disturb the kaimaki already in the cups. Serve hot. Since the grounds are poured into the cup along with the brewed coffee, you must let the coffee stand for a few seconds to allow the grounds to settle. Sip carefully, without disturbing the grounds. Accompany with a glass of cold water.

Note: A *kafetzou* is a fortune-teller who specializes in reading the future from the grounds left in the coffee cup. When you finish your coffee, leave a little liquid in the cup, invert the cup on the saucer, and let it dry upside down for a few seconds. The designs made by the coffee grounds will give a clear picture of your fate to any passing *kafetzou*.

THE POPULAR TEAS OF GREECE

There are two very popular herb teas in Greece. One is called *faskomilo,* which is said to cure colds and stomach ailments. It is very flavorful, and many drink it daily. The other is *hamomilo,* or chamomile tea, which is used to cure stomachaches and headaches.

ALL ABOUT EASTER EGGS
Liya Loyia yia ta Paskalina Avga

Easter is the most important celebration of the Greek Orthodox religion. Eggs are dyed red to symbolize Christ's blood. In general, the eggs are dyed on Holy Thursday. After the midnight Resurrection Service on Holy Saturday, the fast is broken, and the first thing people eat are these red eggs. Each person cracks an egg with a relative or friend, and says, "Christ has risen." The reply is "Truly He has risen." In some areas a little game is played when cracking the eggs: point to point, back to back, the object is to find the person with the strongest egg. The one who has the uncracked egg will have good luck in the coming year.

Imported red dye packages are sold at various Greek specialty shops. (In some church communities, the ladies' auxiliary sells the dye, too.) One package usually is sufficient to dye 18 to 20 eggs.

Dilute the egg dye powder in ½ cup white vinegar. Add this mixture to enough warm water to cover eggs. Bring to a boil and simmer, stirring occasionally, for about 5 minutes. Remove pot from heat and add eggs. The eggs should be at room temperature or they are apt to crack. Return to heat and simmer eggs for 45 minutes. Remove eggs, cool slightly, then rub each egg with an oiled cloth.

HOW TO PREPARE FRESH ARTICHOKES

Ingredients vary depending on size of artichokes. The recipe below is for 6 medium-sized artichokes.

1 tablespoon salt
6 tablespoons fresh lemon
  juice
3 tablespoons all-purpose
  flour

6 medium-sized fresh
  artichokes
2 whole lemons, sliced in
  half
cold water to cover

Fill a large bowl with cold water. Add salt, lemon juice, and flour and blend. Set aside.

(continued)

Remove tough outer leaves of the artichokes and cut off part of the stems. Cut ½ to 1 inch off tips of remaining leaves. Cut artichokes in half lengthwise. Rub all cut surfaces with lemon. Cut and scrape the fuzz, or "choke," from the artichoke hearts. Place the artichokes in the salted water. (Be sure that water covers the artichokes.) This solution helps keep the artichokes green. Keep prepared artichokes in water until ready to use.

HOW TO CLEAN FRESH MUSSELS

To clean mussels, place under cool (not cold) running water to remove surface dirt.

Using a dull knife, scrape the shells to remove any clinging weeds and sand. Pull off the "beard" (a hairlike tuft on the shells at the point where they are joined together); scrub shells well with a hard brush under the running water. Soak in cold water until ready to use, discarding any that are open.

HOW TO PREPARE FRESH SQUID

Use small, tender squid. With a sharp knife, remove the chitinous backbone, ink sac, sand sac, and innards. Chop tentacles and set aside. Cut the body of the squid into small ringlets if you are planning to fry. Otherwise, leave body whole to fill. Wash squid thoroughly and soak for 15 minutes in cold water. Drain and use.

How to Use and Freeze Fresh Grape Leaves

Select young, tender grape leaves from the ends of the vines. (Grapevines grow wild in many parts of the United States. In the East, the best time to pick them is during the month of June.) Trim the stems and wash the leaves thoroughly in cold water. Bring water to a boil in a very large pot. Add the leaves and blanch for about 5 minutes. Remove from the pot, drain well, and rinse in cold water. Layer the leaves, dull side down, in stacks of about 30 (enough for 1 pound of ground meat). Center each stack on a square of plastic wrap and roll the leaves and plastic wrap into cigar-shaped rolls, squeezing out any excess water as you proceed. Place each roll in a plastic bag and freeze. To use, place frozen rolls (still wrapped in plastic) in warm water until thawed. Fresh grape leaves can stay in the freezer for several months, and leftover leaves can be refrozen.

How to Work with Kadaife

Kadaife is pastry that is available in 1-pound packages at various Greek specialty shops. The dough is made out of flour and water, combined into a thick batter. The batter is poured into a perforated tin having about fifteen "teeth." This tin is held over a metal hot plate. As the batter is poured through the tin onto the hot metal, the kadaife partially cooks and dries into long thin strands resembling noodles or shredded wheat. It is tightly rolled up into oblong rolls and packaged.

To use kadaife, separate the oblong rolls and gently pull apart the strands to loosen. This airs it and fluffs it up. Because kadaife tends to dry out if aired too long, the filling, pans, and butter should be ready to use before the package of kadaife is opened.

Kadaife is used to prepare desserts such as Custard Kadaife (see p. 280) or Flat Kadaife (see p. 287). These recipes call for the strands to be used flat in a pan. Divide the kadaife in half and work with one portion; cover the other half with plastic wrap so that it will not dry

out. Gently pull apart the strands to air, and place in a baking pan; set aside. Repeat the procedure with the remaining half of the kadaife. Following the recipe instructions, pour or brush the butter over the kadaife. Proceed with the recipe to complete the dessert.

If you are preparing a recipe such as Kadaife Rolls (see p. 285), then separate the pound of kadaife strands by pulling them apart. Shape into 24 rectangular sections 10 to 12 inches long and 3 inches wide. Place 1 heaping tablespoon of the filling at one narrow end of the kadaife. Roll, jelly roll-fashion, squeezing to make the roll tight. Place rolls close together on a baking pan, and follow the instructions in the recipe for buttering the top of each roll.

Kadaife can be frozen. To use, remove from freezer and let thaw in the refrigerator overnight.

Unused opened kadaife should be tightly wrapped in plastic. It can remain in the refrigerator for one week, or it can be frozen.

How to Work with Phyllo

Phyllo, also spelled *filo,* is a unique, paper-thin, extremely versatile pastry dough that is ubiquitous in Greek cooking. From appetizers to desserts, there are thousands of uses for this remarkable product. Fortunately for Grecophiles, it is now readily available in gourmet and specialty food shops and even in many supermarkets across the country.

Phyllo is sold commercially in 1-pound boxes, each containing 24 to 30 rolled sheets of pastry. An unopened box of phyllo will keep in the refrigerator for several weeks, and several months in the freezer. To defrost, leave the unopened package in the refrigerator overnight and the phyllo will be ready to use the next day. Do not thaw at room temperature because the sheets then have a tendency to stick to each other.

One of the difficulties of working with phyllo is that it tends to dry out very quickly once exposed to air. Thus speed is of the essence. Before unrolling the phyllo, make sure that you have a large area to work on and that all your ingredients and utensils are at hand: baking pans, a feather or pastry brush, the filling, and, most important, the melted, but

not browned, butter that will be used to top each individual sheet. If you are going to bake the phyllo pastry immediately, your oven should be preheated.

Once you have unrolled the phyllo, work with one sheet or a portion of a sheet at a time. Keep the remainder covered with plastic wrap or a damp cloth. (Plastic wrap is preferable because it is easier to handle.) This will prevent the sheets from drying out. Use a feather or other pastry brush to spread an ample amount of butter on the sheet or part of the sheet you are working on, beginning at the edges and working inward. Use broad strokes and work fast to prevent the sheets from drying out. The object is not to saturate the sheet, but to lightly dab it all over.

Note that unsalted or lightly salted butter can be used, depending on the particular recipe. Margarine, but not oil, can be substituted for butter.

Phyllo appetizers such as Bourekakia generally call for the individual sheets to be cut into thirds lengthwise, filled with various ingredients such as spinach, cheese, or meat, and shaped into triangles or rolls. See diagrams 1 and 2. Place each triangle or roll, seam side down, on ungreased baking sheets. Brush each filled triangle or roll with melted butter. Phyllo sheets for such entrées as Chicken Breasts in Phyllo (see p. 102) are usually left whole and amply buttered. The filling is placed on the sheet, which is then folded envelope-style and placed seam side down on a baking sheet. For such desserts as Baklava (see p. 266), whole individually buttered sheets are used. Layer half the amount of phyllo called for, one sheet at a time, in a deep baking pan, spread nut or whatever filling on top, and add remaining phyllo to cover. When phyllo is being baked in a pan, it is best to score the top sheets with a sharp knife (a triangular or diamond design is traditional) to facilitate later cutting. (Optional: To ensure a crisp pastry, sprinkle the top layer of phyllo with cold water before baking; this will also prevent the sheets from breaking.) Baked phyllo items are done when they reach a golden color—not brown. Be careful not to overbake.

One of the great advantages of phyllo is that it freezes extremely well, either baked or unbaked (the latter is preferable). To cook frozen phyllo pastries or dishes, place directly, without prior thawing, into a preheated oven and increase baking time according to directions in the individual recipe. Previously baked and frozen phyllo dishes can be reheated in a 350-degree oven until piping hot.

Do not be afraid of working with phyllo. Once you get the hang of it, it is very simple. Organization, speed, and especially practice are the only prerequisites. The results are certainly worth the effort.

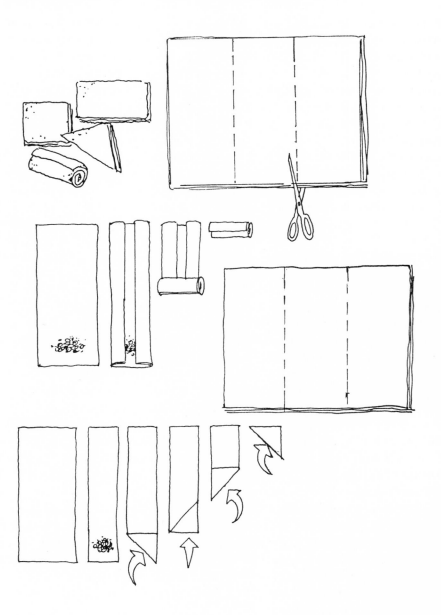

Some Common Greek Cooking Terms and Ingredients

AMIGTHALA: almonds

ANGINARES: artichokes

ANITHO: dill

ARNI: lamb

AVGOLEMONO: an egg and lemon mixture generally used as a sauce or soup base

BAHARI: allspice

BAKLAVA: the most famous dessert of Greece, made of layers of phyllo pastry interspersed with chopped nuts and topped with a honey-flavored syrup

BOUREKI (OR BOUREKAKIA): phyllo puffs made with various fillings

DAPHNE: bay leaf. The distinctive flavor of bay, or laurel, enlivens many Greek stews and meat and fish dishes. In ancient times, a wreath of laurel leaves was awarded to the victor of the Olympic Games.

DOLMADES: grapevine leaves stuffed with meat or rice

DOMATES: tomatoes

ELLIES: olives

FETA: the classic white goat cheese of Greece

FILO (OR PHYLLO): the paper-thin pastry dough essential to Greek cuisine. It is used for appetizers, entrées, and desserts. It can be made by hand, but most purchase it in one-pound packages.

FRAPA: grapefruit

GARIDES: shrimp

GARIFALO: cloves

GLIKANISO: anise. This is the source of ouzo's licorice flavor.

GOUDI: a brass or wooden mortar

GOUVETSI: the Greek word for "casserole," or baked in the oven

HAMOMILO: chamomile. The flowers of this herb are brewed as a tea renowned for its medicinal properties.

KAFES: coffee

KALAMARIA: squid

KANNELA: cinnamon

KASSERI: creamy farm cheese with a mild flavor

KEFALOTIRI: a hard, salty cheese, excellent for grating

KEFTEDES: meatballs

KEIK: cake

KIMONO: cumin

KOURABIEDES: butter cookies topped with confectioners' sugar

KRITHARAKI: tiny oblong-shaped pasta

LADERES: foods braised in olive oil, simmered until done, and served lukewarm or cold

LADOLEMONO: oil and lemon juice dressing

Appendix

MAHLEPI: cherry-flavored seeds used in a variety of Greek cakes and breads. It comes from Syria, and must be finely ground before using.

MAINTANO: parsley

MARANTHO: fennel. Another source of licorice flavor, commonly used in soups, to process olives, and to pickle vegetables

MASTICHA: the sap drawn from the *mastichodenro* bush, grown only on the island of Chios. Masticha is the basic ingredient of chewing gum as well as a flavoring for liqueurs, breads, and cookies.

MATZOURANA: marjoram. Used for flavoring stews and fish dishes; also brewed and used as a medicinal tea

MEZETHAKIA (OR OREKTIKA): small savory appetizers

MOSHARAKI: veal

MOSHOKARIDO: nutmeg

MOUSSAKA: a layered casserole usually made with eggplant and chopped meat, topped with a cream sauce.

OREKTIKA (OR MEZETHAKIA): small savory appetizers

ORZO: tiny almond-shaped pasta

OUZO: a colorless alcoholic drink, flavored with anise. Like Pernod and other anise-based liqueurs, ouzo turns milky white when combined with water or poured over ice.

PASTITSIO: a layered casserole of macaroni and chopped meat, topped with a cream sauce

PHYLLO (OR FILO): the paper-thin pastry dough essential to Greek cuisine

PILAFI: rice boiled in broth, usually with onion and other flavorings

PIPERI: pepper

PSARI: fish

PSITO: baked food

RETSINA: white or rosé wine flavored with pine resin

RIGANI: oregano. The indispensable herb of Greece, oregano grows everywhere and is used in countless dishes.

SKORDALIA: garlic sauce

SKORTHO: garlic

SOUVLA: a skewer used for grilling

SPANAKOPETA: phyllo puffs stuffed with spinach

TAHINI: crushed sesame seed paste

TARAMA: fish roe from the gray mullet

TARAMOSALATA: fish roe spread

THENTHROLEVANO: rosemary

THIMARI: thyme. This aromatic herb is commonly used to flavor fish and meat dishes. It is also the predominant flavor of Greece's most famous honey, produced on Mount Hymettus, near Athens.

THIOSMOS: mint
TIGHANITO: fried
TIROPETES: phyllo stuffed with cheese
TIS SKARAS: broiled food
TSAKISTES: cracked olives marinated in brine

VOTHINO: beef
VOUTIRO: butter
VRASTO: boiled or poached
YIAHNI: stew
YIAOURTI: yogurt
ZESTO: hot
ZOUMI: broth

Appendix

THE CHEESES OF GREECE

Many Greeks consider a meal incomplete without a slab of cheese and a piece of crusty homemade bread. The following is a list of some of the more popular Greek cheeses, all of which are now available in this country.

Anthotyro: A soft (though firmer than cream cheese) white goat's milk cheese, with a mild, sweet taste.

Feta: The most widely known of Greek cheeses, feta is made of a combination of sheep's and goat's milk. Pure white, crumbly, and salty, it is excellent in salads and in a wide variety of baked dishes. To keep it moist, store feta in brine or tightly wrapped in plastic.

Graviera (or kefalograviera): A mild Gruyere-type cheese made of sheep's or cow's milk. A good all-purpose cheese.

Haloumi: A semi-soft cheese, similar to mozzarella but quite salty. Good as a snack with crackers.

Kasseri: A mild, creamy cheese made of sheep's or goat's whole milk. Suitable for baking, kasseri is also a good after-dinner accompaniment for fruit.

Kefalotiri: A light yellow, very hard cheese made of sheep's or goat's milk, salty kefalotiri is widely used in Greek cuisine. It is especially suited for grating.

Manouri: This soft unsalted sheep's and goat's milk cheese closely resembles soft mizithra (see below) and its Italian counterpart, ricotta, and can be used interchangeably with both.

Mizithra: Comes in two types: the first is soft, unsalted, and resembles ricotta. The second is lightly salted and semi-hard. Mildly flavored, this type is a delicious accompaniment for fruits.

Touloumotyri: A semi-hard, flaky white cheese, prepared and aged in animal hides. Similar to feta, but less salty, touloumotyri is excellent with fruit, especially grapes.

WHAT ARE KOLYVA?

A combination of boiled wheat, white raisins, spices, and sugar, Kolyva is the traditional dish made by Greek families forty days after the death of a member of the family, again a year later, and then for the last time three years later. The Kolyva are prepared, decorated, and placed on a tray. The finished tray of Kolyva is brought to the church by the family to be blessed by the priest during the memorial service (called *makaria*) that is held for the soul of the deceased. After the service the church caretaker mixes up the Kolyva and spoons some into little plastic bags, which are distributed to the family, friends, and parishioners at the end of the service. (Kolyva are eaten with a spoon.)

Kolyva are also prepared for the Psychosavata (Saturday of the Souls).

2 pounds whole wheat
1 teaspoon salt
4 cups flour
1 cup white raisins
2 tablespoons ground cumin (optional)
2 tablespoons ground cinnamon
½ to 1 cup sugar

4 cups finely chopped walnuts
¼ cup chopped parsley (optional)
2 cups (1 pound) confectioners' sugar
white Jordan almonds
blanched almonds
silver dragées

Wash wheat with warm water. Place in a saucepan, add water to cover generously and salt, and simmer until wheat is soft, about 4 hours. Add more water as needed. Drain in colander. Spread on linen towel and allow wheat to dry thoroughly.

Put flour in a heavy skillet and cook over very low heat, stirring constantly, until golden. Be careful not to scorch it. Mix wheat with half the flour and add raisins, cumin, cinnamon, and sugar. Blend well. Place mixture on a 15 x 20-inch tray, spreading evenly. Spread chopped walnuts and parsley over mixture. Then spread remaining flour evenly over entire tray. Sift confectioners' sugar over top and carefully press sugar down firmly with wax paper or spatula.

Decorate tray of Kolyva with Jordan almonds, blanched almonds, and silver dragées. Usually a large cross made of silver dragées is placed in the center of the Kolyva and the initials of the deceased are formed with white almonds on each side. Further designs on border and corners are made with remaining almonds and dragées as desired.

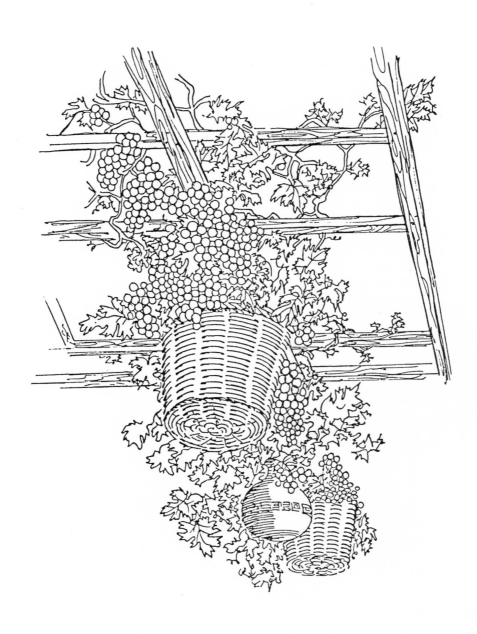

WHAT ABOUT GREEK WINES?

In the last decade, wine production in Greece has changed markedly. The wine makers realized that in order to stay competitive in the world markets, they would have to change their bottling methods and the quality of their wines. For this reason, wine production has moved away from the resin-flavored wines, since most Westerners were unfamiliar with or did not like that particular flavor. The Greeks themselves realized that they wanted a more sophisticated taste to their wines. With the entry of Greece into the Common Market, the wine industry has begun to experiment and improve, making changes in their vineyards, their blending, and their bottling. Modern wine-making techniques and technology are quickly spreading throughout Greece, and as a result, an array of wines is being produced. This is not to say that old standbys such as retsina are not being made; they are, but in lesser quantity.

As a result of modern techniques, wine makers are producing clean-tasting, fresh, fruity, resin-free wines. Furthermore, Greece has recently created a system of appellations, dividing the vineyard lands into twenty-four regions. Similar to the appellation systems of France and Italy, this division guarantees the source of the wines.

Americans have had a stereotyped notion of Greek wines, thinking that they are all resin-flavored and harsh. This is unfortunate, because Greek vintners have been producing a wide variety of other wines, including Achaia Clauss's Domestica, and Santa Helena, and Pendelli.

On the subject of retsina, it must be noted that the word is a generic name that applies to any wine, usually white or rosé, that has been flavored with pine resin. One of the legends about the origin of this wine tells the story of the Athenians trying to save their wine from the invading Persians. The Athenians decided to add resin from the pine trees to their wine to deliberately make it undrinkable. The Persians did not like the wine. After they left, the Greeks opened the jars of wine and were delighted by the flavor. The Greeks have therefore been drinking this wine ever since. Another explanation is that the use of resin (sometimes called pitch) dates back to ancient times, when it was used as a preservative. Resinated wines do not improve with age; they are best when consumed cold. This particular type of wine is said to be an acquired taste, and is certainly not popular with everyone. Some popular resinated wines are made by Boutari, Kourtaris, and Tsantilis.

Among the Greek wines currently available in the States are the following:

WHITE *(with no resin): serve well chilled*

Koutakis Apelia, nonvintage, from savatiano grapes grown near Athens

Calliga Robola, nonvintage, from the island of Cephalonia; smooth, dry, with a touch of fruit flavor

Boutari Santorini, from the assyrtiko grape grown in the Cyclades Islands

Tsantilis Agiorgitikos, made from assyrtiko, athiri, and rhoditis grapes from Mount Athos in the Chalcidice Peninsula

Porto Caras Reserve, from the Chalcidice Peninsula, a limited-quantity wine. Wine making began as a hobby for Mr. Caras; it was so well received by the public that he has greatly expanded his production.

RED *(with no resin): serve at room temperature*

Boutari Naoussa and Grand Reserve, both made from xinomauvro grapes in Thessaly (northeastern Greece). Dry, bright red in color, this wine has medium body, mild taste.

Boutari Cava Boutari, made from grapes of Naoussa and Agiorgitiko. Stored in oak barrels, it has a rich body, aroma, and bouquet.

Caras Cava Caras, from grapes grown in the Chalcidice Peninsula; distinct dry taste and medium body

Naoussa Casa Vaeni, from the Naoussa region; dry and fruity

Paros Paros, made with a combination of deep red mantilanria and white monemvassia grapes, is a dry, mellow-flavored wine.

ROSÉ *(with no resin): serve chilled*

Boutari Rosé and Demi Sec Rosé, made from the varieties of the xinomauvro and agiorgitiko grapes from the mountainous regions of northern Macedonia. The wine has a dry, fruity taste and aroma.

DESSERT WINES *(with no resin)*

Muscat of Samos, nonvintage white dessert wine made from the muscat canneli grapes of Samos. Medium sweet; serve after dinner, chilled.

Muscat of Patras, nonvintage dessert wine made from the muscat canneli grapes of Patras. Also medium sweet; serve after dinner, well chilled.

Mavrodaphne, a sweet, full-bodied red wine. Serve after dinner.

LIQUEURS AND BRANDIES

Liqueurs and brandies have been produced in Greece since 1882. The most famous and frequently exported ones are Metaxa 5 Star and 7 Star, both 92 proof, with a warm, rich color, and Cambas, also 92 proof.

Just as retsina comes to mind when you think of Greek wines, so ouzo comes to mind as the liqueur of Greece. Ouzo is a colorless licorice-flavored liqueur that seems to be ubiquitous in Greece. It is distilled from choice grape extracts and aromatic plants and seeds cultivated in Greece. The drink is served over ice, which makes it cloudy. It is usually served with a glass of water on the side. The Greeks drink it all year round; some drink it straight without water. It is a very strong drink; one often does not realize how potent it is until too late. Many brands are available and they differ only in the proof; the higher the proof, the better the drink. It is interesting to note that many consider ouzo a man's drink. The counterpart for women is a drink called masticha, a soft, slightly sweet anise-flavored liqueur. It is made from the aromatic gum extracted from the masticha bush, which grows exclusively on the island of Chios.

Since there is a new concentrated effort on the part of vintners to export a wider variety of their wines, more are available. They are not all well known here in the United States, but they are gaining. The aforementioned whites, reds, and rosés would be good accompaniments to the various recipes offered. And, when serving a Greek wine or liqueur, remember to say a toast as the Greeks would: *"Eis egian,"* meaning "To your health."

METRIC CONVERSION CHART

CONVERSIONS OF OUNCES TO GRAMS

Ounces (oz)	Grams (g)	Ounces (oz)	Grams (g)
1 oz	30 g *	11 oz	300 g
2 oz	60 g	12 oz	340 g
3 oz	85 g	13 oz	370 g
4 oz	115 g	14 oz	400 g
5 oz	140 g	15 oz	425 g
6 oz	180 g	16 oz	450 g
7 oz	200 g	20 oz	565 g
8 oz	225 g	24 oz	675 g
9 oz	250 g	28 oz	800 g
10 oz	285 g	32 oz	900 g

* Approximate. To convert ounces to grams, multiply number of ounces by 28.35.

CONVERSIONS OF POUNDS TO GRAMS AND KILOGRAMS

Pounds (lb)	Grams (g), Kilograms (kg)	Pounds (lb)	Grams (g), Kilograms (kg)
1 lb	450 g *	5 lb	2¼ kg
1¼ lb	565 g	5½ lb	2½ kg
1½ lb	675 g	6 lb	2¾ kg
1¾ lb	800 g	6½ lb	3 kg
2 lb	900 g	7 lb	3¼ kg
2½ lb	1,125 g; 1¼ kg	7½ lb	3½ kg
3 lb	1,350 g	8 lb	3¾ kg
3½ lb	1,500 g; 1½ kg	9 lb	4 kg
4 lb	1,800 g	10 lb	4½ kg
4½ lb	2 kg		

* Approximate. To convert pounds into grams, multiply number of pounds by 453.6.

CONVERSIONS OF FAHRENHEIT TO CELSIUS

Fahrenheit	Celsius	Fahrenheit	Celsius
170°F	77°C *	350°F	180°C
180°F	82°C	375°F	190°C
190°F	88°C	400°F	205°C
200°F	95°C	425°F	220°C
225°F	110°C	450°F	230°C
250°F	120°C	475°F	245°C
275°F	135°C	500°F	260°C
300°F	150°C	525°F	275°C
325°F	165°C	550°F	290°C

* Approximate. To convert Fahrenheit into Celsius, subtract 32, multiply by 5, then divide by 9.

CONVERSIONS OF QUARTS TO LITERS

Quarts (qt)	Liters (L)	Quarts (qt)	Liters (L)
1 qt	1 L *	5 qt	4¾ L
1½ qt	1½ L	6 qt	5½ L
2 qt	2 L	7 qt	6½ L
2½ qt	2½ L	8 qt	7½ L
3 qt	2¾ L	9 qt	8½ L
4 qt	3¾ L	10 qt	9½ L

* Approximate. To convert quarts to liters, multiply number of quarts by .95.

INDEX